Haggai

Restoring A Work of God
Inspirational, Task-Oriented Leadership

CLINTON'S BIBLICAL LEADERSHIP COMMENTARY SERIES

J. Robert Clinton, D. Miss., Ph.D.
Mike Hannah

BARNABAS PUBLISHERS

Copyright © J. Robert Clinton, January 2001
All Rights Reserved

No Part of this publication may be reproduced, stored in a retrieval system, or transmitted in any form or by any means - electronic, mechanical, photocopy, recording, or any other - except for brief quotations embodied in a critical article or printed reviews, without prior permission of the publisher.

Barnabas Publishers
P.O. Box 6006
Altadena, CA 91003-6006
ISBN No. 1-932814-11-6

Printed in the United States of America

Series & Title Cover Design: D.M. Battermann, R&D Design Servies
Book Design & Layout: D.M. & R.D. Battermann, R&D Design Services

Haggai

CLINTON'S BIBLICAL LEADERSHIP COMMENTARY SERIES

Restoring A Work of God
Inspirational, Task-Oriented Leadership

J. Robert Clinton, D. Miss., PhD.
Mike Hannah

ISBN No 0-9710454-2-9

Copyright © J. Robert Clinton January 2001

Table of Contents

Contents	Page
Abbreviations	v
List of Tables	vi
List of Figures	vii
Introduction to Clinton's Leadership Commentary Series	viii
Preface	x
General Reflection on Haggai	1
Overview	3
Leadership Topics and Leadership Lessons	5
1. TASK ORIENTED LEADERSHIP	5
2. INSPIRATIONAL LEADERSHIP	5
3. TEAM MINISTRY	6
4. INFLUENCE MEANS	7
5. TIMING	8
6. THE RENEWAL FACTOR IN RECRUITMENT	8
7. RESTORING A WORK OF GOD—4 STAGES	9
8. DIVINE AFFIRMATION—AN ESSENTIAL	10
9. EMPOWERING PRESENCE OF GOD	11
10. WORK OF GOD	12
Haggai Commentary	14
For Further Study	25

Leadership Articles (bold faced items appear in other commentaries as well):

1	Civil Leadership—The Missing Ingredient	27
2	Dealing With Personal Discouragement in A Ministry Project	31
3	**Divine Affirmation in the Life of Jesus**	34
4	**Figures and Idioms in the Bible**	38
5	Getting the Job Done—Comparison of Ezra and Haggai	45
6	**God The Promise Keeper**	49
7	**God's Timing and Leadership**	52
8	Haggai—Afterglow Ministry	58
9	Haggai—And Spiritual Authority	61
10	Haggai—And Timing	65
11	Haggai—Calendar And Dating	67
12	Haggai—Delaying God's Work	69
13	Haggai—Dealing With Discouraged Followers	72

14	Haggai—Discouragement, Small Work of God	76
15	Haggai—Leadership Coalition	78
16	Haggai—Lasting Legacies	82
17	Haggai—Profiting From the Past	85
18	Haggai—Prophetic Words	89
19	Haggai—Spiritual Warfare	92
20	Holiness—A Motivating Factor for Leaders	94
21	**Jesus—Sentness**	97
22	**Leadership Functions—Three High Level Generic Priorities**	100
23	**Leadership Levels—A Leadership Continuum**	103
24	Left Hand of God	107
25	Lord of Hosts	110
26	**Macro Lesson, Defined**	114
27	**Macro Lessons, List of 41 Across Six Leadership Eras**	117
28	**Principles of Truth**	120
29	**Promises of God**	125
30	Prophecy Overview	129
32	Prophetic Authority	135
32	Prophetic Crises, Three Major	139
33	**Redemptive Drama, The Biblical Framework**	146
34	Restoration Leaders	162
35	**Six Biblical Leadership Eras--Seeing With Leadership Eyes**	165
36	**Spiritual Authority Defined—Six Characteristics**	179
37	**Spiritual Warfare—Two Extremes To Avoid**	182
38	**Spiritual Warfare—Two Foundational Axioms**	184
	Glossary of Leadership Terms	188
	Bibliography	195

Abbreviations

Bible Books

Genesis	Ge	Nahum	Na
Exodus	Ex	Habakkuk	Hab
Leviticus	Lev	Zephaniah	Zep
Numbers	Nu	Haggai	Hag
Deuteronomy	Dt	Zechariah	Zec
Joshua	Jos	Malachi	Mal
Judges	Jdg	Matthew	Mt
Ruth	Ru	Mark	Mk
1 Samuel	1Sa	Luke	Lk
2 Samuel	2Sa	John	Jn
1 Kings	1Ki	Acts	Ac
2 Kings	2Ki	Romans	Ro
1 Chronicles	1Ch	1 Corinthians	1Co
2 Chronicles	2Ch	2 Corinthians	2Co
Ezra	Ezr	Galatians	Gal
Nehemiah	Ne	Ephesians	Eph
Esther	Est	Philippians	Php
Job	Job	Colossians	Col
Psalms	Ps	1 Thessalonians	1Th
Proverbs	Pr	2 Thessalonians	2Th
Ecclesiastes	Ecc	1 Timothy	1Ti
Song of Songs	SS	2 Timothy	2Ti
Isaiah	Isa	Titus	Tit
Jeremiah	Jer	Philemon	Phm
Lamentations	La	Hebrews	Heb
Ezekiel	Eze	James	Jas
Daniel	Da	1 Peter	1Pe
Hosea	Hos	2 Peter	2Pe
Joel	Joel	1 John	1Jn
Amos	Am	2 John	2Jn
Obadiah	Ob	3 John	3Jn
Jonah	Jnh	Jude	Jude
Micah	Mic	Revelation	Rev

Other

BAS	Basic English Version
CEV	Contemporary English Version
fn	footnote(s)
KJV	King James Version of the Bible
NEB	New English Bible
NLT	New Living Translation
N.T.	New Testament
O.T.	Old Testament
Phillips	The New Testament in Modern English, J.B. Phillips
TEV	Today's English Version (also called Good News Bible)
Vs	verse(s)

List of Tables

		Page
1.1	Civil, Religious, and Peripheral Religious Leaders in the Leadership Eras	28
2.1	A Sampling of Promises to God's Leaders	33
3.1	Four Affirmation Experiences in the Life of Jesus	36
4.2	13 Patterned Idioms	40
4.3	15 Body Language Idioms	42
4.4	14 Miscellaneous Idioms	43
5.1	Ezra and Haggai – A Timeline	46
6.1	God The Promise Keeper—Examples	50
7.1	13 Bible Characters and God's Timing	58
10.1	Some Examples of the Timing Macro Lesson	65
11.1	Restoration Books and Miscellaneous Information	67
11.2	Haggai and Zechariah—Overlap in Ministry	68
12.1	Strong Biblical Illustrations About God's Timing	70
15.1	Possible Coalitions in the Leadership Eras	79
16.1	Ultimate Contribution Categories	82
18.1	Haggai's Prophetic Words	90
22.1	Typical Task Oriented Leadership Functions	101
22.2	Typical Relational Oriented Leadership Functions	101
22.3	Typical Inspirational Leadership Functions	101
24.1	Some Occurrences of the Left Hand of God	108
24.2	God's Left Hand Working Through Cyrus	109
25.1	Frequency of Phrase—LORD of hosts	111
25.2	Bible Translations Rendering of LORD of hosts	111
25.3	Haggai's Use of Lord of hosts—Context By Context	112
26.1	Leadership Eras and Number of Macro Lessons	115
26.2	Top Three Macro Lessons in O.T. Leadership Eras	115
26.3	Top Three Macro Lessons in N.T. Leadership Eras	116
29.1	God The Promise Keeper—Examples	127
30.1	Eight Guidelines for Interpreting Prophecy—Basic Hermeneutics	130
30.2	Two Special Observations on Prophecy—Relating to Fulfillment	133
31.1	Examples of God's Full Backing—Promise of His Presence	138
32.1	Chart—The History Books, Major Content	140
32.1	The Restoration Era Crises And Related Biblical Material	142
32.2	The Restoration Era Crises And Related Biblical Material	143
33.1	Bible Books Related To Chapters of the Redemptive Drama	160
34.1	The Restoration Era Crises And Related Biblical Material	163
35.1	Six Leadership Eras Outlined	166
35.2	Six Leadership Eras in the Bible—Definitive Characteristics	166
35.3	Seven Leadership Genre—Sources for Leadership Findings	167
35.4	Six Leadership Eras in the Bible—Follow-Up Study	173
35.5	Transitions Along the Biblical Leadership Time-Line	176
35.6	Moses' Transition/ Lessons/ Implications	176
35.7	Jesus' Transition/ Lessons/ Implications	177
36.1	Six Characteristics of Spiritual Authority	180

List of Figures

		Page
4.1	11 Common Figures of Speech	39
8.1	The Ministry Time-Line	58
10.1	Haggai's Time-Line for Task of Rebuilding the Temple	66
16.1.	Haggai's Ultimate Contribution Set	84
22.1	3 High Level Leadership Functions	100
23.1	Five Types of Leaders—Sphere of Influence Continuum	103
26.1	Leadership Truth Continuum/ Where Macro Lessons Occur	114
28.1	The Certainty Continuum	122
30.1	3 Types of Prophetic Genre Concerning Jesus Christ	131
33.1	Overview of Redemptive Drama Time Line	147
35.1	Leadership Eras—Approximate Chronological Length In Years	174
35.2	Overview Time Line of Biblical Leadership	174
35.3	Two Major Transitions—The National Transition and The Great Divide	175

Introduction

This leadership commentary on Haggai is part of a series, **Clinton's Leadership Commentary Series.** For the past 11 years I have been researching leadership concepts in the Bible. As a result of that I have identified the 25 most helpful Bible books that contribute to an understanding of leadership. I have done nine of these commentaries to date and am continuing on the rest. I originally published eight of those leadership commentaries in a draft manuscript for use in classes. But it became clear that I would need to break that large work (735 pages) into smaller works. The commentary series does that. Titus was the first in the series. Haggai is the second of the series that is being done as an individual work.

This is a leadership commentary, not an exegetical commentary. That means I have worked with the text to see what implications of leadership are suggested by it. A given commentary in the series is made up of an *Overview Section*, which seeks to analyze the book as a whole for historical background, plan, theme, and fit into the Bible as a whole. In addition, I identify, up front, the basic leadership topics that are dealt with in the book. Then I educe leadership observations, guidelines, principles, and values for each of these leadership topics. This *Overview Section* primes the reader to look with leadership eyes. Then I have the *Commentary Proper*. I use my own translation of the text. I give commentary on various aspects of the text. A given context, paragraph size, will usually have 3 to 4 comments dealing with some suggestions about leadership things.

The *Commentary Proper* suggests *Leadership Concepts* and connects you to leadership articles that further explain these leadership concepts. The emphasis on the comments is not exegetical though I do make those kind of comments when they are helpful for my leadership purposes.

The *Leadership Articles* (in Haggai there are 38 totaling more than 158 pages) in the series carry much of what I have learned about leadership in my 36 years of ministry. In one sense, these articles and others in the series are my legacy. I plan to publish all of the articles of the total series in a separate work, **Clinton's Encyclopedia of Biblical Leadership Insights,** which will be updated periodically as the series expands. I think a leader at almost any level of leadership can be helped greatly by getting leadership perspectives from these articles.

I also include a *Glossary* which lists all the leadership concepts labeled in the comments.

Other books in the series, to be released over the next five years, include:

1,2 Timothy--Apostolic Leadership Picking Up the Mantle
1,2 Corinthians--Problematic Apostolic Leadership
Daniel--A Model Leader in Tough times
Philemon--A Study in Leadership Style
Philippians--A Study in Modeling

John--Jesus' Incarnational Leadership (John)

All of the above were previously done in the large manuscript and used in classes. Now I will break these out as individual commentaries in the series. And then I will do other books anticipated in the series over the next five years. Some of these will be done as I can get to them:

Deuteronomy--A Study in Moses' Inspirational Leadership (Deuteronomy)
Numbers--Moses, Spiritual Authority, and Maintenance Leadership (Numbers)
Mark--Jesus' Power Ministry (Mark)
Luke-Acts--Apostolic Leadership Illustrated (Luke, Acts)
Habbakuk--A Leadership Faith Crisis (Habbakuk)
Jonah--A Study of A Leadership Paradigm Shift (Jonah)
Joshua--Courageous Leadership (Joshua)
Malachi--Renewal Leadership Lessons (Malachi)
Nehemiah--Focused Leadership (Nehemiah)
Mathew--A Study in Leadership Selection and Development (Matthew)
1,2 Samuel--3 Leaders Compared and Contrasted (1,2 Samuel)

I (Bobby) have already done a study of each book in the Bible from a leadership standpoint and have identified and written up a number of leadership topics for each book. This analysis is captured in my book, **The Bible and Leadership Values**.

In an age of relativity, we believe the Bible speaks loudly concerning leadership concepts offering suggestions, guidelines, and even absolutes. We, as Christian leaders, desperately need this leadership help as we seek to influence our followers toward God's purposes for them.

J. Robert Clinton
Mike Hannah
November 2001

Preface

Every Scripture inspired of God is profitable for leadership insights (doctrine), pointing out of leadership errors (reproof), suggesting what to do about leadership errors (correction), for highlighting how to model a righteous life (instruction in righteousness) in order that God's leader (Timothy) may be well equipped to lead God's people (the special good work given in the book Timothy to the young leader Timothy) .
(2 Timothy 3:16,17—Clinton paraphrase--slanted toward Timothy's leadership situation)

The Bible--a Major Source of Leadership Values and Principles

No more wonderful source of leadership values and principles exists than the Bible. It is filled with influential people and the results of their influence--both good and bad. Yet it remains so little used to expose leadership values and principles. What is needed to break this *leadership barrier*? Three things:

1. A conviction that the Bible is authoritative and can give leadership insights;
2. Leadership perspectives to stimulate our findings in the Bible--we are blind in general to leadership ideas and hence do not see them in the Bible;
3. A willful decision to study and use the Bible as a source of leadership insights.

These three assumptions underlie the writing of my leadership commentary series. **Haggai** is one of a series of books intended to help leaders cross the *leadership barrier*.

Leadership Framework

Perhaps it might be helpful to put the notion of leadership insights from Haggai in the bigger picture of leadership in the Bible. Three major leadership elements give us our most general framework (cross-culturally applicable as well) for categorizing leadership insights. The study of leadership involves:

1. **THE LEADERSHIP BASAL ELEMENTS** (The *What* of Leadership)
   a. leaders
   b. followers
   c. situations

2. **LEADERSHIP INFLUENCE MEANS** (The *How* of Leadership)
   a. individual means
   b. corporate means

3. **LEADERSHIP VALUE BASES** (The *Why* of Leadership)
   a. cultural
   b. theological

Preface

It is these elements that enable us to analyze leadership throughout the whole Bible. Using these major notions we recognize that leadership at different times in the Bible operates sufficiently different so as to suggest leadership eras--that is, time periods within which leadership follows more closely certain commonalties than in the time preceding it and following it. This allows us to identify six such eras in the Bible.

Six Bible Leadership Eras

The six leadership eras include,

1. **Patriarchal Era**

2. **Pre-Kingdom Era**
   A. Desert Years
   B. The War Years
   C. The Tribal Years

3. **Kingdom Era**
   A. United Kingdom
   B. Divided Kingdom
   C. Southern Kingdom

4. **Post-Kingdom Era**
   A. Exilic
   B. A Foothold Back in the Land

5. **Pre-Church Era**
6. **Church Era**

For each of these major eras we are dealing with some fundamental leadership questions. We ask ourselves these major questions about every leadership era.[1] Usually the answers are sufficiently diverse as to justify identification of a unique leadership era.

Where does Haggai fit?

The book of Haggai obviously fits in the fourth leadership era, *The Post-Kingdom Era*. In fact, it occurs in part b of that leadership era—*A Foothold Back in the Land*. It is a time of difficulty for leadership. The work of God, which was so glorious at the height of the Kingdom Era was shattered by the exile. This time of restoration seems so small in comparison to that former glorious time. But now God is laying the foundation back in

---

[1]The six questions we use to help us differentiate between leadership eras includes: 1. What is the major leadership focus? 2. What are the influence means used? 3. What are the basic leadership functions? 4. What are the characteristics of the followers? 5. What was the existing cultural forms of leadership? 6. Other? I comment on each of these in the **Clinton's Encyclopedia of Biblical Leadership Insights**.

Preface

the land. And it is a foundation that several hundred years later will result in the coming of Messiah in God's timing.[2] It is the *Times of the Gentiles* referred to by Daniel. Gentile powers are ruling. And God works through them to release his own restoration work back in the land.

What does Haggai say?

Before we can look at leadership insights from Haggai we need to be sure that we understand why Haggai is in the Scriptures and what it is saying in general. Having done our homework, hermeneutically speaking, we are free then to go beyond and look for other interpretative insights--such as leadership insights. But we must remember, always, first of all to interpret in light of the historical times, purpose of, theme of, and structure of the book.

One way of analyzing the structure, that is, the way the author organizes his material to accomplish his purposes would be:

  I.   (ch 1:1-15)   The Task Delayed
  II. (ch 2:1-9)   Discouragement In the Task
  III. (ch 2:10-19)   Patience in the Task
  IV. (ch 2:20-23)   Power for the Task

The overall thematic intent of this short epistle could be represented by a subject, which permeates all of what God is doing through Haggai's leadership. The heart of it is rebuilding the temple and centralizing worship of God through it.

Theme   **God's Work in Rebuilding the Temple** (Under Haggai's Prophetic Impact)
- began when His people back in the land were renewed and reprioritized their lives in response to God's Word,
- initially brought discouragement and was counteracted by God's promise of His presence and blessing as the rebuilders obeyed God's Word,
- continued to be fueled by a God-given vision of what it could be, not what it was, and
- carried with it God affirmation and promise of power to the leadership inspiring this work, in an overwhelming time.

Key words are always helpful in focusing attention on important issues. A number of such key words are repeated in Haggai including: Lord Almighty (13); On the ...day and other time markers (5); house (8); consider (5).

---

[2] Gal 4:4 But when the fullness of time was come, God sent forth His son...This book deals with the earliest foundation of God's work back in the land. It will result in a people in the land to whom Messiah will come.

Preface

It is always difficult to synthesize statements of purpose when the author does not directly and explicitly say them. But it seems reasonable to imply that the following are some of the purposes of this small two-chapter book in the Old Testament.

- to spur the people on to build the temple, the center of hope and inspiration for the returned remnant,
- to give insights on inspirational leadership,
- to show the timeliness and appropriateness of God's revelation to a situation,
- to inspire people of all time to press on in times of discouragement and smallness of the work of God.

General Reflection—Haggai

With this back ground in mind, we can now proceed to the leadership commentary including its *General Reflection*, *Leadership Lessons*, *Commentary notes*, *Articles*, and *Glossary*.

Today, we live in the church leadership era. It is difficult to put ourselves back hundreds of years into the 4th leadership era—Post-Kingdom Leadership. So most modern day pastors and parachurch leaders do not bother to go back and study this period of time in the Bible. A relatively small group of Jewish people have gone back into the land, thanks to Cyrus' decree. God is restoring His work in the land. Why should this relatively unimportant time in Bible history be studied? Let me suggest that four kinds of leaders can profit from the study of Haggai.

1. Leaders who are facing a situation in which the Christian people to whom they are ministering are nominal in their pursuit of Christ and are heavily into secular pursuits?

2. Leaders who are discouraged about getting their followers motivated toward some vision.

3. Leaders who need to know something about how followers react to strong leadership.

4. Leaders who are in small works and are discouraged because they are small.

Further, great leadership lessons are associated with this restoration era that will profit leaders struggling with the complexity of leadership in the Church age. Glance quickly through these leadership topics: importance of team ministry; spiritual authority; gifted power and breakthroughs in ministry; timing of God in ministry; restoration of a sagging work of God; inspirational leadership; vision casting; divine affirmation. We suggest, "Leaders today are in need of these very leadership concepts."

Suggested Approach for Studying Haggai

Read through the overview to get a general feeling of what Haggai is about. Note particularly the *Theme* of the book and its *Plan* for developing that theme, i.e. the outline for developing that theme. Then note the various purposes that we suggest that the book of Haggai is trying to accomplish. Then read through each of the leadership findings that we suggest are in the book. This is all preparation for the first reading of the text.

Read the text itself, both chapters at one sitting, without referring to any of the commentary notes. Just see if you can *see what of the overview information* and the *leadership lessons* are suggested to you as you read the text.

Then reread the text, probably a chapter at a time and note the comments we give.[1] From time-to-time, go back and read a leadership lesson again when it is brought to your mind as you read the text and the commentary. Also feel free to stop and go to the **Glossary** for explanation of leadership terms suggested by the commentary. And do the same thing with the **Articles**. These articles capture what we have learned about leadership over the years as we have observed it, researched it, and taught it. It is these articles that will enlighten your leadership understanding. Obviously because of the unique time in which Haggai ministered there will be some unusual leadership articles.

We have provided some *note space* at the conclusion of the Haggai commentary where you can jot down ideas for future study. Have fun as you work through Haggai, and by all means learn something about *task oriented leadership* and *how a work of God is restored*.

---

[1] From time-to-time in the comments, I will use the abbreviation SRN. SRN stands for Strong's Reference Number. Strong, in his exhaustive concordance, labeled each word in the Old Testament (dominantly Hebrew words but also some Aramaic/ Chaldean) and New Testament (Greek Works mostly) with an identifying number. He then constructed an Old Testament and New Testament lexicon (dictionary). If you have a **Strong's Exhaustive Concordance** with lexicon, you can look up the words I refer to. Many modern day reference works (lexicons and word studies and Bible Dictionaries and encyclopedias) use this Strong's Reference Number.

Overview

BOOK	**HAGGAI** Author: Haggai?[2]
Characters	Haggai, a prophet; Zerubbabel, a governor of Judah; Joshua, high priest;
Who To/For	the actual prophecies were given to Zerubbabel and Joshua, but the written record was for those Jewish exiles who returned to the land to rebuild
Literature Type	narrative record of important revelations from the Lord to Joshua and Zerubbabel and description of responses
Story Line	Zerubbabel had led a group of Jewish people back to Jerusalem upon the issuing of the decree by Cyrus (536 B.C.). They began to settle down and build the temple but had stopped for various reasons: discouragement, resources, and opposition. The time of these prophecies is 16 to 18 years after they had returned. Haggai, a prophet, gets revelation from God, which is used to motivate them to get started on the temple again. The revelation answers all the reasons why the work had been delayed.
Structure	I. (ch 1:1-15) **The Task—Rebuilding the Temple, Delayed** II. (ch 2:1-9) **Discouragement In the Task** III. (ch 2:10-19) **Patience in the Task** IV. (ch 2:20-23) **Power for the Task**
Theme	**God's Work in Rebuilding the Temple** (Under Haggai's Prophetic Impact) • began when His people back in the land were renewed and reprioritized their lives in response to God's Word, • initially brought discouragement and was counteracted by God's promise of His presence and blessing as the rebuilders obeyed God's Word, • continued to be fueled by a God-given vision of what it could be, not what it was, and • carried with it God affirmation and promise of power to the leadership inspiring this work, in an overwhelming time.
Key Words	Lord Almighty (13); On the ...day (time markers, 5), house (8), consider (5)
Key Events	none

---

[2] We are unsure of whether Haggai wrote this or someone else. Some attribute it to Haggai.

Purposes
- to spur the people on to build the temple, the center of hope and inspiration for the returned remnant,
- to give insights on inspirational leadership,
- to show the timeliness and appropriateness of God's revelation to a situation,
- to inspire people of all time to press on in times of discouragement and smallness of the work of God.

Why Important

This book gives valuable insights on inspirational leadership. Stages of reaction by followers to this kind of leadership are illustrated (false satisfaction, false dissatisfaction, false expectation, false fear). Each of these stages is addressed by a timely word from God. Haggai shows the importance of influencing leaders in order to influence the work of God. It also shows how a leader needs to trust God for timely words of intervention. God is continuing to ready Jerusalem for the "fullness of time" and the coming of Messiah. He has not lost sight of that goal even though the people falter.

Where It Fits[3]

Haggai occurs in the Post Exilic phase of era IV. Post-Kingdom Leadership. He is way back at the earliest beginnings of the pre-Messianic period of the Redemptive Drama. It is a time of waiting until the fullness of time was come. It is a time of seeking to rebuild the foundations in the promised land from which Messiah would come.

---

[3] Two frameworks are used to give overall perspective on where a book fits in the totality of the Bible. Framework 1 views the Bible as a whole as a redemptive drama and traces God's working both in what He says and what He does throughout the whole Bible. There is an Introduction, Chapter 1 The Making of a Nation, Chapter 2 The Destruction of a Nation, Chapter 3 Messiah, Chapter 4 The Church, and Chapter 5. Kingdom. Framework 2 views the Bible as a whole in terms of the development of the leadership concept. Six diverse leadership time periods include: 1. Leadership Roots (the patriarchal era); 2. Pre-Kingdom Leadership; 3. Kingdom Leadership; 4. Post-Kingdom Leadership; 5. N.T. Pre-Church Leadership; 6. N.T. Church Leadership. See Articles, *Redemptive Drama, The Biblical Framework*; *Six Biblical Leadership Eras--Approaching the Bible with Leadership Eyes*.

Leadership Lessons

1. TASK ORIENTED LEADERSHIP.

Modern leadership theory has identified three major umbrella-like leadership functions: a. Leaders must move followers to accomplish achievements, that is, there must be an orientation toward task. b. Leaders must provide an environment (community) conducive to accomplishing task. That is, an orientation toward building relationships and a community supportive of God's work. c. Leaders must inspire followers to want to be a part of the endeavor and to accomplish. Normally a given leader is either dominantly a task type leader or a relationship type leader. Rarely is a leader both of these. Either a task leader or a relational leader can inspire. Haggai, a prophetical leader,[4] was a task-oriented leader. His constant thrust was the completion of the task—building of the temple. The book itself is a case study in task-oriented leadership.

Leadership Principles/ Values Suggested by this concept:
  a. A leader who is dominantly a strong task-oriented leader must have supportive leadership to help build the relational aspects of the ministry. Otherwise, many followers will be hurt by the strong leadership and will leave that work of God.
  b. A leader who is dominantly a strong task-oriented leader must have spiritual authority in order to motivate toward the task.
  c. A leader who is dominantly a strong task-oriented leader must have a future perfect orientation in order to motivate toward completion of the task.

See **Articles**, *Leadership Functions, 3 High Level generic Priorities*.

2. INSPIRATIONAL LEADERSHIP.

Haggai, a prophetical leader, was also an inspirational leader. He met each stage of the task, with its discouraging feature, with a positive solution which inspired his followers to rejoin the effort. Of the suggested nine leadership functions of inspirational leadership,[5] the book of Haggai focuses on five of them. But note who of the leadership team (Haggai, Joshua, Zerubbabel, Zechariah) is essentially involved with the function. The five functions seen in the book of Haggai include:

- must motivate followers toward vision (all three but Haggai dominant).
- must encourage perseverance and faith of followers (Haggai dominant).
- are responsible for the financial welfare of the effort (Zerubbabel dominant, implied).
- are responsible for direct ministry along lines of giftedness, which relate to inspirational functions (Haggai dominant; prophetic gift/received revelation).

---

[4] Prophetical leaders, like Haggai, because of their strong corrective bent frequently are task oriented leaders and need real help in relational leading. Haggai got that help through a leadership coalition.

[5] See **Leadership Perspectives**, chapter 1 for the functions listed for task oriented leadership, relationally oriented leadership and inspirationally oriented leadership.

- must model (knowing, being, and doing) so as to inspire followers toward the reality of God's intervention in lives. (Haggai dominant but Joshua very supportive in this).

Note some of the details of this inspirational leadership. In response to the people's obedience and as part of this renewing, God stirs up the spirit of the people. This stirring begins with the leaders (at least in the order mentioned in verse 14) and extends to all the people.

> Haggai 1:14 So the Lord stirred up the spirit of Zerubbabel son of Shealtiel, governor of Judah, and the spirit of Joshua son of Jehozadak, the high priest, and the spirit of the whole remnant of the people. They came and began to work on the house of the Lord Almighty, their God,

Leaders can expect God to stir the hearts of others to join in the task. God speaks to the mind, but He also moves the spirit. This is one form of guidance that God will use to direct people to take part in a project. This principle occurs in other parts of Scripture as well.[6] God is in the business of moving people's hearts. Consider this, if your ministry project does not stir people's hearts, you better reconsider whether God is in it or not.

Leadership Principles/ Values Suggested by this concept:
a. Inspirational leadership is complex and will usually require a range of giftedness not residing in only one leader.
b. The heart of inspirational leadership is the final function—motivating followers to see the hand of God in their situation. The recognition of the reality of God's intervention in a situation is the essential ingredient of restoration.
c. When leading a God-given project in God's timing, expect Got to stir up people to assist. The assistance may take the form of direct work, or indirect support—finances, prayer, etc.

See **Articles**, *Leadership Functions, 3 High Level generic Priorities; Haggai—Task Oriented Inspirational Leadership (motivational principles).*

3. TEAM MINISTRY.

Not being a relational leader, Haggai needed a team. God brought together Zerubbabel, a political leader and Joshua, a Priest. Although only one person's name appears in the title of the book, the task undertaken was not a lone ranger operation. God assembled a team of people to accomplish this task. The two point people for the project appear to be Zerubbabel, the political leader and Joshua, the High priest. Haggai plays a supportive, catalytic role. It appears from the text that Zerubbabel was the primary leader.

---

[6] In 1 Samuel 10:26, we see the newly anointed King Saul "accompanied by valiant men whose hearts God had touched". In a related book Ezra (related to Haggai), we see that "everyone whose heart God had moved--prepared to go up and build the house of the Lord in Jerusalem" (Ezra 1:5). All the way back in Exodus, we see God stirring hearts, "everyone who was willing and whose heart moved him came and brought an offering to the Lord for the work on the Tent of Meeting, for all its service, and for the sacred garments." (Exodus 35:21).

Haggai—Leadership Lessons   page 7

We say this for two reasons. 1) He is always mentioned first (before Joshua) and 2) At the end of the book he alone is recognized in a special way and receives the special promise from God. See also the book of Zechariah, where we see that Zechariah, a contemporary of Haggai, backs these two leaders, and again Zerubbabel is featured.

Leadership Principles/ Values Suggested by this concept:
   a. Expect God to strategically assemble synergistic ministry teams to accomplish significant projects.
   b. An inspirational leader, who is restoring a work of God, ought to concentrate first on inspiring supportive leaders to that work, and then the rank and file followers.
   c. A balance of leadership will be needed to move a people of God—on-going religious leadership, charismatic religious leadership, and civil leadership—to restore a work of God.

See **Articles**, *Haggai—Coalition Leadership; Civil Leadership—The Missing Ingredient.*

4. INFLUENCE MEANS—INTERVENTION OF CHARISMATIC LEADERSHIP.

Leaders often need help to jumpstart a project. The inference from this passage is that Zerubbabel and Joshua were trying to get the building project moving, but the people were resistant. The people did not reject the importance of the project, just the timing ("the time has not yet come"). They didn't see themselves as disobedient, they just kept postponing obedience. The situation came to a stalemate. Something was needed to break things open. That something came in the form of prophetic intervention from God.

Haggai arrives on the scene and stirs things up. God addresses the excuses head on. He points out the price they are paying by delaying – drought, famine, leanness. He then offers an opportunity to turn things around by turning toward Him and beginning work on his house. God uses Haggai, not just to get things started, but also to keep them going. At strategic times through the process, Haggai steps in and offers hope, encouragement, blessing.

Haggai did not have positional political authority, like Zerubbabel, or religious priestly authority, like Joshua. His major means of influence was charismatic (dint of strong personality) and spiritual authority. He dominantly acted with gifted power—getting an authoritative word and then applying it to the situation. In his first leadership act (1:2-11) he overcame the excuses that were given about building the temple (there had been a delay of almost 16 years). His authoritative word gave a divine perspective on what was happening to them economically and why. It was a word with spiritual authority (1:12 ...people obeyed the voice of the Lord their God and the message of the prophet Haggai, because the Lord their God had sent him. And the people feared the Lord).

This same pattern of influence means prevails throughout all the stages. Haggai is able by a word from God to head off the excuses at each stage and to inspire both the people and the team leaders.

Leadership Principles/ Values Suggested by this concept:
   a. Leaders doing God's work ought to see the need for and expect powerful interventions to jumpstart ministry projects and reenergize stalled ones.
   b. Prophetic ministry and other forms of gifted power frequently can offer the impact needed to provide breakthroughs in ministry.

See **Articles**, *Haggai—Task Oriented Inspirational Leadership (motivational principles)*.

5. TIMING

A macro lesson seen early on in the first leadership era, The Patriarchal Leadership Era, and then repeated in other eras is powerfully emphasized in the book of Haggai. And that is the timing macro lesson. *God's timing is crucial to the accomplishment of God's purposes*. The issue of timing is crucial in accomplishing God's work, the right project at the wrong time can add up to trouble. Scripture is full of references of people who get ahead of God.

In Haggai we find an example of people who fall behind. God is ready to go but the people say "not now." In Haggai 1:3 God says, "These people say, 'The time has not yet come for the Lord's house to be built.' " They believe it's something that needs to be done, just not right away. Their reply, "The time has not yet come". What they were waiting for? What would have been the sign that now is the time? Their statement has the tone of someone who has surveyed the situation and come to the official conclusion that now is not the time for this to happen. Through Haggai, God challenges their time table and, not just their time table, but the underlying priorities that result in their contention that "now's not a good time".

Leadership Principles/ Values Suggested by this concept:
   a. Leaders must discern God's timing for a project. This may mean slowing down or speeding up the workers and the work.
   b. Followers often do not have a correct perspective on timing.
   c. Followers tend to fall behind in the timing of God. Strong directive leaders tend to move ahead of the timing of God. Both need corrective perspective. Frequently, this can only come via revelatory ministry.

See **Articles**, *Macro Lesson Defined; Macro Lessons—List of 41 Across Six Leadership Eras*.

6. THE RENEWAL FACTOR IN RECRUITMENT

God addresses the lack of interest in the building project not as a recruitment problem, but as a priority problem. God doesn't send Haggai to do a talk about using spiritual gifts in ministry, God calls the people to put him first. At the heart of the problem is a heart problem. People got so busy rebuilding their own lives they moved God to the back burner. Haggai calls people to put God first. The result is people are stirred to serve. The goal is not for each person to "do their part," but for each person to honor God. God calls people to build: "so that I may take pleasure in it and be honored

(Haggai 1:8)." When people reprioritize and reconnect with God, the overflow is involvement in service. All things begin equal we see renewal first – recruitment second.

Leadership Principles/ Values Suggested by this concept:
 a. When people reprioritize and reconnect with God, the overflow is often involvement in service. Do not underestimate the power of renewal in recruitment.
 b. A priority that puts God in first place is always needed in order to bring restoration into a work of God.

See *recruitment*, **Glossary**.

7. RESTORING A WORK OF GOD—4 STAGES

This particular task, rebuilding the temple, had four stages to it as the work unfolded:

(1) The Task Delayed—Getting the Task initiated; timing is critical. Haggai overcame the inertial lag with a strong authoritative word from God. It will often take gifted power to break through and get the task oriented.

(2) Discouragement—after initial momentum, enthusiasm usually wanes, some excuses for pulling back occur. The leader must then re-fire up the people. In this case, the work seemed so small and puny (especially compared to the temple that had once been there). Haggai's answer from God is simple. God reaffirms that it is not the size of a work of God that makes it important but the presence of the living God in it. And He strongly promises that His presence will be there and will accomplish the great things He wants through it. The people again responded.

(3) Patience in the Task—having been promised that God would be in this the people immediately look for His blessing. They do not see it and hence could easily become discouraged. Haggai gets a word from God which says blessings will come but are basically conditioned on obedient response. The people again respond.

(4) Power for the Task—finally the real issue arises, the need for God's power and protection. Haggai again gets a word from God and convinces the followers of God's provision of power and protection. Frequently, tasks will pattern themselves like this. The major lesson to see is that gifted power is needed to answer objections. Objections will come at each stage. Spiritual authority is needed to convince and overcome. Complementary functions (in this case relational leading) are often needed. It is probably significant that Haggai headed off each of the objections before they were full bloom. He in fact identified the objection for the people (similar to word of knowledge used today in some charismatic circles). Further, it should be noted that commitment all along the 4 stages was based on *careful thought* not emotional stirrings. In long-term projects, which are labor-intensive, time intensive, and money intensive, leaders should call for commitment based on "careful thought" not emotional stirrings. Note also Haggai's appeal to the followers was primarily on a basis of God-honoring obedience.

Leadership Principles/ Values Suggested by this concept:
a. When people reprioritize and reconnect with God, the overflow is often involvement in service. Do not underestimate the power of renewal in recruitment.
b. Leaders should base calls to commitment on careful reasoned thought rather than emotional appeals.
c. Leaders should expect various follower reactions to a task and counter them early with an authoritative Word from God.

See *restoration (corporate)*, **Glossary**. See **Article**, *Restoration Leaders*.

8. DIVINE AFFIRMATION—AN ESSENTIAL FOR ONGOING LEADERSHIP

All leaders need affirmation from God in their ministry. Haggai gives a special message from God to the point person on the team—Zerubbabel.

> Haggai 2:23 " 'On that day,' declares the Lord Almighty, 'I will take you, my servant Zerubbabel son of Shealtiel,' declares the Lord, 'and I will make you like my signet ring, for I have chosen you,' declares the Lord Almighty."

Four types of affirmation are embedded in this climactic ending of the book. (1) God affirms Zerubbabel's **obedience**. God calls Zerubbabel His "servant." A servant is someone who obeys, and Zerubbabel had been obedient in his God-given role of leadership. (2) God's affirmation of Zerubbabel's **future role** in God's plan – "I will take you" and "I will make you". This points to future plans that God has for Zerubbabel. Zerubbabel was faithful in his task, and now he will be used in even a greater way. This is a form of the Luke 16:10 principle: when we're faithful in small things, often we're given bigger things. God's promise to "take" and "make" Zerubbabel points to God's future shaping and development in his life. God has a hope and a future for His faithful servant. (3) God's affirmation of Zerubbabel as one with **authority and approval**. God promises to make Zerubbabel like His signet ring. This speaks of authority, God's instrument of authority, bearing God's approval – someone who is backed by God's power, authority and position. (4) God's affirmation of His **sovereign selection** of Zerubbabel, "I have chosen you". What an encouraging thing to know that you are hand-selected by God. Leaders need to know that God has called and placed them in ministry. During tough times, it is helpful to be reminded that this whole leadership thing is God's idea. And if God has chosen a leader, we can look with faith that He will support that leader. For Zerubbabel this must have been a destiny incident in his life. It was a powerful motivating benchmark for his leadership.

Leadership Principles/ Values Suggested by this concept:
a. Leaders should expect sovereign times of divine affirmation.
b. Leaders need to be reminded of their place and importance in God's plan.
c. God's sovereign affirmations bring hope for the future.

d. To combat discouragement, leaders must seek personal strengthening that comes from experiencing divine affirmation and the personal application of the promises of God.
   e. Leaders who ride point on difficult projects ought to seek special encouragement from God.

See *divine affirmation*, Glossary. See Article, *Divine Affirmation in the Life of Jesus.*

9. EMPOWERING PRESENCE OF GOD

An important macro lesson identified in the first leadership era and seen throughout all eras is,

> The essential ingredient of leadership is the powerful presence of God in the life and ministry of a leader.

God affirms that notion very forcefully in this book of Haggai. At a point of discouragement, God supernaturally encourages and empowers both the leaders and the followers.

> Haggai 2:4 "But now be strong, O Zerubbabel," declares the Lord. "Be strong, O Joshua son of Jehozadak, the high priest. Be strong, all you people of the land," declares the Lord, "and work. For I am with you."

God doesn't give one general, "be strong," to the entire group. He says it three times: first to Zerubbabel, second to Joshua, and third to all the people. It's as if God is going around the table and personally strengthening each person. People need to know that the promises of God are more than general wishes, they apply personally to people. God's Word needs to hit home in the heart. God's three-fold charge to "be strong" leaves the listeners with the feeling that God is speaking directly to them.

Notice that God singles out the two leaders, Zerubbabel and Joshua, for personal attention. They are ones who are carrying the burden of this project. As leaders, they need special encouragement. This reminds them that God knows them by name and that God is for them.

After the charge to "be strong", He sends a reminder of His presence – "I am with you". This is one of the most powerful statements in Scripture. Leaders need to know that God is with them. Remember that important macro lesson—*the essential ingredient of leadership is the powerful presence of God in the life and ministry of the leader.* There are many things we can do without in ministry—but God's empowering presence is not one of them. During tough times, an affirmation of God's presence diminishes the doubts and fans into flame our faith.

Haggai—Leadership Lessons

Leadership Principles/ Values Suggested by this concept:
a. To combat discouragement, leaders must seek personal strengthening that comes from experiencing divine affirmation and the personal application of the promises of God.
b. Leaders who ride point on difficult projects must seek special encouragement from God.
c. Before engaging in any major project, a leader ought to receive confirmation that God is in the project. Like Moses, the prayer of a leader should be, "If your Presence does not go with us, do not send us up from here." (Exodus 33:15)

See **Article**, *Macro Lesson Defined; Haggai—And Spiritual Authority*.

10. WORK OF GOD

No work of God, if initiated by Him is small (2:1-9). And any work of God will require His power and presence in it. And the promise of His presence is enough. We cannot judge the significance of our efforts whether small or big. God will work through it and bless it according to His purposes. It is enough for us to know that God has called us and He will empower us and will use the work for His purposes. Note Haggai's approach to this. He deals directly with the discouragement due to the smallness of the work. Then instead of focusing on what is (in their mind – nothing), he focuses the people on what can be. He casts a vision of what the temple will become. They were looking at a pile of rubble, but God helps them see a temple filled with the glory of the Lord – people from all over the world coming to worship. This is future perfect thinking. For those old timers who longed for the past, he even gives a special encouragement at the end of verse 9 by promising them that the glory of this present temple will be greater than the former.

Leadership Principles/ Values Suggested by this concept:
a. During times of small beginnings, leaders must cast a compelling picture of the finished project.
b. During times of small beginnings, leaders should find encouragement not by what is, but by what can be.
c. Leaders should provide *big-picture-meaning* to people's individual efforts. Vision casting provides the meaningfulness of ministry.

See **Article**, *Haggai—Discouragement, Small Work of God*.

Haggai

CLINTON'S BIBLICAL LEADERSHIP COMMENTARY SERIES

**Restoring A Work of God
Inspirational, Task-Oriented Leadership**

Verse By Verse Commentary

I. (ch 1:1-15) The Task—Rebuilding the Temple, Delayed

1 On the first day of the sixth month in the second year[1] of King Darius,[2] Haggai the prophet[3] received a Word from the Lord.[4] It was a Word to be given to Governor Zerubbabel, the son of Shealtiel, and to Joshua the high priest, the son of Josedech.[5]

---

[1] The year is 520 B.C., approximately 18 years after Cyrus had let the first group of Israelites to return to Jerusalem. Note the detailed timing indicated (first day of the sixth month). Other timing indicators let us pinpoint when Haggai gives his several encouraging revelatory words from God. The messages of Haggai were given during a four-month period. See **Article**, *Haggai—And Timing; Prophetic Crises, Three Major; Haggai—Calendar and Dating; God's Timing and Leadership*.

[2] Darius the Great became king of Persia in 522B.C. (See Ezr 4:1-5,24). Darius was interested in the religions of people in his empire and encouraged their religious efforts. Haggai and Zechariah began to preach in his second year, 520 B.C. Darius fully supported the Jews in their religious restoration. See **Article**, *Left Hand of God*.

[3] There were two prophets operating during this time—Haggai and Zechariah. Of the two Haggai seems to be the practical one—urging the completion of the task. Zechariah was the more mystical of the two—getting revelation in terms of apocalyptic visions. Both encouraged the work of God through Zerubbabel and Joshua. Haggai does not appear to hit spiritual warfare head on as Zechariah does. See *Restoration Leaders*, **Glossary**. See **Article**, *Restoration Leaders; Civil Leadership—The Missing Ingredient; Getting the Job Done—Comparison of Ezra's and Haggai's Roles; Haggai—Spiritual Warfare*.

[4] Haggai receives revelatory information concerning the situation four times. See 1:1, 2:1, 2:10 and 2:20. His information speaks to the situation in terms of what people are thinking, feeling, and what God says about their thoughts and feelings. See **Article**, *Prophetic Authority*.

[5] Notice the first word is given to two specific leaders, not the people as a whole. It is through these leaders that God will work. There is actually a group of leaders, which includes Haggai and Zechariah (outsiders to the actual recognized leadership) and Zerubbabel, and Joshua (the recognized leaders). At strategic times in ministry a leader should expect God to speak in ways that are needed to see the ministry move forward. Sometimes God will speak directly to the recognized leader(s). At other times, as in the case of Haggai, through some outside influence. God sent Haggai along at a divinely appointed time. Things break open. Notice the interesting team of people God assembles to lead this building project. Joshua held a spiritual office. Zerubbabel held a civil office. Haggai operated without office but with spiritual authority. Haggai doesn't appear to have any supervisory role in the project. He came along side of Zerubbabel and Joshua to provide catalytic prophetic input. See **Article**, *Haggai—Leadership Coalition; Civil Leadership, the Missing Ingredient; Restoration Leaders*.

Haggai 1:2-4

2 The Lord Almighty[1] warns, "Your people are saying, that this isn't the right time[2] to rebuild the Lord's temple."[3]

3 Then came the Word of the Lord by Haggai the prophet, saying, 4 "Is it right for you[4] to have nice expensive homes[5] while my temple lies in ruins?[6]

---

[1] See Haggai 1:2, 5, 7, 9; 2:4, 6, 8, 9, 11, 23 (twice). *Lord Almighty* is Haggai's favorite name for God. See also Isaiah 13:4 where the title for God, *Lord Almighty*, is further clarified with the phrase *mustering an army for war*. The Hebrew for army (SRN 6635) is the singular form of the word for Almighty. The NIV study Bible captures it well. "God is the head of the armies of Israel (1Sa 17:45), of angelic powers (1Ki 22:19; Lk 2:13)" and in the Isaiah passage of the armies that will destroy Babylon as predicted also by Habakkuk. The Contemporary English Version (CEV) translates *Lord Almighty* by the title, *Lord All Powerful*. Note the special significance of this title, *Lord Almighty*. It is dominantly a *captivity title* for God. It occurs 23 times referring to God's activity prior to captivity times. It occurs 211 times with reference to God's captivity activity. God frequently reveals Himself in terms of who He needs to be for His people in terms of their situation and their need. See **Article**, *Lord of Hosts*.

[2] *Time* (SRN 6256) is also translated *season*. Notice carefully again. The people are not saying that this is a wrong project, just the wrong time. This group has returned from captivity, basically with just what they could carry. They are into rebuilding homes, rebuilding businesses, and rebuilding their lives. When things settle down they will turn their attention to building God's house. But a good time never comes. So a prophetic challenge is needed. See **Article**—*Haggai and Timing; Haggai—Delaying God's Work*.

[3] "Your people are saying." God immediately addresses the same kinds of rationalizing excuses that Joshua and Zerubbabel were themselves hearing. Sometimes leaders feel like, "God, do you hear what these people are saying?" In this case, God shows that He does. God is letting these two leaders know that He is fully aware of what they are up against.

[4] That is, is it time for you to build nice homes? Vs 4 powerfully compares, the people's excuse of no time for God's house with their efforts for their own homes. Notice the contrast in the description of their houses as paneled, while God's house is in ruinsSee **Article**, *Haggai—Materialism, Getting Sidetracked*.

[5] The KJV uses ceiled (paneled) houses. *Cieled* (SRN 5603) indicates a more lavish finish. This is contrasted with the rubble of the temple.

[6] *Ruin* (SRN 2720) means a *waste* or *desolate*. The fact that 18-20 years later the temple site is still in *ruins* while the people are living in paneled houses, shows the priority of public worship among these people—after all this time there is still no temple. In captivity, they had no temple. Perhaps they just got used to not having a temple, so that lack of a central place for worship was no longer a priority for some.

Haggai 1:5-8

5 This is the Lord Almighty talking. Give careful thought. Consider what is happening to you.[1] 6 You plant a lot but reap very little. You don't have enough to eat or drink. You don't have enough clothing to keep you warm. What you earn isn't enough to meet your needs."[2]

7 This is the Lord Almighty talking. Have you thought why this is so? Think about it. 8 Get up to the mountain and get wood.[3] Rebuild my temple. Then I will be pleased and will be recognized for who I am.[4]

---

[1] "Give careful thought," is repeated in Haggai. It comes from two Hebrew words—*fix or direct* (SRN 7760) and *take to heart* (SRN 3824). It is often used to refer to one's inner life. God is saying, "Sit down and think about this deeply. Search your hearts."

[2] In vs 5-6, God put into words the very frustrations that these people had been experiencing. Life was not working out like they thought. They never had enough. They were never happy. As the people listened to the prophecy of vs 5-6. They may have been nodding in agreement, "That's right! That's exactly what life has been like these last years. We don't have enough money, no matter how hard we work. We don't have enough food." These may well be the very excuses given for not getting started on the construction of God's house. Things were tight. Life was hard. There was famine, poverty, and hunger. And money was going out faster than it came in. I have captured the figurative language—*purses with holes in them* by the phrase, *what you earn isn't enough to meet your needs*. In the verses which follow, they will soon find out these tough times were the result of neglecting God's house. See *capture*, **Glossary**. See **Article**, *Figures and Idioms in the Bible*.

[3] Notice that vs 8 is an action step—it calls for a specific response. The goal of this opening prophecy is not simply to create guilt—it's to motivate to action. God gives them a step of obedience—a starting point. This step of obedience is accompanied by the possibility of pleasing and honoring God.

[4] Literally, "take pleasure in it and be honored." The motivation for change is a call to please and honor God. Honored connotes being *recognized for who I am*. Notice there are two dynamics in this text. God is using both negative experiences and a positive call. God has lit a fire under them with the famine. He brings their *unhappiness* factor up to a motivating boil. He then extends an upward call to please and honor God. In calling them to obedience, God's appeal is not "Go up into the mountains and bring down timber and build the house, so that I may remove the famine," but "so that I may be pleased and honored." It's a higher calling. One task of a leader is to call people to please and honor God. The word *pleasure* (SRN 07521) is a word that speaks of delighting. In the KJV, it is most often translated *accept*. It also is translated *approve* and *affection*. It is a word picture of pleasing God in ways that finds His acceptance, His approval and His affection. This is a powerful motivation for the person who has a heart for God.

Haggai 1:9-11

9 You expected[1] rich harvests but instead got poor ones.[2] And then when you brought these small harvests home, I blew them away. You know why? My temple is in ruins.[3] Let me remind you again who is telling you this--the Lord Almighty. You are busily[4] building your own fine places.[5] 10 That is why there is no rain and the crops are poor. 11 I have caused this drought. I have caused the crops to be poor. The drought has affected your new wine, your olive oil, your cattle, and everything you have worked so hard to get.[6] All of you have been affected.[7]

---

[1] Unmet expectations can be a powerful motivating force. God often creates dissatisfaction with existing conditions to make us uncomfortable enough to change. This is a form of negative processing. See *negative processing*, **Glossary**.

[2] Vs 9 –sums up and reiterates the *not enough* dynamic of verses 5-8. He says "You expected much, but see, it turned out to be little." This lack wasn't an accident—God *blew* it away. This is a strong complex metaphor. It is referring to the winnowing process with grain. The wind takes away the chaff. God has been bringing judgment on them by taking away the rich harvests they wanted. Leaders must help people see what God is doing in life's circumstances. Here is a picture of people working hard to make a better life. But their prosperity is out of reach. The harder they try, the less they seem to have. And God is in it. And it is because they are prioritizing their own materialistic desires ahead of obedience to God.

[3] Notice the contrast between my house, and your houses. There is a distinction between what God was concerned about, and what they were concerned about. God wasn't helping them build their houses, because they were not helping to build God's house. When followers don't include God in their worlds, then their problems really do become their problems.

[4] This word *busily* means to run around (SRN 7323). They are scrambling around trying to hold life together, but neglecting the one thing that was needed.

[5] In vs 9 God tells them *why*. "Because of my house, which remains a ruin, while each of you is busy with his own house." This is a classic challenge through out the Bible – the challenge to put God first. In this case, everybody loses – God's house loses – it remains in ruins, the people lose because all their work comes to nothing. The word *house* at the end of verse 9 is probably speaking of more than physical houses—their houses were already *paneled*. Instead, it is probably a metonomy standing for household and their life including making a life and making a living. See *figurative language, metonymy*, **Glossary**. See **Article**, *Figures and Idioms in the Bible*.

[6] In verse 10-11, God shows the severity of the problem. Their disobedience has shut up the floodgates of heavens. This seems almost the opposite of Malachi 4, where generous giving resulted in financial floodgates being opened. This connection between generosity and drought is taught in both of these post-exilic books. Malachi, like Haggai, is a call to put God first, a call to give God the first and best, not the leftovers.

[7] In Deuteronomy 28 we have a description of the blessings that will follow obedience to God, look at Deuteronomy 28:8 "The Lord will send a blessing on your barns and on everything you put your hand to. The Lord your God will bless you in the land he is giving you." Through disobedience, they of course were experiencing the reversal of this.

Haggai 1:12-14

12 Then Zerubbabel the son of Shealtiel, and Joshua the son of Josedech, the high priest, with all the remnant of the people, obeyed the voice of the LORD their God. They responded to Haggai's prophetic words. They recognized that the LORD their God had sent him.[1] The people feared the Lord.[2]

13 Haggai then gave this Word from the Lord. "I am with you!"[3]

14 Governor Zerubbabel was really fired up.[4] So was Joshua, the high priest. And the people themselves were highly motivated to do the work.[5] They came and began to seriously rebuild the house of

---

[1] Notice the interesting language in verse 12 "whole remnant of the people obeyed the voice of the Lord their God and the message of the prophet Haggai, because the Lord their God had sent him. And the people feared the Lord." Haggai, had no title, no position, no history, but He did have a word from God. It's interesting that the people recognized that God was speaking through Haggai. Historically, listening to prophets was not always the case. Probably, what helped, was that the leaders obeyed first. God confirmed this prophecy by a witness in the hearts of the hearers. There is an outward call to obedience and then an inward response of the people to obey. This is then followed by an inward stirring of the spirit by God. See *spiritual authority*, **Glossary**. See **Article**, *Haggai—And Spiritual Authority*; *Spiritual Authority Defined, Six Characteristics*.

[2] *Feared* (SRN 3372) is a word containing both the English notion of fear (to be afraid) and also the notion of have an awe and respect for. These people had a responsive heart to hear God's word. Their response is similar to that which God is looking for in Isaiah 66:2 "This is the one I esteem: the one who is humble and contrite in spirit, and trembles at my word." Trembles at my word—that is, fearfully respects me and obeys.

[3] Verse 13 has a short, but very powerful statement. "I am with you." Here is the powerful promise of God's presence. Notice that even after the people's initial obedient response, God graciously confirms that small step of obedience—by a promise of His presence. Remember the crucial macro lesson, *The essential ingredient to leadership is the powerful presence of God in the life and ministry of that leader*. This is true of a leader. It is also true of a corporate group representing God. *The essential ingredient to success in a ministry project is the powerful presence of God in that project*. If God is not in it—neither should leaders and followers be in it. One of the most powerful motivators for a ministry task is to know that God is in it. This one phrase alone can launch an army into the purposes of God. See **Article**, *Macro Lessons, Defined*.

[4] Note the translation, *really fired up* which literally means an emotional *stirring* (SRN 5782). It means to wake up, to lift up, arouse, to incite, to excite. When God moves in people's hearts, that's when they start getting excited. Notice that the excitement was the result of a willful decision to obey. Note the result—the emotional excitement (stirring) followed a *carefully thought through* decision—"Give careful thought." For more on this, see leadership lesson 6, **The Renewal Factor in Recruitment**.

[5] God stirs up both the leaders and the followers. Sometimes a leader is excited about a project but the followers are not. But the best situation is when everybody is excited about what God is doing. This is another mark of a God-driven project—God rallies the troops.

Haggai 1:15-2:4   page 19

the Lord Almighty.[1] 15 This occurred in the second year of Darius's reign, on the 24th day of the sixth month.[2]

II. (ch 2:1-9)   Discouragement In the Task

1 On the twentieth day of the seventh month.[3] God gave another Word to the prophet Haggai.[4] 2 "Speak to Governor Zerubbabel,[5] the son of Shealtiel, and to Joshua the high priest, the son of Josedech and to the remnant of the people who have come back to the land. 3 Ask the following questions.[6] "Do any of you remember how splendid Solomon's Temple really was?[7] And now look at what you are building? Not much, is it?"[8] 4 But don't be discouraged. Be strong, Zerubbabel. Be strong, Joshua. Be strong all you

---

[1] The proof of repentance is the fruit. In this case the people followed through on their commitment and began to work.

[2] It took twenty-three days from the first prophecy, until work began. After taking time to give *careful thought*, they began to work relatively quickly. This verse, like the next (Haggai 2:1) is one of the time markers in Haggai. See **Article**, *Haggai—And Timing*.

[3] This further prophecy comes about a month after the work begins, and close to two months after the original prophecy. See **Article**, *Haggai—And Timing*.

[4] As noted earlier, Haggai, doesn't appear to have a direct leadership role in the project, He came along side of Zerubbabel and Joshua to provide catalytic prophetic input.

[5] Notice the order throughout this book. The Lord speaks first to the leaders, then to the people. In this case, he particularly, singles out one leader—probably the point leader in the project, Zerubbabel. Although Joshua is important, we can tell by the final context of this book that Zerubbabel plays the lead role.

[6] God likes questions—notice in verse three that He asks three questions. Sometimes the best way to address an issue is do it through questions, not statements, not proclamations. Here is a leadership observation based on God's method here. *As a leader, sometimes the best way to drive home a point is to draw it out.* See *figurative language; rhetorical question*, **Glossary**. See **Article**, *Figures and Idioms in the Bible*.

[7] These would be very old persons, indeed. Some think that Haggai himself was one of them. Respect for Haggai's word was rooted in his long walk with God. It's hard not to compare the present with the past. Here God addresses those who were longing for the *good old days*. There may be times when older leaders need special encouragement by God to throw in their hand and work with the new generation toward a new work of God. See **Article**, *Profiting From the Past*.

[8] God asks them a question, but before they get a chance to answer, God gives them His opinion. God Himself initiates the comment "Not much, is it?" God is speaking out loud what is on the older leaders' minds. God anticipates what everyone is thinking. A leader needs to anticipate questions and address them head on. A leader needs a finger on the pulse of the people. Are we doing well? Are we discouraged? In this case God deals with the discouragement head on. Ignoring problems seldom helps. The new project looks like *nothing*. Imagine the discouragement—they had been at work on the project for close to a month and they feel that *nothing* has been accomplished. So there are two issues here. Some would wish for the past. Others would look at the present and experience real discouragement. See **Article**, *Haggai—Afterglow Ministry; Haggai, Dealing with Discouraged Followers; Discouragement, Small Work of God*.

Haggai 2:5-6

people.[1] Rebuild this temple! For I, the Lord Almighty,[2] am with you.[3] 5 I made a covenant with you long ago when you came out of Egypt.[4] And I am still with you. So don't be afraid or discouraged.[5]

6 I the Lord Almighty am going to shake[6] the heavens, and the earth—land and sea.

---

[1] How do you as a leader deal with discouragement? God sees that some encouragement is needed – He charges the two main leaders and the group to be strong. Do the work! And there is the accompanying promise, "I will be with you!" This is the second time so far in the book in which God says this. Notice how God singles out the leaders with His charge to *be strong*. Leaders who carry the burden of a ministry project need personal encouragement from the Lord. God doesn't give one sweeping, *be strong*, to the entire group. He says it three times: first to Zerubbabel, second to Joshua, and thirdly to all the people. It's as if God is going around the table and personally strengthening each person. That personal encouragement from God is crucial during tough times and difficult assignments. Notice that God addresses both the *being* and the *doing*. God addresses the *being* in His charge to *be strong*. That is an inward attitude thing, a being component. God addresses the *doing* in his charge to *work*. Both being and doing are important to a leader, especially one involved in a task-oriented inspirational project. Here God gives strength not just for personal affirmation but to spur accomplishing His purposes. The *be strong* is not just to help them feel good. It is also to help them do good.

[2] The Lord Almighty–Haggai's name for God—is still powerful. What He did in Egypt, He can repeat here for these exiles who have returned.

[3] Here again is this powerful promise of His presence. When engaged in ministry, you can't hear this too often. God reminds them that His presence with them is based on a promise. In spite of present discouragements, leaders can always count on God's promises. Leaders must know God as the Promise Keeper. What God promises He will keep. Note again the most important macro lesson in the O.T. *The essential ingredient of leadership is the powerful presence of God in the life and ministry of a leader*. See **Article**, *Macro Lessons, Defined; God The Promise Keeper*; *Promises of God*.

[4] God brought them out of Egypt. God brought them out of captivity a second time, this time from Babylon. This captivity was fresh enough on their minds. This reference to Egypt, reminded them of God's power and faithfulness. An implication for this project is that God is powerful enough to finish what He starts. Some listeners may have remembered the prophecy from Jeremiah, before the Babylonian captivity, that deliverance would come. Jer 16:14 "However, the days are coming," declares the Lord, "when men will no longer say, 'As surely as the Lord lives, who brought the Israelites up out of Egypt,' 15 but they will say, 'As surely as the Lord lives, who brought the Israelites up out of the land of the north and out of all the countries where he had banished them.' For I will restore them to the land I gave their forefathers." See **Article**, *God The Promise Keeper*.

[5] This is a powerful comment, "So don't be afraid or discouraged!" What might these people have feared? That God would abandon them, that they would not be able to accomplish the task, that this *nothing* project was a waste of time, that the rubble was overwhelming and the workers and resources few. This was a reminder to let faith, not fear dominate their hearts.

[6] The *Lord Almighty*, Haggai's name for God, is powerful enough to shake nations.

Haggai 2:7-9

7 And I will shake all nations and their treasure will be brought here. And this temple shall be filled with wealth. 8 All the silver and the gold of the world belongs to me, [1] the Lord Almighty. 9 This new temple shall be better than Solomon's temple[2] for my glory will be seen in it.[3] And I, the Lord Almighty,[4] will bring peace[5] to my people.[6]

---

[1] "All the silver and the gold of the world belongs to me." The *Lord Almighty* is able to provide any resources needed to accomplish His purposes. This reminds us that financially, God is in control. God actually does move on the hearts of foreign kings to provide for this building project. In their recent past, these followers have seen that. First Cyrus, King of Persia, aided them financially.

> Ezr 1:3 "In the first year of Cyrus king of Persia, issues a decree to provide him (the remnant returning to Jerusalem) with **silver** and **gold**, with goods and livestock, and with freewill offerings for the temple of God in Jerusalem." Later Artaxerxes, king of Persia, will provide resources for the building the temple. Ezr 7:19 Deliver to the God of Jerusalem all the articles entrusted to you for worship in the temple of your God. 20 And anything else needed for the temple of your God that you may have occasion to supply, you may provide from the royal treasury. 21 Now I, King Artaxerxes, order all the treasurers of Trans-Euphrates to provide with diligence whatever Ezra the priest, a teacher of the Law of the God of heaven, may ask of you-- 22 up to a hundred talents of **silver**, a hundred cors of wheat, a hundred baths of wine, a hundred baths of olive oil, and salt without limit. 23 Whatever the God of heaven has prescribed, let it be done with diligence for the temple of the God of heaven. Why should there be wrath against the realm of the king and of his sons?

[2] For those old timers who longed for the past – He gives a special promise that the glory of this present temple will be greater than the former. For those that thought the best was behind them, God tells them that the best is yet to come. Just like the wine at Cana – God has saved the best for last. See **Article**, *Profiting From the Past*.

[3] This *nothing* project will one day soon (*little while*) be a house filled with glory. God encourages the workers by casting vision of the work in His big picture plan. He encourages them by calling them to focus not on what is, but on what can be. Right now they are looking at a pile of rubble, but God helps them see a temple filled with the glory of the lord, and people from all over the world coming to worship Leaders must have eyes of faith to see beyond the present into what God will do (see Leadership Lesson 10. Work of God). See **Article**, *Prophecy Overview*.

[4] Notice how many times, Haggai's favorite term for God, *Lord Almighty*, is used in verses 6-9. It is used five times. There is a real sense of Divine purpose in these verses. This is something God has purposed, and His purposes will stand. His purposes will prevail. This project will play a part.

[5] *Peace,* Shalom (SRN 07965). God promises peace and prosperity. Notice the contrast between the shaking of the nations, and the peace of God's house.

[6] This section 2:6-9 is an illustration of futuristic prophecy. The other prophetic words are corrective for the situation in Haggai's day. See **Article**, *Prophecy Overview*; *Haggai—Prophetic Words*.

Haggai 2:10-18

III. (ch 2:10-19) Patience in the Task

10 On the twenty fourth day of the ninth month during the second year of Darius' reign,[1] The Word of the Lord came again to Haggai the prophet.

11 "I, the Lord Almighty, have a question to ask the priests about the law. 12 Suppose a priest takes a piece of consecrated[2] meat, from a sacrifice. And suppose that person carries it in a fold of the robe being worn. If he happens to touch his robe on other cooked food or bread, or wine, or olive oil or any other kind of food, Will this consecrated meat make the other food consecrated?"
And the priests answered correctly, "No!"

13 Here then is a second question. "Suppose someone is defiled by touching a dead body? If that one touches these foods, will that defile them?"
And the priests said, "That would make those foods unclean also."

14 Then Haggai responded further, the Lord says, "The same thing applies to these people. They are defiled and what they produce is defiled. What they offer me on the altar is defiled."[3]

15 Think back. Can't you see what has happened to you?[4] Before you began to rebuild the temple, 16 you would look at a pile of grain and expect to get twenty bushels out of it. But you only got ten. And you would expect to get fifty gallons of wine from the wine press. But you would only get twenty. 17 I sent hot dry winds and I sent hail to ruin your crops. But you didn't respond to me and repent.[5] 18 Think again.[6]

---

[1] We are now three months into building project. See **Article**, *Haggai—And Timing*.

[2] *Consecrated* (SRN 6944) is often translated *Holy*. See **Article**, *Holiness—A Motivating Factor*.

[3] God is giving them an analogy that has a two fold purpose. 1) It will sum up the dynamics of why, in the past, everything they touched went bad. 2) It will prepare them, by way of contrast, for the blessing God will give them in verse 19. One point of this analogy is: When people are not right with God, every area of their lives are effected. Because of their disobedience, they were under God's judgment, and subsequently everything they touched was affected by this judgment. Notice in verse 12 the word *touches* and in verse 13 the word *contact*. Every area of life they had contact with, was affected by this cycle of disobedience. This is why they planted much but harvested little. It wasn't a coincidence. This is why God called for a drought (1:11), Why the little they had, God blew away (1:9). This is a good reminder to us as leaders and our people too. When we are not right with God, every area of our lives are affected. God will often use an area of our life we do care about (Money, Health, Job) to get us to focus on an area we do not care as much about, in many cases—spiritual matters. Obedience and disobedience have a spill-over affect.

[4] Here again is the call for *careful thought*. This is not an emotional appeal. Reasoned thought will see God's teaching points in these analogies.

[5] God's message through their circumstances did not cause them to turn to God. They needed Haggai's prophetic message. God will use circumstances to get our attention. Sometimes this works. But at other times we need a more direct approach. See **Article**, *Haggai—Prophetic Words*.

[6] In verses 15-18 God says to *think again* (literally give careful thought) twice. The repetition is emphatic. They must discern conceptually the hand of God in their daily lives.

Haggai 2:19-22

This is the 24th day of the ninth month, since the foundation was completed. Watch what will happen to you from now on.[1] 19 Even though there is no grain left and your vines are barren and your fig trees and pomegranate trees are not bearing fruit and no olive oil has been produced,[2] still I will bless you.[3]

IV. (ch 2:20-23) Power for the Task

20 Later that same day, the twenty fourth day of the month, another[4] Word of the Lord was revealed to Haggai. 21 "Give the following word to Governor Zerubbabel.[5] I will shake the heavens and the earth. 22 I will overthrow kingdoms and end their powerful reigns. I will dismantle their chariots and strand the

---

[1] God is being very intentional in setting a spiritual benchmark. This time reference will serve as a milestone to use as a future point of reference.

[2] God is doing something really interesting. God says, I want you take one more look in the barn and notice it's empty, because I'm going to fill it – and when I do, I want you to remember that it was me that did it. He is calling them to test His faithfulness to bless. God says I want you to watch—because I'm going to start blessing. You know what's its like to be under my judgment, now I want you to pay attention to what it is like to be under my blessing. He sends them into this season of blessing with a reminder of what they don't want to go back to. This contrast of the empty vats and the beginning of blessing, only makes one appreciate the blessings more when they come. There is no doubt, that God did it. This call to look at the empty barns provokes thoughts on another related book—Malachi. In Malachi 3, God plainly tells the people to test Him. If they become obedient in their financial giving, God will open the floodgates of heaven and fill their barns. Malachi 3:10 "Bring the whole tithe into the storehouse, that there may be food in my house. Test me in this," says the Lord Almighty, "and see if I will not throw open the floodgates of heaven and pour out so much blessing that you will not have room enough for it."

[3] Here is an encouraging observation. God doesn't wait until the construction project is over to begin blessing them. God blesses even small steps of obedience. At this point in the story, all they had done was the foundation. The truth that God blesses small steps of obedience is seen throughout this story. When they initially obeyed, God blessed them with a sense of His presence. One month into the work, He blesses them with strength and a second reminder of his presence. Now three months into the project, God withdraws the judgment on their businesses and households and blesses them. God blesses even small steps of obedience. New Christians sometimes fear that God won't be pleased with them until they are perfect. The truth is that God blesses small steps along the way.

[4] *Another Word*, referring to a second time on the same day. This prophecy was on the same day as the "I will bless you" prophecy. The intentional reference to a *second time* clarifies that this must be seen as a separate prophecy. This is the last prophecy of Haggai.

[5] Unlike all the previous prophecies this was personal in nature. It was directed only to Zerubbabel. Joshua and the remnant of Israel are not addressed in this closing prophecy.

soldiers riding in them. They will fight with one another and kill one another.[1] 23 On that day, I the Lord Almighty, will take you, Zerubbabel, my servant,[2] and will appoint[3] you as my authoritative representative to rule.[4] You are the special one I have chosen.[5] The Lord Almighty has spoken.[6]

---

[1] God once again reiterates His earlier "shaking" comments of Haggai 2:7-8. But here it comes in even a stronger form. Perhaps God is personally preparing Zerubbabel for this coming *shaking*. So when God starts shaking, Zerubbabel won't be shaken.

[2] In this last verse God gives Zerubbabel a strong personal affirmation, it comes in four areas. First is God's affirmation of Zerubbabel's **obedience**—God calls Zerubbabel his *servant* a servant is someone who obeys, and Zerubbabel had been obedient in his God-given role of leadership.

[3] God's affirms Zerubbabel's **future role** in God's plan. "I will take you" and "I will make you." God is not done with Zerubbabel yet. Zerubbabel was faithful in his task, now he will be used in continuing ways. God's promise to "take" and "make" Zerubbabel points to God's future shaping and development in his life. God has a hope and a future for His faithful servant.

[4] I have captured the phrase *make you a signet ring* (SRN 2368) and replaced it with its emphatic meaning—*you as my authoritative representative to rule*. God's promise to make Zerubbabel like His signet ring indicates God's affirmation of Zerubbabel as God's instrument of **authority**. It sets apart Zerubbabel as one bearing God's **approval**, someone who is backed by God's power, authority and position.

[5] God's affirmation of His **sovereign selection** of Zerubbabel. "I have chosen you". What an encouraging thing to know that you are hand selected by God. A leader needs to know that God has called and placed them in ministry. During tough times it is helpful to be reminded that this whole leadership thing is God's idea.

[6] Notice how the book closes. Haggai's favorite phrase for God is used. The Lord Almighty has spoken. Its meaning is clear. God can and will do what He says. Haggai is a task oriented inspirational leader. He is masterful at motivating his hearers. He leaves behind a legacy, a model of inspirational leadership. See **Article**, *Haggai—Lasting Legacies*.

For Further Leadership Study
1. Study each of the two contexts as leadership acts: a. 1:2-15, b. 2:10-19. Particularly note leadership styles involved in the influence.
2. What is the significance of the two words coming so close together on the same day (2:10; 2:20)?
3. See also the Bibliographical Section for Major Materials for further study.

Special Comments

The following time-line is helpful in catching the flow of the timely revelations. Notice the whole book takes place in about four months.

Haggai Time-Line for Task of Rebuilding The Temple

Time Reference--------------4 months -->

2nd Year 6th month 1st day	2nd Year 6th month 24th day	2nd year 7th month 21st day	2nd year 9th month 24th day	2nd year 9th month 24th day
1st Word challenge to move motivation	Response Began work	2nd word Countering Discouragement	3rd word Countering reward	4th word Encouraging trust in God for power
stage 1 false satisfaction		stage 2 false dissatisfaction	stage 3 false expectation	stage 4 false fear

Haggai

CLINTON'S BIBLICAL LEADERSHIP COMMENTARY SERIES

**Restoring A Work of God
Inspirational, Task-Oriented Leadership**

Commentary Articles

Article 1

Civil Leadership—The Missing Ingredient

Introduction

To have impact on a society, a broad spectrum is needed which includes civil leadership, mainstream religious leadership, and peripheral religious leadership. Let me define these terms.

Definition *Civil leadership* refers to followers of God, sold out on following God, yet impacting the society via two types of roles often needed—1. Governmental or political roles sanctioned by the society and 2. Military roles sanctioned by the society.

They are not considered religious workers.

Definition *Mainstream religious* leadership refers to officially recognized religious roles sanctioned by the society and religious structures.

Priest and various ordained ministry roles (e.g. pastor) would be mainstream religious roles.

Definition *Peripheral religious* leadership refers to those roles, mostly outside the mainstream religious structures, which attempt to speak for God to bring about change in religious groups, structures, and society in general.

These sometimes fringe leaders are frequently needed because mainstream religious leaders go nominal in their pursuit of God. God raises these types of leaders up in an *ad hoc sort of manner*, as and when needed. The oral and writing prophets of the O.T. and those exercising prophetic ministries and some apostolic ministries in the present *Church Leadership* Era typically would be examples of peripheral religious leaders.

Typically, all three of the above types of leadership are needed to accomplish God's work in our world. Table 1.1 lists the six Biblical leadership eras and shows how these roles played out in the various eras.

Table 1.1 Civil, Religious, and Peripheral Religious Leaders in the Leadership Eras

Leadership Era	Civil a. political b. military/ Example	Mainstream Religious/ Example	Peripheral Religious/ Example
1. Patriarchal	The family head served as civil political, and military when needed. / Abraham	The family head served to interceded in a priestly way with God for the family. / Abraham, Job	The family head received revelation from God for situations. / Abraham, Job
2. Pre-Kingdom a. Desert	Civil done by an apostolic type leader raised up by God for the time/ a. political—Moses (supported by Miriam as adviser) b. Military—Joshua under Moses control.	God initiated a specific religious role the Priesthood (supported by the Levites)/ Aaron	Moses served to receive revelatory word for the people.
2. Pre-Kingdom b. Conquering the Land	Civil done by succession leader appointed by Moses/ a. political—Joshua b. Military—Joshua	Aaron's successor was appointed by Moses/ Eleazar, head priest	Joshua served to receive revelatory word (less frequently than Moses)
2. Pre-Kingdom b. Conquered by the Land	No overall civil head; Joshua did not appoint a successor; Military heads were the Judges who were raised up according to need.	Not clear who was the head priest; none apparently coordinating priestly effort for all the tribes; Eli had some sphere of influence but not clear how wide his range of influence. Samuel performed this function toward the end of the Judges era.	Occasional prophets arose like Deborah; Samuel performed this function toward the end of the Judges era.
3. Kingdom	Civil done by the King; kings generally by succession—oldest family member or one appointed by king; Various advisory posts supplemented civil leadership (Nathan and Gad); Military appointed by king	Priests; not clear how head priest was chosen;	Oral prophets raised up by God outside the normal priestly structures to correct civil and military leadership/ Elijah and Elisha are typical examples. Writing prophets raised up to correct both Northern and Southern Kingdoms/ Amos, Micah, et al

4. Post-Kingdom a. As Kingdom was crumbling	None; the people were subservient to conquerors	Not clear how priestly families survived or a head priest appointed; Impact of leadership unknown; Ezekiel was a priest;	Jeremiah and Ezekiel were typical of those who received revelatory information and corrective information for civil and military leadership as the kingdom was being dismantled; Daniel would be typical of one receiving
b. In exile	Not clear;	None mentioned;	
c. Return to Land	Civil: leaders like Zerubbabel and Nehemiah Military: none	Joshua and Ezra were priests who impacted	Haggai, Zechariah, and Malachi
5. Pre-Church Leadership Era	None; Sanhedrin some influence; ruled by appointed leadership from Rome; Roman military garrisoned Palestine	There were high priests and a priestly line; not sure how succession was done	John the Baptist; Jesus
6. Church	Civil missing; No military leadership	Pastors, elders, deacons were formally appointed by formal Apostolic leadership or local church leadership	Apostolic leaders and prophets (itinerant leaders)

Civil Leadership An Important Key

Some observation on synergistic functioning of civil, military, formal religious and peripheral religious leadership include the following:

1. When civil and priestly leadership were spiritually strong there was little need for peripheral religious leadership.
2. Civil leadership that is spiritual is needed to control military. Only two military leaders in O.T. were strong spiritually—David and Joshua (who both wore two hats—civil as well; and David had weak moments in which prophetic leadership exercised corrective action).
3. The strongest synergistic efforts are seen in the Post-Kingdom leadership era in two different times: a. Rebuilding the temple—Haggai, Zechariah, Joshua, and Zerubbabel; b. Building the wall around Jerusalem—Nehemiah, Ezra (who wore two hats—priestly and prophet's).
4. In the church leadership era the emphasis, structure wise, is units, local churches, which will fit into any culture or society anywhere as a religious influence on the society (correcting wrongs of society and bringing people in the society into relationship with God). The place of military and civil leadership is not directly related to the religious structure. The peripheral religious function occurs both within these local churches (apostolic, prophetic and exhortive ministries) and without (apostolic, prophetic and exhortive ministries).
5. Civil leadership is exercised outside the jurisdiction of local church structures.
6. Military leadership is exercised outside the jurisdiction of local church structures.

7. Priestly leadership that was spiritual directly affected civil leadership for the good several times in the kingdom era.
8. Kingly leadership which was spiritual directly affected the whole nation several times.
9. Spiritual leadership, whether kingly, priestly, or peripheral religious prolonged the life of the southern Kingdom well beyond that of the northern kingdom which had no spiritual leadership throughout. Spiritual leadership makes a difference.

Closure

Because of the dispersed nature of local churches in various geographical and cultural areas all over the world there is no formal coalition leadership made up of civil political, military, formal religious and peripheral religious leadership. What is needed are leaders in the civil sphere and military spheres who are out and out believers and followers of God and who work closely with formal religious structures and heed peripheral leadership as they seek to work together to protect and improve society.

Leadership in our complex world today needs godly influence no matter what the direct sphere of influence. Especially needed is at least a quasi-coalition effort among the diverse leadership.

See **Article**, *Leadership Coalition*.

Article 2

Dealing With Personal Discouragement During A Ministry Project

Introduction
Every leader faces discouragement –Often in ministry things don't happen as quickly as hoped for. At other times the smallness of the project can discourage a leader. Often the people that initially committed to help out, one by one (and sometimes all at once!) begin to pull out. People quit, progress is slow, problems pop up, and resources run low. As a leader, what can you do when discouragement sets in? How can you stay motivated and focused when after your best efforts it feels like "nothing" has been accomplished? A visit to the book of Haggai may provide just the cure for discouraged leaders.

Help from the Book of Haggai
In the book of Haggai, the people make a commitment to build God's house, they roll up their sleeves and with the excitement that accompanies the start of something new, they begin the rebuilding process. Haggai 2 gives a snapshot of their activity about thirty days later. A month into the project they stood back to gauge the progress that was made. Imagine their discouragement when the scene before them was perhaps best summed up in the word God uses—"nothing." (Hag 2:3)

At times the work of ministry can be overwhelming. This is especially true when, like in Haggai, you're taking on a rebuilding project. Perhaps it's rebuilding a church that feels like it's best years are in the past, or rebuilding hope in people who feel defeated, perhaps it's rebuilding a ministry that has lost its effectiveness, perhaps it's something as personal as rebuilding trust in a relationship. Often times visible progress in ministry is slow, yet reasons for discouragement appear daily. Often a leader's personal sense of purpose and progress is tied into the success of the project. Every leader has experienced how emotions can rise and fall with things like attendance and financial resources.

In a ministry setting the leader is usually expected to inspire the followers and provide encouragement during seasons where enthusiasm sags. But the reality is:

> **As the leader, the most difficult discouragement to deal with may be your own.**

People look to the leader for help, but sometimes the point person is more discouraged than the people he/she is supposed to lift up. A leader's greatest leadership challenge may be getting to a place where he/she can find fresh hope and help from God.

Four Things to Count on When Attempting a God-Given Project
A leader must learn to find personal encouragement from the one unchanging source of hope – God. During seasons of discouragement a leader needs to meet God in personal ways that make His presence and promises real. The book of Haggai provides an example

of one such interaction between a gracious God and weary workers. In Hag 2:4-5 God encourages the leaders by breaking into their lives and personally applying His promises to their project. From this text we can draw out four things a leader <u>can</u> count on when attempting a God given project.

> "But now be strong, O Zerubbabel," declares the Lord. "Be strong, O Joshua son of Jehozadak, the high priest. Be strong, all you people of the land," declares the Lord, "and work. For I am with you," declares the Lord Almighty. 5 "This is what I covenanted with you when you came out of Egypt. And my Spirit remains among you. Do not fear." Hag 2:4

1. Count on God giving you the strength you need. Vs 4 "be strong"

In Hag 2:4 God comes to workers and says – "be strong." Instead of giving one general—"be strong" to the entire group, God takes a more personal approach and calls out the leaders by name. He actually says *be strong* three times, first to Zerubbabel, second to Joshua, and thirdly to all the people. It's as if God is going around the table at a meeting He has called and is personally strengthening each person.

Seasons of weariness are a normal part of ministry. Often times the leader is working hard with little help. Most in ministry are not strangers to long hours. Leaders know they should press on, but the physical and emotional energy just isn't there. A leader wonders, "How am I going to make it?" In Hag 2:4 God's answer to one group of people was, "with my strength." God says, "be strong and work." In other words, don't give up, I'm with you and will give you strength. Leaders need that fresh touch from God to find strength when reserves are running on low. Be encouraged, if God has called you to a task—rely on the promise of His strength to do it.

2. Count on God being with you as you trust and obey. Vs 4 "I am with you"

Haggai's friends were working hard, without much to show for it. Some appeared discouraged by the smallness of the project. Every leader faces times when the easiest thing to do is quit. Things don't progress as hoped for. People that initially committed to help don't follow through. They back out. It's easy to feel all alone and overwhelmed. It's at a time like that, when a leader most needs to hear God's powerful promise to leader. - "I am with you."[1] When obeying God, a leader can find encouragement from the fact that the awesome, powerful king of the universe is with him/her. Do you feel like quitting? Ask God to send a reminder of His presence your way in your needy moment.

3. Count on God helping you by the Holy Spirit. Vs 5 "My Spirit remains among you"

It's one thing to stay "be strong," "hang in there," and "don't give up." But where does a leader find strength for the task? Where does a leader find the faith, the hope, and the love to keep going in spite of difficult opposition? Where do these inner resources come from? Answer—from the Spirit of God. The Holy Spirit is God's source of love, joy, peace, patience…(Gal 5:22). The Holy Spirit supplies us with the grace and gifts needed for ministry. The Holy Spirit provides us with God's power to be and do. In Hag 2:5 God reminds them of the promised help of the Holy Spirit. He says to the discouraged leaders *"My Spirit remains among you. Do not fear."* The Christian Leader can count on the promised help on the Holy Spirit.

---

[1] One of the macro leadership lessons of the Bible is found in Moses encounter with God during the Pre-Kingdom Era — The essential ingredient of leadership is the powerful presence of God in the leader's life and ministry.

Dealing With Personal Discouragement in A Ministry Project

4. Count on God's promises being true – vs. 5 "This what I covenanted with you".

Every leader must manage change. So much about ministry is an ever-moving matrix of people, resources, momentum, windows of opportunity, etc. Enthusiasm for a project changes. The roster of workers change; relationships change. During difficult times of uncertainty, a leader needs something that doesn't change with the ups and downs of attendance. In Hag 2:5 God reminds the leaders of an unchanging source of strength they can always rely on – His covenant promises. In verse 5, God reminds the workers that the promises He is making are based on something they can count on – His word "This is what I covenanted with you when you came out of Egypt." When God makes a promise He keeps it. Do you need a promise from God? Here are some promises that leaders in the Bible found helpful

Table 2.1 A Sampling of Promises to God's Leaders

Bible Reference	Scriptural Promise	Leader Given To
Gen 22:17	I will surely bless you and make your descendants as numerous as the stars in the sky and as the sand on the seashore. Your descendants will take possession of the cities of their enemies	Abraham
Gen 28:15	I am with you and will watch over you wherever you go, and I will bring you back to this land. I will not leave you until I have done what I have promised you."	Jacob
Ex 33:14	The Lord replied, "My Presence will go with you, and I will give you rest."	Moses
Jos 1:9	Be strong and courageous. Do not be terrified; do not be discouraged, for the Lord your God will be with you wherever you go."	Joshua
Jer 29:11	For I know the plans I have for you," declares the Lord, "plans to prosper you and not to harm you, plans to give you hope and a future.	Jeremiah
Isa 41:10	So do not fear, for I am with you; do not be dismayed, for I am your God. I will strengthen you and help you; I will uphold you with my righteous right hand.	Isaiah
Mt 16:18	I will build my church, and the gates of Hades will not overcome it.	Peter

Conclusion

Leaders need to find personal encouragement from God. Are you a leader in need of encouragement? Look again quickly at the four things to count on when attempting a God-given project. Which of the four do you most need right now. Ask God to meet you in a personal and powerful way that will bring the help you need to continue in His work.

See **Article**, *God The Promise Keeper*.

Article 3

Divine Affirmation in the Life of Jesus

Introduction

Leaders need encouragement. Jesus' leadership has long been a model of encouragement. All leaders need affirmation. When God gives that affirmation there is renewed hope. Jesus models this too. This article shows the importance of affirmation in the life of a leader. Jesus needed it. We do too. Four things should result.

1. You should recognize some of the facets of affirmation and hence be more sensitive to it when God gives it.
2. You will be able to go back over your past leadership and identify affirmation times; you will be re-encouraged.
3. You will not see it as a weakness because you need affirmation.
4. You will recognize that emerging leaders whom you influence need affirmation. You should learn to give affirmation.

Defining Affirmation—Two Kinds

Over a lifetime of ministry there will be times when a leader will need reassurance from God. This involves a psychological need for acceptance as a person loved by God, as well as approval regarding ministry. God meets this need through a special shaping activity called *divine affirmation*. God shows up and touches the heart of a leader giving the acceptance that is needed.

Definition *Divine affirmation* is a special kind of sense of destiny experience in which God gives approval to a leader so that the leader has a renewed sense of ultimate purpose and a refreshed desire to continue serving God. This is a major motivating factor to keep one serving the Lord.

Divine affirmation can come through:
1. an inner voice or other direct revelation,
2. an angelic visitation,
3. a vision,
4. a miraculous sign,
5. a prophetic word,
6. a dream,
7. a sense of God's blessing on a life as attested to by external testimony (see Joseph, Gen 39:2,3 39:21-23).
8. sovereign arrangement of circumstances.

Divine Affirmation in the Life of Jesus

God uses divine affirmation to:
1. renew a leader's desire to serve God,
2. give confirmation of acceptance, especially when there is a sense of rejection due to ministry or personal circumstances.
3. give external support for ministry purposes.
4. expand the spiritual authority power base.

A second related shaping activity God uses to encourage a leader is *ministry affirmation*. Over a lifetime of ministry, many lessons are learned via negative experience. These lessons are valuable when seen in terms of an overview of a lifetime of development. But in the midst of ministry that overall perspective is often hard to see. And these negative lessons can be discouraging. Leaders need to be encouraged concerning proper leadership which is pleasing to God. The ministry affirmation shaping activity provides that needed encouragement. It is a special form of the more general divine affirmation process item. It encourages a leader and gives a renewed sense of ultimate purpose in leadership. It is God's *pat on the back*.

Definition *Ministry affirmation* is a special kind of destiny experience in which God gives approval to a leader in terms of some ministry assignment in particular or some ministry experience in general which results in a renewed sense of purpose for the leader. This is a major motivating factor to keep one serving the Lord.

Ministry affirmation can come through a number of means such as:

1. a vision,
2. sign,
3. inner voice,
4. inner conviction,
5. successful ministry incident,
6. human expressions of appreciation,
7. inner satisfaction in reflection on some aspect of ministry history,
8. a word of knowledge or wisdom, or prophecy,
9. promotion, or expansion of sphere of influence.

God uses ministry affirmation primarily as encouragement. Secondarily, it often serves as confirmation of guidance.

Both divine affirmation and ministry affirmation can be internal (perceived inwardly by the person alone), external (witnessed by others also), or a combination of internal/external. When it is external, the shaping experience is probably validating spiritual authority as well as encouraging the leader.

Affirmation Examples of Divine and Ministry Affirmation

O.T. examples abound showing God's use of this shaping activity. From Gen 12:1-3 onward for more than 25 years Abraham was affirmed by God. God repeatedly gave, a-periodically,[2] divine affirmation to Abraham. See especially Gen 15 where God renewed Abraham's purpose and also revealed great truth. Another O.T. example, Samuel, illustrates this shaping activity. 1 Sam 12:13-19 is a great passage illustrating divine affirmation of Samuel's ministry which is primarily external. One of the most beautiful examples of divine affirmation is seen in Daniel's life. God sends an angelic visitor to give affirmation about His view of Daniel's personhood (see Dan 10:11,19). The N.T. also has

---

[2] Aperiodic indicates not on a strict time cycle. It comes repeatedly but not on some regular time schedule.

Four Major Affirmations in the Life of Jesus

At least four times in Jesus' life and ministry, God openly gave affirmation to Jesus—both divine and ministry. Table 3.1 gives these references and explanation about them. Notice that both divine and ministry affirmations occur. Notice too that three of these experiences were audible voices—some heard by others, some not. Notice carefully the uses of these—most were dominantly for followers benefit and for Jesus. One is dominantly for Jesus benefit and secondarily for followers. Most important note that Jesus needed these affirmations. They come at critical junctures in his ministry—The beginning, at the moment when Jesus must set his will to go to the Cross, at the height of rejection by Jewish leaders, and in the final moment when Jesus needs to know the Cross is the only answer. Jesus needed these affirmations. Do leaders today need such affirmation any less? The affirmation experiences in Jesus life particularly affirmed Jesus by giving encouragement and confirmation of guidance.

Table 3.1 Four Affirmation Experiences in the Life of Jesus

Where	Type	Kind/Use	Actual Verses/ Explanation
Mt 3:17	Divine affirmation: External	Audible voice; symbol of dove seen/ All four uses seen but use 3 is dominant.	17 Then a voice from heaven said, "This is my beloved Son; in whom I am fully satisfied."/ Jesus obeys God and is baptized by John. He receives God's personal approval and John the Baptist recognizes and affirms his divine mission.
Mt 17:5	Divine affirmation and ministry affirmation: External / dazzling brightness	Audible voice; dazzling cloud—awesome presence of God/ Uses 1, 2, and 4 seen. Use 2 is dominant.	5 While Peter was speaking, a bright cloud enveloped them. They heard a voice from the cloud, "This is my beloved Son; I am fully pleased with him; listen to him."/ At the Mount of Transfiguration Jesus gets personal approval that his mission, going to the cross, is right. The three with him are convinced of his spiritual authority. Peter remembers this incident in old age.
Jn 11:38-44	Ministry Affirmation: External: validating power from God	Supernatural power/ resurrection of Lazarus/ All 4 uses evident; 2, 3, and 4 more prominent with 4 in focus.	41 ...Jesus looking heavenward, said, "Father, Thank you for hearing me. 42 I personally know that you always hear me. But I have publicly said this for the sake of these people listening, that they may believe you have sent me."/ In the most powerful ministry affirmation given Jesus, God backs his ministry claims, especially sentness,[3] with resurrection power. Lazarus is raised from the dead as predicted by Jesus.
Jn 12:27,	Ministry Affirmation:	Audible voice; awesome noise/	27 "My heart is nearly breaking. What can I say? Father, get me out of this. No! This is the

---

[3] See **Article, Jesus:Sentness**. Sentness, a major concept in John, is a term capturing the divine backing of Jesus' intervention in the world to represent and reveal God to our world. It carries the notion of anointing and appointment by God for a mission, but in Jesus' case—more since it was the incarnation of God in human form. The closest functional equivalent for leaders today is divine appointment.

| 33 | External/Internal: Awesome sound to others; audible voice to Jesus | Uses 1,2, and 3 seen; Uses 2 and 3 equally in focus. | very reason why I came. 28 Father, bring honor to yourself." Then God spoke, "I have honored and revealed myself through you. And I will continue to do so." 29 The people heard something sounding like thunder. Some said, "An angel spoke to him." 30 Jesus said. "More than to affirm me, this voice came so that you may be assured of God's backing for me. This voice came not because of me, but for your sakes."[4]/ At a crisis moment, Jesus personally needs God's assurance that the Cross is the only way; in addition, the rejection of Jesus by the Jews (religious leaders) has steadily grown. Jesus needs reassurance that what he is doing is God's way. And people following him need to know he is God's representative. |

Conclusion

Jesus models for us, as leaders, the need to get affirmation from God concerning our selves and our ministry. No leader can alone determine if his/her ministry is exactly what God wants. Each leader needs affirmation from God about that ministry. All leaders need to know that God accepts them and loves them. At critical junctures in his ministry, God met Jesus. He will do no less for us, leaders in this complex Church Leadership Era.

Because we as leaders are also involved in God's leadership selection and development process of other leaders,

>**Effective leaders view leadership selection and development as a priority function,**

we can use this model, being affirmed, to give affirmation to those we are selecting and developing. They will need it. And we, as more mature leaders, who can sense God's ways and see what He is doing in their lives, can be significantly used by God to encourage them along the way in their development.

See *sense of destiny, destiny processing, destiny pattern, word of knowledge, word of wisdom, prophecy,* **Glossary**. See **Article**, *Destiny Pattern*

---

[4] Literally, This voice came not because of me, but for your sakes. Probably an absolute for the relative. That is how I have translated it. An absolute for the relative is an idiom having the pattern, Not A but B. It really means Yes A but much more B. See *absolute for the relative*, **Glossary**. See **Article**, *Figures and Idioms in the Bible*.

Article 4

Figures and Idioms In The Bible

Introduction to Figures

All language is governed by law—that is, it has normal patterns that are followed. But in order to increase the power of a word or the force of expression, these patterns are deliberately departed from, and words and sentences are thrown into and used in unusual forms or patterns which we call figures. A figure then is a use of language in a special way for the purpose of giving additional force, more life, intensified feeling and greater emphasis. A figure of speech is the author's way of underlining. He/She is saying, "Hey, take note! This is important enough for me to use a special form of language to emphasize it!" And when we remember the fact that the Holy Spirit has inspired this product we have—the Bible—we are not far wrong in saying figures are the Holy Spirit's own underlining in our Bibles. We certainly need to be sensitive to figurative language.

Definition   A *figure* is the unusual use of a word or words differing from the normal use in order to draw special attention to some point of interest.

For a figure, the unusual use itself follows a set pattern. The pattern can be identified and used to interpret the figure in normal language. Here are some examples from the Bible. I will make you fishers of people. Go tell that fox. Quench not the Holy Spirit. I came not to send peace but a sword. As students of the Bible we need to be sensitive to figures and know how to interpret and catch their emphatic meaning.

Definition   A figure or idiom is said to be *captured* when one can display the intended emphatic meaning in non-figurative simple words.

One of the most familiar figures in the Bible is Psalm 23:1. The Lord is my shepherd. I shall not lack. *Captured*: God personally provides for my every need.

E.W. Bullinger, an expert on figurative language, lists over 400 different kinds of figures. he lists over 8000 references in the Bible containing figures. In Romans alone, Bullinger lists 253 passages containing figurative language. However, we do not need to know all of those figures for the most commonly occurring figures number much less than 400. Figure 4.1, below, lists the 11 most common figures occurring in the Bible. If we know them we are well on our way to becoming better interpreters of the Scripture. In fact, you can group these 11 figures under three main sub-categories, which simplifies learning about them.

Figures and Idioms In The Bible

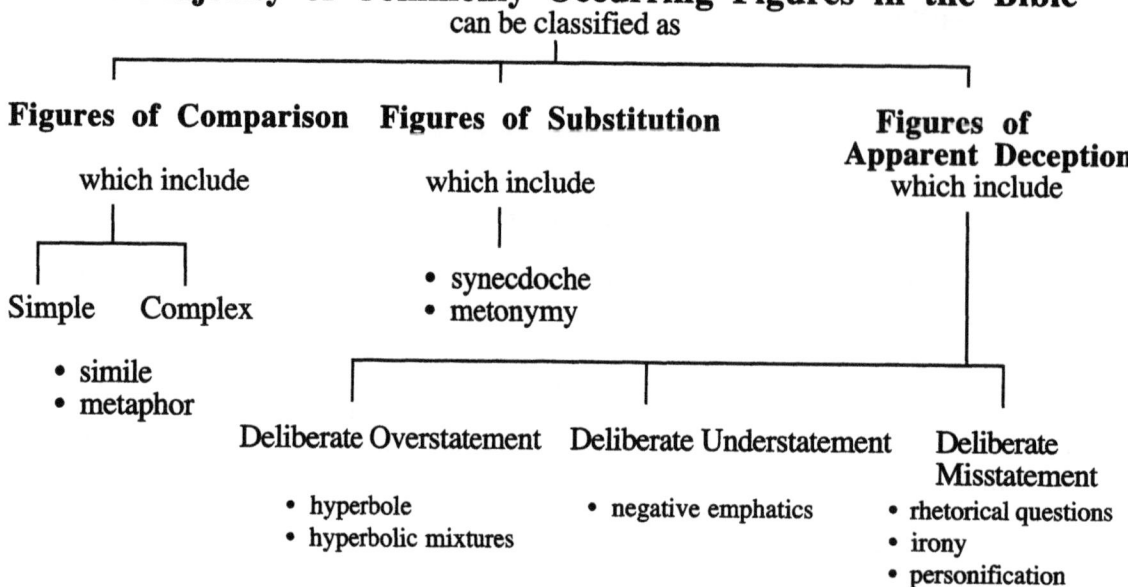

Figure 4.1   11 Common Figures of Speech

Table 4.1 below gives these 11 figures of speech, a Scriptural reference containing the figure, and the basic definition of each of these figures.

Table 4.1 11 Figures in the Bible Defined

Category/ Figure	Scriptural Example	Definition
Figures of Comparison: 1. Simile 2. Metaphor	simile—Isa 53:6 metaphor—Ps 23:1	A <u>simile</u> is a stated comparison of two unlike items (one called the real item and the other the picture item) in order to display one graphic point of comparison. A <u>metaphor</u> is an implied comparison in which two unlike items (a real item and a picture item) are equated to point out one point of resemblance.
Figures of Substitution 3. Metonymy 4. Synecdoche	metonymy—Ac 15:21 Moses for what he wrote synecdoche—Mt 8:8 roof for the whole house.	A <u>metonymy</u> is a figure of speech in which (usually) one word is substituted for another word to which it is closely related in order to emphasize something indicated by the relationship. A <u>synecdoche</u> is a special case of metonymy in which (again usually) one word is substituted for another to which it is related as, a part to a whole or a whole to a part.
Figures of Apparent Deception— Deliberate Overstatement: 5. Hyperbole 6. Hyperbolic	hyperbole—1 Co 4:14-16 ten thousand instructors hyperbolic mixture—2 Sa	A <u>hyperbole</u> is the use of conscious exaggeration (an overstatement of truth) in order to emphasize or strikingly excite interest in the truth. Hyperbole is sometimes combined with other figures such as comparison and substitution. When such is the case it is called a <u>hyperbolic mixture</u> figure.

mixtures	1:23 swifter than eagles, stronger than lions	
Figures of Apparent Deception— Deliberate understatement: 7. Negative emphatics	negative emphatics—Mk 12:34 not far = very near	A figure of <u>negative emphasis</u> represents the deliberate use of words to diminish a concept and thus call attention to it or the negating of a concept to call attention to the opposite positive concept (I have deliberately merged two figures, litotes and tapenosis into one because of the basic sameness of negative emphasis).
Figures of Apparent Deception— Deliberate Misstatement: 8. Rhetorical questions 9. Irony 10. Personification 11. Apostrophe	rhetorical question—1Ti 3:5 irony—2Co 12:13 personification —Heb 4:12 apostrophe—1 Co 15:55	A <u>rhetorical question</u> is a figure of speech in which a question is not used to obtain information but is used to indirectly communicate, (1) an affirmative or negative statement, or (2) the importance of some thought by focusing attention on it, or (3) one's own feeling or attitudes about something. <u>Irony</u> is the use of words by a speaker in which his/her intended meaning is the opposite of (or in disharmony with) the literal use of the words. <u>Personification</u> is the use of words to speak of animals, ideas, abstractions, and inanimate objects as if they had human form, character, or intelligence in order to vividly portray truth. <u>Apostrophe</u> is a special case of personification in which the speaker addresses the thing personified as if it were alive and listening.

I have developed in-depth explanations for all of the above figures. I have developed study sheets to aid one in analysis of them. Further I have actually identified many of these in the Scriptures and captured a number of them.[5]

Introduction to Idioms

Idioms are much more complicated that figures of speech.

Definition An <u>idiom</u> is a group of words which have a corporate meaning that can not be deduced from a compilation of the meanings of the individual words making up the idiom.

What makes idioms difficult is that some of them follow patterns while others do not. For the patterned idioms, like figures, you basically reverse the pattern and capture the idiom. Table 4.2 lists the patterned idioms I have identified in the Bible.

Table 4.2 13 Patterned Idioms

Idiom	Example	Definitive principle/ Description
Three Certainty Idioms: 1. Double certainty (pos/neg)	double certainty—1 Ki 18:36 fulfilled— Ge 15:18	<u>double certainty</u>—a negative and positive statement (in either order) are often used to express or imply certainty. <u>fulfillment</u>—in the fulfillment idiom things are spoken of as given, done, or possessed, which are only promised or proposed.

---

[5] See my self-study manual, **Interpreting the Scriptures: Figures and Idioms**.

Figures and Idioms In The Bible

2. Fulfilled (promised/proposed) 3. Prophetic past	prophetic past—Jn 13:31	prophetic past—in the prophetic past idiom the past tense is used to describe or express the certainty of future action.
4. Superlative (repetitive superlative)	Ge 9:25 servant of servants Isa 26:3 peace, peace = perfect peace 2Ti 4:7	The Hebrew superlative is often shown by the repetition of the word. Paul uses a variation of this by often using the noun form and a verb form of the same word either back to back or in close proximity. (the good struggle I have struggled).
5. Emphatic comparisons	1Pe 3:3,4	This takes three forms: absolute for relative: one thing (importance or focus item) is emphasized as being much more important in comparison with the other thing (the denial item). The form not A but B really means A is less important than B. relative for absolute: One thing is positively compared to another when in effect it is meant to be taken absolutely and the other denied altogether. abbreviated emphatic comparisons: Half of the comparison is not given (either the focus item or denial items). Half of the statement is given. The half missing is an example of ellipsis and is to be supplied by the reader.
6. Climactic arrangement	Pr 6:16-19 Ro 3:10-18	To emphasize a particular item it is sometimes placed at the bottom of a list of other items and is thus stressed in the given context as being the most important item being considered.
7. Broadened kinship	Ge 29:5	Sometimes the terms son of, daughter of, mother of, father of, brother of, sister of, or begat, which in English imply a close relationship have a much wider connotation in the Bible. Brother and sister could include various male and female relatives such as cousins; mother and father could include relatives such as grandparents or great-great-grandparents, in the direct family line; begat may simply mean was directly in the family line of ancestors.
8. Imitator	Ge 6:2, 11:5	to indicate that people or things are governed by or are characterized by some quality, they are called children of or a son of. or daughter of that quality.
9. Linked noun	Lk 21:15	Occasionally two nouns are linked together with a conjunction in which the second noun is really to be used like an adjective modifying the first noun.
Indicator Idioms: 10. City indicator 11. List indicator 12. Strength Indicator	city indicator La 1:16, daughter of Zion list indicator Pr 6:16, these 6 yea 7 Strength indicator 1Sa 2:1,10	city indicator—idiomatic words, daughter of or virgin of or mother of. list indicator—2 consecutive numbers—designates an incomplete list of items of which the ones on the list are representative; other like items could be included. strength indicator—a horn denotes aggressive strength or power or authority.

Figures and Idioms In The Bible

| 13. Anthropomorphism | Lk 11:20 | In order to convey concepts of God, <u>human passions, or actions, or attributes are used to describe God.</u> |

In addition, to the patterned idioms there are a number of miscellaneous idioms which either occur infrequently or have no discernible pattern. I have labeled 32. Their meaning must be learned from context, from other original language sources, or from language experts' comments, etc.

Table 4.3 15 Body Language Idioms

Name	Word, Phrase, Usually Seen	Example	Meaning or Concept Involved
1. Foot gesture	shake off the dust	Mt 10:14, Lk 9:5 et al	have nothing more to do with them
2. Mouth gesture	gnash on them with teeth; gnashing of teeth	Ps 35:16; 37:12 Ac 7:54 et al	indicates angry and cursing words given with deep emotion and feeling
3. Invitation	I have stretched forth my hand(s)	Ro 10:21; Pr 1:24; Is 49:22	indicates to invite, or to receive or welcome or call for mercy
4. New desire	enlighten my eyes, lighten my eyes	Ps 13:3; 19:8; 1Sa 14:29; Ezr 9:8	to give renewed desire to live; sometimes physical problem, sometimes motivational inward attitude problem
5. Judgment	to stretch forth the hand; to put forth the hand	Ex 7:5; Ps 138:7; Job 1:11	to send judgment upon; to inflict with providential punishment
6. Fear	to shake the hand, to not find the hand, knees tremble	Is 19:16; Ps 76:8	to be afraid; to be paralyzed with fear and incapable of action.
7. Increase punishment	to make the hand heavy	Ps 32:4	to make the punishment more severe
8. Decreased punishment	to make the hands light	1Sa 6:5	to make punishment less severe
9. Remove punishment	to withdraw the hands	Eze 20:22	to stop punishment
10. Repeat punishment	to turn the hand upon	Is 1:25	to repeat again some punishment which was not previously heeded
11. Generosity	to open the hand	Ps 104:28; 145:16	to generously give or bestow
12. Anger	to clap the hands together	Eze 21;17; 22:13	to show anger; to express derision

Figures and Idioms In The Bible

13. Oath	to lift up the hand	Ex 6:8; 17:16; De 32:40; Eze 20:5,6	to swear in a solemn way; take an oath; an indicator of one's integrity to consider worthy to be accepted; to accept someone or be accepted by someone
14. Promise	to strike with the hands (with someone else)	Pr 6:1; Job 17:3	become a co-signer on a loan; to conclude a bargain
15. Accept	to lift up the face	Nu 6:26; Ezr 9:6; Job 22:26	to consider worthy to be accepted; to accept someone or be accepted by someone

Table 4.4   14 Miscellaneous Idioms

Name	Word, Phrase, Usually Seen	Example	Meaning or Concept Involved
1. Success	tree of life	Pr 3:18; 11:30; 13:12; 15:4	idea of success, guarantee of success, source of motivation to successful life
2. Speech cue	answered and said	Mt 11:25; 13:2 and many others	indicates manner of speaking denoted by context; e.g. responded prayed, asked, addressed, etc.
3. Notice	verily, verily	Many times in Jn	I am revealing absolute and important truth; give close attention (this is a form of the superlative idiom)
4. Time	___ days and ___ nights	Jn 1:17; Mt 12:40; 1Sa 30:11; Est 4:16	any portion of time of a day is indicated by or represented by the entire day
5. Lifetime	forever and ever	Ps 48;14 and many others	does not mean eternal life as we commonly use it but means all through my life; as long as I live
6. Separation	what have I to do with you	Jn 2:4; Jdg 11;12; 2Sa 16:10; 1Ki 17;18; 2Ki 3;13; Mt 8:29; Mk 5:7; Lk 8:28	an expression of indignation or contempt between two parties having a difference or more specifically not having something in common; usually infers that some action about to take place should not take place
7. Reaction	heap coals of fire	Ro 12:20; Pr 25:21	to incur God's favor by reacting positively to a situation in which revenge would be normal
8. Orate	open the mouth	Job 3:1	to speak at great length with great liberty or freedom
9. Claim	you say	Mt 26:25,63,64	means it is your opinion
10. Excellency	living, lively	Jn 4:10,11 Ac 7:38; Heb 10:20; 1Pe 2:4,5;	used to express the excellency of perfection of that to which it refers

		Rev 1:17	
11. Abundance	riches	Ro 2:4; Eph 1:7; 3:8; Col 1:27; 2:2	used to describe abundance of or a great supply
12. Preeminence	firstborn	Ps 89:27; Ro 8:29; Col 1;15, 18; Heb 12:23	special place of preeminence; first place among many others
13. Freedom	enlarge my feet; enlarge	2Sa 22:37; Ps 4:1; 18:36	freed me; brought me into a situation that has taken the pressure off, taken on to bigger and better things
14. Reverential respect for	fear and trembling	Ps 55:5; Mk 5:33; Lk 8:47; 1Co 2:3; 2 Co 7:15; Eph 6:5, Php 2:12	describes an attitude of appropriate respect for something. The something could be God, could a person, or could be a combination including some process. Sometimes indicates confronting a difficult situation or thing with a strong awareness of it and possible consequences

Again I would recommend you refer to my manual **Figures and Idioms** to see the approach for capturing the patterned idioms.

Figures and Idioms should be appreciated, understood, and should be interpreted with emphasis. Hardly any passage which is any one of the seven leadership genre will be without some figure or idiom.

Article 5

Getting the Job Done—Comparison of Ezra's and Haggai's Roles

Introduction
In the book of Haggai God calls the returned Israelites to engage in the long-delayed rebuilding of the temple. The re-energized workers obey God, start construction and the project is off and running. Haggai records this exciting beginning. The narrative in Haggai then brings us four months into the process, up to the laying of the foundation. At the end of Haggai, things are going well, but the book doesn't tell us if the Temple was ever finished. To find out what becomes of the project the reader needs to turn to another post-exilic book of the Bible—the book of Ezra.

In studying Haggai, the book of Ezra is helpful for five reasons.

1) It provides a narrative setting in which to understand the prophetic message of Haggai.
2) It is the only other book in the Bible where Haggai is mentioned by name.
3) It shows Haggai's continued leadership influence on the project.
4) It shows Haggai functioning as part of a leadership team.
5) It records the completion of the temple

Reason 1 Explained
Ezra provides a narrative background for understanding Haggai's message and ministry.

The historical period covered in Ezra reaches before and after the brief slice of time mentioned in Haggai. The book of Haggai covers only four months—August thru December in 520 BC. Ezra records events beginning in 537 B.C and ending in 457 A.D.—a span of 80 years. Haggai has a public presence for at least four of these years – 520-516 BC[6]. The book of Ezra in helpful in that it covers 17 years of history leading up to Haggai's ministry and 59 years after the last recorded appearance of Haggai in the Bible[7]. This broader context gives us a background to understand the challenges Haggai

---

[6] Inserting the events of Haggai into the timeline of Ezra is made relatively simple in that both books contain dated time markers, and like Ezra, Haggai follows a progressive, sequential storyline. As a side note—Haggai shares several other similarities with the book of Ezra. Like Ezra, Haggai shows the importance of renewal—but renewal for a purpose, in this case a building project. It illustrates how doing flows out of being—how task is important to God, but that it flows out of right relationship with God.

[7] While mentioned in the same book, Haggai and Ezra did not share public ministry together. In fact Ezra did not show up in Jerusalem until 58 years after the last scriptural mention of Haggai. While not contemporaries, both Ezra and Haggai had a powerful public ministry. Haggai's was prophetic, Ezra leaned more toward teaching. He was a scribe, well-versed in God's word. The people whose lives bridged both their ministries had the best of both worlds—powerful prophetic messages under Haggai, and powerful public teaching under Ezra

faced going in, and also the impact of his ministry afterwards to the long term success of the project. The timeline in Table 5.1 will provide an overview of key dates.

Table 5.1 Ezra and Haggai – A Timeline

Description of Event	Scriptural Reference in the book of Haggai	Scriptural Reference in the book of Ezra	Date of Event (all dates are B.C.)
Zerubbabel and Joshua the high priest led the return of exiles from captivity to Jerusalem		Ezra 1:11 -	537+-
Work on the temple begins		Ezra 3:8	536
Opposition from enemies		Ezra 4:1-5	536-530
Construction of the temple ceased		Ezra 4	530-520
Haggai's first message	Hag 1:1-11,	Ezra 5:1	August 520
Rebuilding of the temple resumes	Hag 1:12-15	Ezra 5:2	September 520
Haggai's second message	Hag 2:9		October 520
Beginning of Zechariah's preaching		Zechariah 1:1-6	Oct/Nov 520
Haggai's third message	Haggai 2:10-19		December 5:20
Haggai's fourth message	Haggai 2:20-23		December 520
Temple Completed		Ezra 6:15	March 516
Ezra Arrives in Jerusalem		Ezra 7	August 458
End of the Historical period covered in the book of Ezra		Ezra 10	457

Reason 2 Explained
Haggai appears twice in the book of Ezra.

Ezra is the only book in the Bible (outside the book of Haggai) that mentions Haggai by name. These two references in Ezra occur as bookends to his four years of public ministry recorded in scripture. Ezra 5:1 marks Haggai's influence in restarting the rebuilding of the temple (520 BC). The reference in Ezra 6:14 occurs at the end of the four year construction process and the completion of the temple (516 BC). Here are the two verses.

> Ezra 5:1 Now Haggai the prophet and Zechariah the prophet, a descendant of Iddo, prophesied to the Jews in Judah and Jerusalem in the name of the God of Israel, who was over them.

> Ezra 6:14 So the elders of the Jews continued to build and prosper under the preaching of Haggai the prophet and Zechariah, a descendant of Iddo. They finished building the temple according to the command of the God of Israel and the decrees of Cyrus, Darius and Artaxerxes, kings of Persia.

Reason 3 Explained
Haggai had a continued leadership role in the project.

Ezra is also helpful in showing that Haggai played a prominent role not just in initiating the building project, but in bringing it to completion. From the book of Haggai, we see that Haggai's message was used to stir the people to begin building, in Ezra 6:14 we see Haggai's ongoing public ministry encouraged the workers as they continued to build.

> "So the elders of the Jews <u>continued</u> to build and prosper under the <u>preaching</u> of Haggai the prophet.."

The content of this ongoing preaching is not recorded. But if the prophecies recorded in Haggai are an indicator, we might guess that God used Haggai to:

1) Bring perspective to a large-scale and often overwhelming project.
2) To step in with words of encouragement when enthusiasm sagged.
3) To counteract the tendency towards discouragement as progress was slow at times.

Observation—In some cases God may use a prophetic leader to catalyze a work, but not to provide ongoing influence. In this case Haggai stayed at it until their God-given task was completed. Haggai's influence was used by God to get the job done.

Reason 4 Explained
Haggai served as part of a leadership team.

In both books, Haggai and Ezra, the prophet Haggai served as part of a leadership team. In Ezra 6:14 it's alongside another post-exilic prophet,[8] Zechariah[9]. Rebuilding the temple was a complex, multi-year task. During this four year process God works through a coalition of leaders to contribute to the task.[10] This team consisted of Zerubbabel the governor, Joshua the high priest, Haggai and Zechariah —both prophets[11].

---

[8] The other two post-exilic prophets are Zechariah and Malachi. There are seventeen books of prophecy in the Old Testament. These prophets cluster around three crises: (1) The Assyrian threat which eventually cut off the northern kingdom; (2) The Babylonian threat which eventually cut off the southern kingdom; (3) The return from exile—in which Jerusalem was reoccupied, the wall built and the temple rebuilt. Haggai deals with this third crisis. He falls in the post kingdom, post-exilic period. In fact Haggai is the first prophet to prophesy after the captivity. See the **Article**, *Prophetic Crises, Three Major*.

[9] Note the two times Haggai's name appears in Ezra. Both are alongside Zechariah

[10] See the **Article**, *Leadership Coalition*.

[11] Even between the two prophets, Zechariah and Haggai, each brought a unique perspective. Haggai's prophecies came largely in the form of pronouncements from God. Zechariah on the other hand was more visionary. Much of Haggai's comments are directed toward re-engaging in the task. Zechariah gives us a peek into the spiritual warfare going on behind the scenes

Reason 5 Explained
God used Haggai to see the project to completion.
   In Haggai we see that they started rebuilding the temple, in Ezra we see that they <u>finished</u> building the temple. Many leaders have seen projects get off to a great start, only to fizzle out along the way. It's encouraging to know that a good start was followed by a strong finish.

Conclusion
The book of Ezra, along with the book of Haggai, provides a helpful case study for successfully bringing a project to completion. A leader can profit from studying the principles involved in completing a God-given task.

Article 6

God The Promise Keeper

Introduction

Have you been to a *Promise Keepers'* event? That is an oft asked question these days. I smile and answer that question with another one. Do you know **The Promise Keeper**? Great as those promise keepers' events are they are nothing when compared to **The Promise Keeper** meeting with you.

Promises of God

When I was a little boy my friends and I would often say, "I promise." And the other person would say, "Cross your heart and hope to die?" The meaning was, "Do you really mean it?" Now little boys make and break promises about as fast as can be. But with God it is not so. One, He does not promise helter-skelter-like. And when He does promise He can be trusted. Our problem is learning to hear Him promise and being sure what we heard was a promise from Him, for us.

Definition   A *promise from God* is an assertion from God, specific or general or a truth in harmony with God's character, which is perceived in one's heart or mind concerning what He will do or not do for that one and which is sealed in our inner most being by a quickening action of the Holy Spirit and on which that one then counts.

There are three parts to the promise:

1. the cognitive part which refers to the assertion and its understanding, and
2. the affective part which is the inner most testimony to the promise, and
3. the volitional act of faith on our part which believes the assertion and feelings and thereafter counts upon it.

A leader can err in three ways, concerning promises. One, the leader may misread the assertion. That is, misinterpret what he/she thinks God will do or not do. Or two, the leader may wrongly apply some assertion to himself/herself which is does not apply. It may even be a true assertion but not for that leader or that time. Or the leader may misread the inner witness. It may not be God's Spirit quickening of the leader.

Sometimes the assertion comes from a command, or a principle, or even a direct statement of a promise God makes. The promise may be made generally to all who follow God or specifically to some. It may be for all time or for a limited time. Commands or principles are not in themselves promises. But it is when the Holy Spirit brings some truth out of them that He wants to apply to our lives that they may become promises. Such truths almost always bear on the character of God.

One thing we can know for certain, if indeed we do have a promise from God, then He will fulfill it. For Titus 1:2 asserts an important truth about God.

God can not lie.

He is **The Promise Keeper**. This is an image of God that all leaders need.

Examples of God As The Promise Keeper

God keeps his promises. He is the Promise Keeper. Table 6.1 gives some examples to shore up our faith in **The Promise Keeper**. I could have chosen 100s of promises.[12]

Table 6.1 God The Promise Keeper—Examples

To Whom	Vs	Basic Promise/ Results
Abraham	Gen 12:1,2	Bless the world through Abraham. Give descendants. Spawn nations. Give a land. / This has happened and continues to happen.
Nahum	Whole book	Judgment on Nineveh/ Assyria. Promises fulfilled.
Obadiah	Whole book	Judgment on Edom. Promises fulfilled.
Habakkuk	Ch 2	Judgment on Babylon. Promises fulfilled. See Da 5.
Zechariah	Lk 1:13	Birth of John the Baptist. Promise fulfilled.
Mary	Lk 1:35	Birth of Jesus. Promise fulfilled.
Hezekiah	Isa 39:1ff, especially vs 5-7	Babylonian captivity. Royal hostages taken (Daniel was one of these). Promise fulfilled.
Daniel	Ch 2	The broad outlines of history/ nations and God's purposes. Promise fulfilled in part with more to come.
Daniel	Ch 9	Messiah and work of cross. Promise fulfilled.
Daniel	Ch 10-11:35	Again the broad outline of history particularly with reference to Israel. Everything up to 11:35 has taken place in detail as promises. The rest is yet to come.

Conclusion

The dictionary defines a promise as giving a pledge, committing oneself to do something, to make a declaration assuring that something will or will not be done or to afford a basis for expectation. Synonyms for promise include: covenant, engage, pledge, plight, swear, vow. The central meaning shared by these verbs is *to declare solemnly that one will perform or refrain from a particular course of action*. God is **The Promise Keeper**. As children of His we should learn to hear His promises and to receive them for our lives. As a leader you most likely will not make it over the long haul if you do not know God **as The Promise Keeper**.

One of the six characteristics[13] of a leader who finishes well is described as,

---

[12] Over the years I have kept a listing of promises I felt God has made to me and my wife. Many of these have been fulfilled. In December of 1997 I reviewed all of these—an encouraging faith building exercise.

[13] The six characteristics include: 1. They maintain a personal vibrant relationship with God right up to the end. 2. They maintain a learning posture and can learn from various kinds of sources—life especially. 3. They manifest Christ-likeness in character as evidenced by the fruit of the Spirit in their lives. 4. Truth is lived out in their lives so that convictions and promises of God are seen to be real. 5. They leave behind

> **Truth is lived out in their lives so that convictions and promises of God are seen to be real.**

A leader who has God's promises and lives by them will exemplify this characteristic.[14] Paul did. Paul, the model N.T. church leader knew God as **The Promise Keeper**. Do you?

---

one or more ultimate contributions. 6. They walk with a growing awareness of a sense of destiny and see some or all of it fulfilled.

[14] One of the symptoms of a plateaued leader is failure to get new fresh truth from God—especially failure to get new promises from God. Such a leader will also lack faith to see old promises fulfilled.

Article 7

God's Timing and Leadership

Introduction
What do these verses have in common?

Joseph's birth:
22 And God remembered Rachel, and God hearkened to her, and opened her womb. 23 And she conceived, and bare a son; and said, God hath taken away my reproach: 24 And she called his name Joseph; and said, The LORD shall add to me another son. Gen 30

Jesus Ministry:
4 But when the fullness of the **time** was come, God sent forth his Son, made of a woman, made under the law, 5 To redeem them that were under the law, that we might receive the adoption of sons. Gal 4:4

From John Quoting Jesus:
John: Jesus said unto her, Woman, what have I to do with thee? my **hour** is not yet come. Jn 2:4

Then Jesus said unto them, **My time** is not yet come: but your time is always ready. Jn 7:6

I am not going to the feast, yet; for **my time** is not yet full come. Jn 7:8

Then they sought to take him: but no man laid hands on him, because his **hour** was not yet come. Jn 7:30

These words spoke Jesus in the treasury, as he taught in the temple: and no man laid hands on him; for his **hour** was not yet come. Jn 8:20

And Jesus answered them, saying, The **hour** is come, that the Son of man should be glorified. Jn 12:23

Now is my soul troubled; and what shall I say? Father, save me from this **hour**: but for this cause came I unto this **hour**. Jn 12:27

Now before the feast of the Passover, when Jesus knew that his **hour** was come that he should depart out of this world unto the Father, having loved his own which were in the world, he loved them unto the end. Jn 13:1

All have to do with God's timing. One of the major macro lessons first seen in *the Patriarchal Leadership Era* and then in every other leadership era thereafter states,

God's timing is crucial to the accomplishment of God's purposes.[15]

Effective leaders are increasingly aware of the timing of God's interventions in their lives and ministry. They move when he moves. They wait. They confidently expect. Leaders must learn to be sensitive to God's timing. God's direction includes *What, How, and When*. All are important.

This is a leadership lesson that all leaders must learn. Strong leaders, such as apostolic leaders desperately need to learn this. Such leaders usually have a strong sense of destiny. Such leaders usually have a strong vision they want to accomplish. Often these strong leaders tie their vision to some prophecy or other revelatory word. While they may know the *what* and even the *how* of the vision they may well be off in the *when*. They often move ahead of God's timing. God's timing is crucial. Less bold and forceful leaders also need to learn about God's timing. Frequently, they lag behind God's timing. What can we learn from some Bible characters about God's timing?

Thirteen Bible Characters and God's Timing

Table 7.1 lists thirteen Bible characters and implications about God's timing.

Table 7.1 13 Bible Characters and God's Timing

Character	Leader-ship Era	Timing Issue	Observations/ Lessons
Abraham/ Sarah	Patriarchal	Birth of Isaac/ Israel's deliverance 400 years later	*Isaac: The promises of God include what, how, and when.* Abraham and Sarah only knew what. The how they tried to manipulate. The when—they went ahead of God. God was true to his promise. The what, how, when all came together. God's timing was crucial. *Israel's Promised Deliverance from Egypt: Sometimes God's timing is well beyond a leader's own lifetime. Such a promise can enable one to live with hope and faith though they may never see the fulfillment of that promise.*
Jacob/ Rachael	Patriarchal	Birth of Joseph	Joseph's birth, as to timing was important. The birth order was necessary to God's purposes for him—both favored status and his brothers jealousy. The time of birth was important; he was to deliver in 39 years. *Manipulation of God's timing can bring problems. Manipulation begets manipulation.*
Joseph	Patriarchal	Fulfillment of Certainty Guidance— 2 Dreams	Throughout the Joseph narrative timing is important (dreams at 17; caravan; in jail with two of Pharaoh's servants; God's dreams about drought, etc.) Most important lesson. *The way up is often down and may take a long time for God to accomplish.*
Moses	Pre-	Deliverance	Deliverance from Egypt: Moses was a strong

---

[15] See **Article**, *Macro Lessons—Defined; Macro Lessons—List of 41 Across Six Leadership eras.*

God's Timing and Leadership

	Kingdom	of Israel from Egypt	leader who went ahead of God to deliver Israel from Egypt. He learned a major lesson that strong leaders often learn—The Death of a Vision. *A strong ego leader must surrender a vision and give it back to God. God will bring it about in his own way and timing. Don't move ahead of God. Make sure the how of guidance is God's how.* Crossing the Red Sea: *The when of God's guidance is crucial. It takes faith to believe in exact timing of God's intervention.* Failure to Enter the Land: *Failure to heed God's intervention time can bring long term ramifications—* *40 years in the desert, loss of a generation* Going in to the land: *God's progressive timing has underlying reasons behind it. Development of an armed force takes time.*
Joshua	Pre-Kingdom	Generational leadership/ Capture of Jericho/ Gibeon (flesh act)	Desert Wandering: *A leader often pays a price due to followership. A leader needs time to enculterate and be enculterated to a new generation of followers.* Crossing the Jordan: They could have crossed in non-flood season without God's help. They needed this God intervention for courage and to give Joshua spiritual authority. The three days they camped beside the flood waters built anticipation and fearfulness. Fall of Jericho: *The How and When must be obtained from God in a major achievement.* Gibeon: *Moving ahead of God, making a decision in the flesh with hearing from God and then asking God to approve your decision often results in major negative ramifications that you must live with.*
Caleb	Pre-Kingdom	Generational Leadership; Fulfillment of Promise	Desert Wandering: *Leaders who model whole hearted obedience to God can impact a new generation with the importance of believing God and obeying Him.* Land: *The promises of God will be fulfilled in His timing. Respond with courage.*
Samuel	Pre-Kingdom	Moving from decentralized leadership to a Kingdom	Sons: *The what of God's intervention is as important as the when and how. Samuel's sons were not God's answer to the leadership need.*: Saul: *Obedience to God's timing is necessary. Failure to obey God as to His timing may well imply lack of integrity and an eventual setting aside by God.*
David	Kingdom	Made King	Uniting the Kingdom: *Time is involved even*

			when the what is known.
Hezekiah	Kingdom	Sickness Unto Death/ Babylonian Envoy (flesh act)	**Changing God's Timing:** *Hezekiah's prolonged life brought ramifications he probably didn't foresee. The birth of Manasseh occurred in this time.* **Babylonian envoy:** *To move ahead of God, make a decision without consulting God, can bring ramifications (later Babylonian captivity). To be safe in one's own generation may well bode problems for future generations.*
Daniel	Post-Kingdom	70 Years Captivity Fulfilled	**Learning Posture:** *Daniel's maintaining a learning posture, studying the Scriptures, brought out the what and when and hints as to the how of God's plans. God's timing is exact. He will fulfill His promises on time.*
Jesus	Pre-Church	The Cross	**World Scene:** *The timing was perfect for Jesus birth.* **Sensitivity:** *Jesus was sensitive to God's timing for his life, throughout his ministry. He never went ahead; he never lagged behind. Jesus models perfectly the whole notion of what, when, and how in following God's plans.*
Peter	Church	Impulsive Actions; Coming of Holy Spirit	**Impulsive:** *Peter's tendencies to move too quickly throughout the disciples training serves as a negative model. See Jesus' reactions and training of Peter.* **Pentecost:** *God's promise of power was fulfilled exactly on time. Waiting was involved.* **Lagging Behind:** *The church failed to expand. God brought persecution to get them to expand.*
Paul	Church	Reaching of Gentiles/ Kings	**Antioch Call:** *A leader may be called upon to do something at a time (when is clear). But the what and how are hazy. The what and when may be revealed over time.* **Macedonian call:** *God's timing may involve pre-preparation about the what and how. The move to Europe involved a pre-prepared receptive group ready to hear and respond.*

Four Reasons For Delay In Timing

In a number of the Biblical examples given above God delayed what He was going to do. Some possible reasons for delay include:

1. **Dealing With a Strong Ego Leader**—The *Death of a Vision* as seen in Moses' case involved dealing with the right vision but the wrong motivation, wrong power base, and wrong timing.
2. **God's Working out of other purposes**—In the promise to Abraham (400 years) God pointed out that He was dealing with the nations in the land and that

their iniquity was not yet full. That is, He was giving them time to repent. That time wasn't up yet when Moses made his first attempt at deliverance.
3. **Foundational Character Shaping**—Moses' isolation period brought about a humility in character (Nu 12:3) which made him a pliable vessel in God's hands. He would need this humility because God would reveal power through his ministry which could be dangerous with a strong unfettered ego leader.
4. **Remedial Training**—God is doing remedial training. He is giving time for certain disciplines to be built in the life of the leader. Moses was a desert leader. He learned about desert disciplines as a shepherd wandering over desert land taking care of sheep.

Three Reasons To Move Fast in God's Timing

Just as some leaders have a tendency to move too fast and God has to delay their actions, some leaders move to slowly. Why should leaders move faster? Here are some reasons:

1. **Windows of Opportunity**—God knows that sometimes the needed action must take place within a certain time period or an opportunity to accomplish something may be lost.
2. **Networks/ onward guidance**—Sometimes the timing is such that obedience will connect to other things God has set up. The next piece of guidance will open up after obedience. To not move will be to miss it. Following an unusual apparently hurried intervention may lead to a series of people or events and give guidance that would not previously have been dreamed of.
3. **God's Doing**—Sometimes God moves a leader to action before things are apparently ready because He wants all to know that He alone is responsible and He alone will get credit for the results. That is, sometimes God has something happen fast because it would be impossible for it to happen unless God alone brought it about.

Four Implications of the Timing Lesson

Four observations can be drawn from a comparative study of God's timing with the leaders listed above:

1. **Ramifications.** Moving ahead of God's timing in guidance or in carrying out some aspect of ministry may accomplish the task; it will most certainly bring ramifications which will require remedial training and the repetition of incidents to teach us the dependence lesson.
2. **Guidance.** The *what*, *how*, and *when* are the major elements of guidance. We need clarity on all three. It is the *when* that is most in focus on the timing macro lesson.
3. **Sensitivity.** We must be sensitive to the Spirit in our lives. Timing can refer to daily interventions or long term guidance decisions. In either case we need to be sensitive to the Spirit. Seemingly small issues may turn out to be pivotal points. This implies that we as leaders especially need to develop the Spirit Sensitivity component of the Spirituality model.
4. **Negative Preparation and Flesh Act.** We need to be thoroughly familiar with these two process items including the various illustrations of them in Scripture so we will respond more quickly and carefully to incidents which God is using for this kind of processing. A *flesh act* means making a decision based on fleshly wisdom and moving ahead without getting God's guidance. *Negative preparation* refers to numerous negative happenings in the life. These may well be used by God to move a leader out of a situation.

Conclusion

Look again at the basic lesson.

God's Timing Is Crucial To Accomplishment Of God's Purposes.

Moses learned this lesson the hard way. But he learned it well. The latter stages of his desert leadership reflect his increased sensitivity to God's timing. The question is,

Are You Sensitive To God's Timing In The Little Things Of Daily Ministry As Well As The Big Things Of Major Guidance?

Some final advice should be noted, especially for major guidance decisions.

1. **Triple Confirmation.** Where possible never make a major decision unless you are clear on the *what*, the *how*, and the *when* of the issues. Should you be unclear on any, then it may be best to wait. Certainty guidance via double confirmation or divine contact should be sought on all three issues: what, when, how.
2. **Presumption.** Be careful of presuming to know God's intents on some aspects of ministry without clearing with Him first. Simply attempting to get His approval after the fact may prove fatal in the long run.
3. **Patterns.** Study the concept of timing in the Bible and identify patterns of sensitivity to God's timing. Note what to avoid as well as what to assert. Go back through the vignettes associated with the leaders given in Table 7.1. Study them carefully and learn first hand what you need to know about God's timing and your leadership.

Let me repeat in closing. Effective Leaders Are Increasingly Aware Of The Timing Of God's Interventions In Their Lives And Ministry. They Move When He Moves. They Wait. They Confidently Expect. Leaders must learn to be sensitive to God's timing. God's direction includes *What*, *How*, and *When*. All are important.

See *flesh act; negative preparation; pivotal point; double confirmation; divine contact;* **Glossary**.

Article 8

Haggai—Afterglow Ministry

Introduction

Figure 8.1 below introduces the ministry time line we currently use when teaching lifelong development of a leader.

```
Phase I      Phase II              Phase III      Phase IV      Afterglow
|------------|---------------------|--------------|-------------|---------|
A.  B.       A.   B.    C.         A.    B.       A.   B.
```

Where:

Phase I, **Ministry Foundations**, is made up of:
A. Sovereign Foundations (13-20 years)
B. Leadership Transition (3-6 years)

Phase II, **General Ministry**, is made up of:
A. Provisional Ministry (2-6 years)
B. Growth Ministry (6-8 years)
C. Competent Ministry (2-6 years)

Phase III, **Focused Ministry**, is made up of:
A. Role transition
B. Unique Ministry
(A and B together total from 3-12 years)

Phase IV, **Convergent Ministry**, is made up of
A. Special Guidance (time???)
B. Convergence (time???)

Figure 8.1 The Ministry Time-Line

And then there is *Afterglow*. What a beautiful picture. One sees in one's mind the picture of a fire whose coals are red hot and glowing. There is still a warmth radiating from such a fire, even though the flames themselves are not leaping up. And so it is with a life well lived. Leaders in *Afterglow* may be retired from formal positions but not from influencing others for the Kingdom.

Definition
Afterglow is that special time in a leader's life when the leader has no formal role but has extended influence in the lives of others because of a life well-lived and a recognized spiritual authority.

Definition
Spiritual authority is
1. the God-given right to influence followers toward accomplishments for God,
2. which is conferred on a leader by followers because of the leader's
   a. personal experiences with God,
   b. exemplary Godly character,
   c. demonstration of gifted power in ministry.

It is that almost intangible characteristic of a God-anointed leader developed upon an experiential power base which enables a leader to influence followers through persuasion, force of modeling and moral expertise toward God's purposes.

It is authenticated and recognized in a leader by followers in one or more of three ways.

1. They see a Godly life—that is, character which emulates their perception of what Godliness ought to be like.
2. They see demonstration of power in the leader's giftedness in ministry.
3. They recognize that the leader has deep experiences and hence knowledge of God which they don't have.

In *Afterglow* ministry, spiritual authority is prominent, as usually no other kind of authority is available.

Haggai and Afterglow
Haggai was a very successful prophet. The people responded to his ministry. In fact, it is amazing that they did so. The work on the temple had been stalled for about 18 years. Then we have these words of Haggai. Almost immediately the work begins again. And in about 4 years the project is finished. Why such a response? Well, obviously from the response alone, it is clear that Haggai had spiritual authority. Two prominent leaders, Zerubbabel and Joshua, listen to his words and heed them. These experienced leaders are not going to be taken in by some fly-by-night self-appointed prophet. Haggai is listened to and heeded.

Some commentators view the words below from Haggai and suggest that Haggai, himself, was one who saw the original temple. That is why he can so empathetically give this message on discouragement about the small work of God.

> 1 On the twentieth day of the seventh month. God gave another Word to the prophet Haggai. 2 "Speak to Governor Zerubbabel, the son of Shealtiel, and to Joshua the high priest, the son of Josedech and to the remnant of the people who have come back to the land. 3 Say this, "Do any of you remember how splendid Solomon's Temple really was? And now look at what you are building? Not much, is it?" 4 But don't be discouraged. Be strong, Zerubbabel. Be strong Joshua. Be strong all you people. Rebuild this temple! For I am with you, the Lord Almighty. 5 I made a covenant with you long ago when you came out of Egypt. And I am still with you. So don't be afraid nor be discouraged. Haggai 2:1-5

I think that makes sense. Haggai was probably a very old prophet. One who had lived a long time under the shadow of the Lord Almighty. When he spoke, he was listened to because of his age, wisdom, and testimony of a long life with the Lord Almighty. He had seen the original temple. He had seen the Babylonian captivity. He had seen God bring the people back from captivity. He had seen the left-hand of God at work through the pagan rulers—Cyrus, Darius, Xerxes. He could see God's future perfect view of this work, small though it was. It was *Afterglow* time for Haggai.

Closure

Spiritual authority, from the standpoint of the follower is the right to influence, conferred upon a leader by followers, because of their perception of spirituality in that leader. From the leader's perspective *Spiritual Authority* is that characteristic of a God-anointed leader, developed upon an experiential power base (giftedness, character, deep experiences with God), that enables him/her to influence followers through persuasion, force of modeling, and moral expertise. Haggai had it. Such spiritual authority is very compatible with the *Afterglow* period of ministry. I think it highly likely that Haggai was in *Afterglow*.

Some cultures respect older people. The Jewish culture in the O.T. was such a culture. Our western culture is a bit weak in this. Older leaders do not always see *Afterglow* ministry. May I challenge you if you are a younger leader to recognize *Afterglow* leaders and seek them out for mentoring help. And may I challenge all of you to finish well and have an *Afterglow* ministry.

See **Article**, *Haggai—And Spiritual Authority; Left Hand of God.*

Article 9

Haggai—And Spiritual Authority

Introduction
How can a leader, without an official title, without an organizational office, be powerfully used to effectively call people to engage in a difficult ministry project? Especially a project that requires followers to radically re-orient their lives?

An Old Testament Case Study on Spiritual Authority
Such a project was the post-exilic rebuilding of the temple, and the leader was the prophet Haggai. Haggai stepped into a stalled out building project and *authoritatively* injected a word from God to jumpstart the rebuilding of the temple. But where did that authority come from? Why did the people listen to Haggai? Unlike the other leaders on the scene, Haggai was the only one who held no office, and possessed no title. He was not part of the religious or civil leadership. So where did his authority come from? From God! Haggai is an excellent example of a leader who operated from a primary leadership base of spiritual authority.

The importance of Spiritual Authority in Haggai's Influence
In the book of Haggai God uses a leadership team of four to launch the temple rebuilding project – Joshua, Zerubbabel, Zechariah and Haggai.[16] Likely all four operated with a measure of spiritual authority, but unlike Joshua – who was the high priest, or Zerubbabel who had a position as governor, Haggai had no formal office, title or position. Void of such cultural or organizational support Haggai depended solely on spiritual authority as a means of influence.[17]

4 Reasons To study spiritual authority in the life of Haggai
Before jumping into a study of spiritual authority in the life of Haggai, perhaps it is fair to ask the question. Why is this important today? What help does it offer today's leaders. A study of Haggai is valuable, because just like in Haggai's time...

- We need leaders who can step into a situation and bring a word from God that will break things open and move a ministry forward.

- We need leaders who can face a ministry challenge with the unshakeable confidence that flows from being authorized by God

- We need leaders who experience the Holy Spirit's empowering of their words to reach the hearts of women and men.

- We need leaders who can receive insight from God that provides compelling vision for followers desperately in need of hope and encouragement

---

[16] See the **Article**, *Haggai- Leadership Coalition*.
[17] Neither did Zechariah. However, in this article we are focusing on Haggai.

What is Spiritual Authority?[18]

Before observing spiritual authority in the life of Haggai, it would be helpful to pause and consider a definition of spiritual authority.

Definition—Viewed from Followers Standpoint
1. *Spiritual Authority* is the right to influence conferred upon a leader by followers because of their perception of spirituality in that leader.

Definition—Viewed from Leader's Standpoint
2. *Spiritual Authority* is that characteristic of a God-anointed leader, which is developed upon an experiential power base that enables him/her to influence followers through: 1. Persuasion, 2. Force of modeling, and 3. Moral expertise.

A leader with spiritual authority is someone who operates with the God-given, God-authenticated spiritual resources needed to effectively influence followers towards God's purposes. Ultimately spiritual authority is a result of God's work in a leader's life. As opposed to positional authority, spiritual authority comes from the calling, giftedness and other spiritual resources that God has worked and/or placed in the leader. A leader walking in spiritual authority carries a certain deposit of leadership grace entrusted by God for use in leading His people.

Six Examples of Spiritual Authority from Haggai's Life

One of the best ways to understand spiritual authority is to see at work in the life of a leader. Our case study is Haggai. If Haggai operated with spiritual authority, what are evidences of it? There are several things we can point to. A good place to start is with a verse from Haggai that perhaps best captures the people's recognition of this type of authority.

> Hag 1:12 Then Zerubbabel son of Shealtiel, Joshua son of Jehozadak, the high priest, and the whole remnant of the people obeyed the voice of the Lord their God and the message of the prophet Haggai, because the Lord their God had sent him. And the people feared the Lord.

1. God authenticated Haggai's Leadership.

Haggai's authority was recognized from top to bottom by both leaders and followers alike. All the people, beginning with Zerubbabel and Joshua saw God's hand on Haggai's leadership. In obeying Haggai, the people recognized that they were in fact, obeying God. The people obeyed "the message of the prophet Haggai", because in it they heard "the voice of the Lord their God". This is a component of spiritual authority.[19] A follower correctly recognizing spiritual authority does so with a desire to obey God. Like many other leaders in the Bible, Haggai saw God confirm his ministry in the hearts of the hearers.

2. Haggai served with a sense of Sentness.

Haggai operated with a clear sense of *sentness*.[20] That is – he was recognized as someone sent from God. In verse 12 we read that "the Lord their God had <u>sent</u> him" A leader with spiritual authority enjoys a supernatural sense of security in their leadership. They have a confidence that comes from knowing that in using that authority, they are acting as ambassadors of the Lord God Almighty.

---

[18] See the **Article**, *Spiritual Authority* for expanded study.
[19] This is gifted power, one of the ways folks know God is in it.
[20] See the **Article**, *Jesus—Sentness*.

3. God defended Haggai's leadership.

The verse above says that the people obeyed Haggai because God sent him and "the people feared the Lord." The people quickly recognized that refusing to follow Haggai's message, would result in consequences from God. While God did not have to actively defend Haggai against a challenge to leadership, Haggai's listeners realized that God was ready and willing to back up and enforce Haggai's prophetic message. And in fact the way they responded to Haggai's message did experience consequences – good ones. In this case the people obeyed and enjoyed God's blessings!

4. Haggai's effectiveness in bringing a corrective message.

A fourth evidence of spiritual authority in Haggai was His effectiveness at courageously bringing a "hard to hear" message. Haggai brought what was probably a very unpopular message. No one wants to hear that their priorities are all messed up. Yet Haggai didn't shy away from bringing a heavily corrective and directive prophecy. Like Paul, Haggai was not shy in exercising "the authority the Lord gave me.... for building you up" (2 Co 13:10). Haggai speaks as one speaking the very words of God (1 Pe 4:11).

5. Haggai was not hindered by lack of organizational position.

Haggai was a leader because God made him a leader. Titles and positions can be a helpful and biblical part of leadership. But ultimately God is the one who makes or breaks a leader. Haggai could not fall back on organizational avenues to ensure compliance with his leadership. Yet, lack of a name plaque on the organizational chart in no way detracted from Haggai's leadership influence. Haggai should be an encouraging example to emerging leaders wondering if they can make a difference when not yet having a title or position. Embracing the Biblical concept of spiritual authority would seem to suggest two personal convictions for both emerging and existing leaders.

1) While titles are helpful, no amount of titles can make me something that God had not made me and conversely,
2) If God grants a measure of spiritual authority to my leadership- lack of titles or position would not take that away.

While followers can recognize spiritual authority, it is ultimately a result of God's work in a leader. The source of spiritual authority comes not from the outside, but from God's work on the inside.

6. The results of Haggai's leadership.

Prior to Haggai the building project was going no where quick. Despite the current leadership of two good and Godly leaders – Joshua and Zerubbabel, this project lagged for twenty some years. Yet this one prophet, in short time, motivated followers to rearrange their lives and make God's work a priority. This is the difference the right person, at the right time, can bring when God is powerfully working through their life. There are examples of equally called leaders who saw less than favorable responses to their ministry – including other prophets, but in the case of Haggai, the spiritual authority was recognized by the followers and brought a much needed breakthrough.

Relevance for Today

Spiritual leadership was foundational for Haggai's leadership. But that was over two thousand years ago. Is it still relevant to leaders at the beginning of the third millennium?

> **Our increasingly postmodern culture offers a fresh reason to revisit the importance of spiritual authority.**

Haggai—And Spiritual Authority

Leaders today face a world where people are no longer delivered to the front door of the church eager to follow someone simply because of their position. We live in an culture where simply wearing the title "leader" brings little "built-in" credibility, even less so with the title "church leader'. Like Haggai, in order to have impact, today's leaders may find an increasing need for a God-authenticated authority that stands up well – whether or not accompanied by a name tag.

It might not surprise us to see that the churches and ministries that will prevail will be led by those who understand the a deepening need to walk before God in dependency and allow God to build spiritual authority into their lives.

Two suggestions for personal growth

Do you desire to grow in your understanding and experience of spiritual authority? Here are two suggestions

> **Suggestion #1 – As you look forward** - Ask God to work spiritual authority into your life. Be on the look out for ways God is developing character, developing sensitivity to His Spirit, and supernaturally equipping you for life and service.

> **Suggestion #2 – As you look backwards** – Ask God to show you ways He's been working to develop spiritual authority in your life. Find encouragement by noting ways God has already been at work in this important area. Be challenged to cooperate even more fully as God works in and through you.

Spiritual authority will no doubt look different on everyone, but here are a few questions that may be helpful for identifying ways God has developed and demonstrated spiritual authority in your life.

Questions to Probe for Spiritual Authority

- What are examples from my past where God has defended my leadership?

- What are instances that point to God's hand of favor on my life and leadership?

- What might people point to in my ministry as examples where God has worked through me?

Closure

Effective leaders value spiritual authority as a primary power base. Are you pursuing spiritual authority? What role does spiritual authority play in yor life? Think of Haggai. What God did for him, he can do for you.

Article 10

Haggai—And Timing

Introduction
One of the important leadership macro lessons[21] learned in the very first leadership era and then repeated so forcefully in the second and then frequently throughout all the other leadership eras is the timing macro.

Timing Macro-Lesson
God's Timing Is Crucial To Accomplishment Of God's Purposes.

Notice the following examples.

Table 10.1 Some Examples of the Timing Macro Lesson

Era	Example(s)
I. Patriarchal Era	Abraham/ birth of child; Genesis 15, deliverance 400+ years later in Egypt
II. Pre-Kingdom Era: a. Desert Phase	Deliverance from Egypt, Exodus; Crossing the Red Sea; Failure to Enter the Land; 40 years in the desert; Going in to the land, Deuteronomy
b. Conquering the Land Phase	Crossing the Jordan, 3 days, flood season; Fall of Jericho
c. Conquered by the land	Deliverers, e.g. Gideon, Jephthah
III. Kingdom Era	Samuel, transition to Kingdom leadership
IV. Post-Kingdom Era	Daniel 9, Praying in the Return
V. Pre-Church Era	Galatians 4:4, Luke 1,2; Matthew 1,2
VI. Church Era	Pentecost; Macedonian call

God's will includes direction for what, how and <u>when</u>.

The book of Haggai illustrates this important timing macro lesson very explicitly. In this short little two chapter book, God emphasizes repeatedly how crucial timing is—in two different ways.

1. The overall timing of this thrust to rebuild the temple. The work had been started almost 18 years ago and fizzled. Now God wants to put a fire under these people and motivate them to work on the temple. He also wants to show them how the things happening to them have been engineered by God for His purposes.

2. The repeated timing of the various prophetic utterance given to Haggai the prophet.

---

[21] See **Articles**, *Macro Lesson Defined and Macro Lessons; List of 41 Across Six Leadership Eras.*

Haggai—And Timing

The timing of each of the utterances is clearly indicated in the text. Figure 10.1 shows this timing emphasis.

Time Reference		← 4 months total →		
2nd Year 6th Month 1st Day	2nd Year 6th Month 24th Day	2nd Year 7th Month 21st Day	2nd Year 9th Month 24th Day	2nd Year 9th Month 24th Day (a second time)
1st word was a challenge to move	People responded and began work	2nd word comes to counter discouragement	3rd word comes countering expectation of rewards	4th word comes encouraging trust in God for power to do job
Stage 1 False Satisfaction		Stage 2 False Dissatisfaction	Stage 3 False Expectation	Stage 4 False Fear
1st Word a Corrective Prophetic word Given to two leaders for the people		2nd Word a Corrective Prophetic word Given to two leaders for the people	3rd Word a Corrective Prophetic word Given to leaders and people	4th Word a Futuristic Prophetic word Given to Zerubbabel

Figure 10.1 Haggai's Time-Line for Task of Rebuilding The Temple

Some Observations

1. Note, God anticipates the various reactions (stages of the project) and gives a Word to offset each issue.
2. Haggai's ministry is very practical. Contrast his prophecies with Zechariah, his fellow prophet. Haggai's prophecies are to inspire the civil and religious leaders and motivate the people to build the temple. Timing is thus critical in order to head off the various stages. Haggai must be obedient and respond immediately as each word is given. See **Article**, *Haggai—Prophetic Words*.
3. Note the intervals between words. From the time the people began work until the dissatisfaction—about 3 and 1/2 weeks. From the time of the dissatisfaction word to the time of the false expectation word—about 8 weeks. The 3rd word and the 4th word came on the same day.
4. Sensitivity to God's timing and word were crucial to Haggai's ministry.
5. Prophetic ministry frequently depends on situational issues which condition the hearers; hence, timing is crucial.

Conclusion

The book of Haggai is a good book to teach the timing macro lesson.

God's Timing Is Crucial To Accomplishment Of God's Purposes.

The timing macro lesson is one of the top five macro lessons in the Bible. All leaders need to learn this valuable lesson. Seeing illustrations of the timing macro in the Bible helps sensitize one to discerning them in real life. And leaders must discern God's timing.

See **Article**, *God's Timing and Leadership*.

Article 11

Haggai—Calendar and Dating

Introduction

It is helpful when studying any of the restoration era books—Haggai, Zechariah, Malachi, Ezra, Nehemiah—to recognize the order in which the occur. Table 11.1 puts these books in order.

Table 11.1. Restoration Books and Miscellaneous Information

Item	539 B.C.	536 B.C.	520-516 B.C.	486-465 B.C.	465-424 B.C.	430 B.C.
Restoration Activity	Daniel Prays	Work on Temple Begun	Work on Temple begun again and Completed	Israelites Preserved due to Esther and Mordecai's activities	Wall is constructed around Jerusalem—Ezra and Nehemiah bring about restoration movement	Malachi again engenders restoration movement
Bible Indication	Daniel 9	Ez 3:12	Ez 6:13-15 Haggai (whole book) Zechariah	Esther	Nehemiah; latter part of Ezra	Malachi
Left Hand of God	Cyrus		Darius	Xerxes	Artaxerxes	
Restoration Leaders	Daniel		Haggai, Zechariah, Zerubbabel, Joshua	Mordecai, Esther,		

Table 11.2 correlates Haggai's ministry with Zechariah's.

Table 11.2 Haggai and Zechariah—Overlap in Ministry

Order	Date[22] (using modern calendar)	Prophetic Message/ Or Other Activity	Bible Passage (or other reference to dating)
1	Aug 29, 520 B.C.	Haggai gives 1st message to Zerubbabel (civil leader) and Joshua (religious leader); message talks about timing of rebuilding temple; compares temple and peoples homes	Hag 1:1-11; Ez 5:1
2	Sep 21, 520 B.C.	Work begun again on temple. Opposed or hindered from 536-530 B.C. Stopped altogether from 530 to 520 B.C.	Hag 1:12-15; Ez 5:2 Ez 4:1-5, 24
3	Oct 17, 520 B.C.	Haggai's 2nd Message given to counter discouragement of people.	Hag 2:1-9
4	Oct/Nov 520 B.C.	Zechariah exhorts; His ministry begins	Zec 1:1-6
5	Dec 18, 520 B.C.	Haggai's 3rd message concerning patience in the task; God will reward	Hag 2:10-19
6	Dec 18, 520 B.C.	Haggai's 4th message concerning power for the task—to Zerubbabel; futuristic message and empowerment predicted	Hag 2:20-23
7	519-518 B.C.	Tattenai's letter to Darius; about rebuilding the temple	Ez 5:3-6:14)
8	Feb 15, 519 B.C.	Zechariah's night visions; eight of them	Zec 1:7-6:8
9	Feb 16 (maybe) 519 B.C.	Joshua crowned	Zec 6:9-15
10	Dec 7, 518 B.C.	Message exhorting to repentance; blessings promised	Zec ch 7,8
11	Mar 12, 516 B.C.	Dedication of the temple[23]	Ez 6:15-18
12	?	Zechariah's final prophecies	Zec ch 9-14

Conclusion

When reading the various passages about restoration activity, keep in mind the overall timing of what was going on. When reading Haggai and Zechariah's words, remember the ordering as suggested above and note how Zechariah's ministry supplemented Haggai's and carried the temple on to completion. Remember also that Haggai is the practical prophet while Zechariah is the more mystical prophet—also dealing with spiritual warfare.

See **Article**, *Haggai—Afterglow Ministry*; *Getting the Job Done—Comparison of Ezra and Haggai's Role*.

---

[22] Modern dating suggested by NIV study Bible and corroborated in other study Bibles.
[23] One wonders if Haggai was around for this. If I am right about Haggai's Afterglow ministry, then he probably wasn't.

Article 12

Haggai— Delaying God's Work

Introduction
Notice Haggai's accusing words.

Hag 1:2-5
2 The Lord Almighty warns, "Your people are saying, that this isn't the right time to rebuild the Lord temple."

3 Then came the Word of the Lord by Haggai the prophet, saying, 4 "Is it right for you to have nice expensive homes while my temple lies in ruins? 5 This is the Lord Almighty talking. Consider what is happening to you. 6 You plant a lot but reap very little. You don't have enough to eat or drink. You don't have enough clothing to keep you warm. What you earn isn't enough to meet your needs."

Notice the contrast given. You seem to think it isn't the right time to build God's temple but you seem to think it is all right to build your own homes—nice one's at that.

God's Timing
In the study of characters and situations in the Bible two major problems concerning timing occur.

1. People and leaders want to go ahead of God's timing. That is, they want to do something or react to some situation before God is ready for them to do so.

2. People and leaders want to lag behind God's timing. That is, they do not want to do something or react to some situation when God wants them to. They want to delay in doing what God wants. Or worse still, they do not want to do it altogether.

Why is this so?

In the case of moving ahead of God's timing, Moses is a good example. In terms of leaders, if we use Moses as an example, we can tentatively identify at least 3 reasons why Moses was wrong in attempting to deliver the Israelites as seen in Exodus 1,2.

1. **Death of a vision**—right vision, wrong motivation, wrong power base, wrong timing. Moses had a right vision. God wanted to deliver the Israelites from the Egyptian bondage. But his power base was wrong. Moses was on his way up in the Egyptian hierarchy of leadership. God was not going to use that positional leadership as His means for delivering. God alone was going to receive the honor and glory of this deliverance. And God's timing (as seen in

Gen 15) involved complicated things He was doing in the land with its various peoples. Moses was about 40 years ahead of God's 400 years plan.

2. **God's working out of other purposes**. In Moses case, God was working to give people in the land time to repent. In Biblical phraseology, their iniquity was not yet full.
3. **Foundational character shaping**. Moses returned from his 40 years of desert experience a very humble person (Num 12:3). He would need this character trait, since God would invest Moses ministry with great power.

In the case of lagging behind God's will several Biblical illustrations suggest reasons.

1. **Fear**—In the case of Israel not wanting to go into the land after hearing the report of the spies, fear gripped the people.
2. **Idolatry**—In the O.T. frequently people were worshipping other gods. God was not first and uniquely only their God. Hence, His frequent calls through the prophets to return to His ways went unheeded.
3. **Self-Interest**—Putting one's own interest ahead of God's priorities. It is this reason that is seen in the book of Haggai.

Materialistic pursuits as is the case in Haggai can easily detract from hearing and doing God's will in His timing. In the case of the followers in Haggai, it wasn't as if what God wanted done was wrong (rebuilding the temple). It was just not the right timing. And these followers rationalized it away. They needed to be taking care of their own materialistic pursuits. And it was this situation that God spoke into. He pointed out that the reason they were having financial problems was due to their lack of obeying Him.

The amazing thing is that the leaders, Zerubbabel and Joshua, discerned that God's word through Haggai was true. They were able to influence the followers to put God first—to rebuild the temple. And then Haggai gave them a word that God would amply reward them in His timing.

We need to be impressed with the timing macro lesson.

God's Timing Is Crucial To Accomplishment Of God's Purposes.

It is not just in the book of Haggai that God's timing is seen as important. This timing lesson is seen in every leadership era in the Bible.

Table 12.1 Strong Biblical Illustrations About God's Timing

Era	Example(s)
I. Patriarchal	Abraham/ birth of child; Genesis 15, deliverance 400+ years later in Egypt
II. Pre-Kingdom: a. desert	Deliverance from Egypt, Exodus; Crossing the Red Sea; Failure to Enter the Land; 40 years in the desert; Going in to the land, Deuteronomy
b. conquering the land	Crossing the Jordan, 3 days, flood season; Fall of Jericho
c. conquered by the land	Deliverers, e.g. Gideon, Jephthah

III. Kingdom	Samuel, transition to Kingdom
IV. Post-Kingdom	Daniel 9, Praying in the Return
V. Pre-Church	Galatians 4:4, Luke 1,2; Matthew 1,2
VI. Church	Pentecost; Macedonian call

Conclusion

What can we learn from this example in Haggai?

1. In terms of N.T. language, you cannot serve two masters simultaneously (God or pursuit of financial goals). Jesus put it succinctly in his Sermon on the Mount address. God must be first in priority in a life.

2. People, even committed followers, will tend to rationalize their situation so as to back their plans, whether or not their plans adhere to God's timing.

3. Leadership is the key to staying on target as to timing. Discerning leaders are needed to understand God's timing and to influence God's people toward acting in accordance with God's timing.

In our modern western world, all three of these observations are easily seen in almost any given church situation. In general, people are putting their own materialistic pursuits first in their lives. Yes, they are serving God but it is one among many things they are doing. And they easily rationalize what they are doing. And where there are exceptions to this general trend it is because of influential godly leaders who are helping people see God's priorities.

But what are needed are more leaders like Haggai, Zerubbabel and Joshua. Leaders who can discern God's will and timing. And leaders who can influence God's people to see and follow God's will and timing.

See **Article**, *God's Timing and Leadership; Haggai—And Timing; Macro Lesson, Defined.*

Article 13

Haggai— Dealing With Discouraged Followers

Introduction

How can a leader help discouraged workers stay focused and encouraged during a God-given task? Every ministry project hits bumps in the roads. Those in ministry know that visible progress is sometimes slow in coming. Even projects that start out with excitement sometimes fizzle as the energy drops and discouragement sets in. No leader wants to watch as along the way people get tired and quit. How can a leader best help when followers get discouraged? The book of Haggai provides help for those leaders learning to encourage those they serve along side.

In the book of Haggai, the people make a commitment to build God's house, they roll up their sleeves and with the excitement that accompanies the start of something new -they began the rebuilding process. In Haggai 2 we catch up with them about thirty days into the ministry project. At this point the initial excitement wears off. And like a month into membership at a health club, reality sinks in that this is plain old hard work. And to make matters worse the visible progress was not too impressive – God leads the way in saying "Does it not seem to you like nothing?" (Hag 2:3)

God, through the prophet Haggai sees that the people's enthusiasm is sinking and so a fresh touch from God is injected into the situation. God's breaks into the scene and brings the inner resources needed to move forward in the project. In watching how God deals with these discouraged workers we learn 6 principles for dealing with discouraged followers.

1) Deal Directly With Discouragement

How might a leader best handle discouragement among the ranks? Some leaders ignore it. Some put a smile on their face and pretend everything is all right. In Hag 2:3, God takes a different approach. The people begin the building project but become discouraged by the small beginning. They look at the progress made and it's not too impressive. Instead of ignoring the situation, God says what's on everyone's mind, "Does it not seem to you like nothing?" By putting it out in public, followers know they are not the only ones feeling that way. Followers find confidence in a leader who is aware of their feelings. Followers lose confidence in a leader who seems out of touch. So God asks the question:

"Who of you is left who saw this house in its former glory? How does it look to you now?
    Does it not seem to you like nothing?" (Hag 2:3)

Instead of letting discouragement go underground, Haggai brings it into the light. God (using three questions) draws out the feelings of discouragement and deals with it publicly. Different situations require different approaches, but whether publicly or privately, Leaders usually do best to address underlying discouragement head on.

2) Find Personal Encouragement From God.

As a leader, the most difficult discouragement to deal with may be your own. God's first work may need to begin in you. As a leader, people look to you hope and encouragement, but it's hard to share something you yourself do not have. In Haggai 2, before turning attention back to the task, God addressed the leaders and workers need for personal encouragement. Calling them out by name, God encourages the leaders by giving them

- A. A promise of His strength **"be strong" Vs 4**.
- B. A promise of His Presence, **"I am with you" Vs 4**.
- C. A promise of the Holy Spirit's help **"My Spirit remains among you" vs. 5**.
- D. A reminder that these promises are based on something we count on – His covenant **"This what I covenanted with you". vs. 5.**

Expect God to work encouragement in you, before He works encouragement through you. Then you can turn around and encourage those you serve along side.[24]

The next thing God does is point people back to the project, but He gives them a new perspective on it. In Haggai chapter two, verses six through nine – God gives them hope by helping them look past what is, to what will be. When we are up to our elbows in rubble, it's hard to see the forest for the trees, at times like that we need God's perspective on ministry. The difference between leaders and followers is perspective. Hag 2:6-9 shows us practical ways for a leader to bring God's perspective into a situation. The following suggestions flow from the approach that God uses to bring the project into a new perspective.

3) Remind people that success is not limited by what we can do, but what God will do. *"I will shake...I will fill...I will grant"*

In large ministry projects, the amount of work can be overwhelming. There is usually too much to do and not enough time, to much work and not enough workers, to many opportunities and not enough energy. When we think of all the work that needs to be done it's easy to get overwhelmed. The reality sets in, that if success is based on us alone – the project is in trouble!

Up to this point much of the book of Haggai is about what the people need to do – "go up the mountains", "bring down timber", "build my house" etc. Hag chapter 2 verses six through nine have a different feel. It's all about what God will do; *"I will shake...I will fill...I will grant"*. When faced with a God-sized project, leaders and workers alike will become overwhelmed if convinced that success is dependent solely on them. The good news is that ultimately – success in ministry is based on what God will do. If God is in the project ordinary people will become powerful tools in the hand of extraordinary God. During large projects a leader should remind workers that God is actively at work and that nothing is impossible for God.

---

[24] For more, see **Article**, *Dealing With Personal Discouragement*.

Haggai—Dealing With Discouraged Followers

4) Help people see that their efforts, however small, play an important part in God's Big picture plan for the future. Vs 6-7 *"I will fill this house with glory..."*

In verse 6-9 God talks about a powerful and important work that He will do "In a little while." The workers find encouragement in knowing their efforts (which seem to be accomplishing "nothing") will play a part in this house filled with riches and glory. God is going to do something "greater" (vs. 9) than anything in the past, and they get to be a part of it. This project will bring "glory" to God. Discouraged leaders and workers can remember that God can use even small steps of obedience to make a big difference and bring glory to Him. Even small efforts can make a lasting difference in the eternal purposes of God. Leaders need to remind that no work of God, however small lacks significance. Efforts of obedience are never wasted, but instead become acts of worship to God who will reward those faithful with an eternity-lasting "well done".

5) Remind people that their efforts will supported by the God who can provide for us. Vs 8. *"the gold is mine and silver is mine"*

In Hag 2:8 God reminds the people that "the gold is mine and silver is mine." God had given the workers a giant task – rebuilding the temple. The materials required for the construction of the temple, even a much smaller one than Solomon's temple, would still stretch these followers. This raised the question "Where are we going to get the money?" Finances were tight for Haggai's listeners, crops were failing, money was put into pockets with "holes" in them. In general, life was difficult. Lack of finances offered one more reason to be discouraged. These people are looking at this "nothing" pile of rubble and thinking of all the expenses needed to get from where they were, to the finished temple.

Money is always a reality in ministry. Ministry is often about large projects and little resources. But leaders can not let the size of the resources determine the size of the vision. Hag 2:8 reminds leaders that they serve a powerful God who is able to provide any resources needed to accomplish His purposes. Hag 2:8 reminds leaders that, financially, God is in control. If God has called a leader to do something, the corresponding good news is that God has the resources to get the job done.

6) Cast vision by looking past what is, to what will be. Vs 7-9 *"The glory of this present house will be greater than the glory of the former house"*

God encourages them not by what is, but showing them what will be. God says "I will fill <u>this</u> house with glory." What house? God says the glory of this present house" What house? They had not even completed the foundation! They were looking at a pile of rubble, but God helps them see an already completed temple filled with the glory of the Lord, and people from all over the world coming to worship. God acknowledges that it may look like "nothing" now, but if the people are willing to trust, to obey and believe His promises – this "nothing" project will one day soon ("little while") be a house filled with glory.

Conclusion

Look again at the Haggai encouragement principles.

1. **Deal directly with discouragement.**
2. **Find personal encouragement from God.**
3. **God is the one who is doing this.**
4. **We are partnering with God so Remember what success is: little is big if God is in it!**
5. **God will provide the resources.**
6. **Look to the future in faith for what this work can become.**

Followers need a vision-painted picture of what God can do. As a leader ask God to give you a vision of God's future for your life and ministry. Do you have a God's vision for your ministry? If not, get it. If so, share it.

Are you a leader with some discouraged followers? Use these principles from the book of Haggai to bring new life to the people and projects under your leadership.

Article 14

Haggai— Discouragement, A Small Work of God

Introduction

Haggai challenges us afresh concerning our evaluation of our work as leaders. Note his words.

> 1 On the twentieth day of the seventh month, God gave another Word to the prophet Haggai. 2 "Speak to Governor Zerubbabel, the son of Shealtiel, and to Joshua the high priest, the son of Josedech and to the remnant of the people who have come back to the land. 3 Say this, "Do any of you remember how splendid Solomon's Temple really was? *And now look at what you are building? Not much, is it?"*

The people are discouraged about the work. The temple foundation is laid. But compared to Solomon's temple this is a puny work. And the people are discouraged with it. Haggai is just voicing what they are saying to themselves. And folks who believe that what they are doing is insignificant and won't count are just a step away from quitting. But the challenge comes.

> 4 But don't be discouraged. Be strong, Zerubbabel. Be strong Joshua. Be strong all you people. Rebuild this temple! *For I am with you, the Lord Almighty.* 5 I made a covenant with you long ago when you came out of Egypt. And I am still with you. So don't be afraid nor discouraged.

God is affirming their work. God is in it. God's presence is enough in any work of God. And it is the Lord Almighty, who is voicing this affirmation of His presence. Not only the Lord Almighty but God the Promise Keeper. This is the covenant God who empowered the mighty exodus from Egypt. He keeps His promises. He has the power to do so. And then comes the further challenge.

> 6 I the Lord Almighty am going to shake the heavens, and the earth—land and sea. 7 And I will shake all nations and their treasure will be brought here. And this temple shall be filled with wealth. 8 All the silver and the gold of the world belongs to me, the Lord Almighty. 9 This new temple shall be better than Solomon's temple for my glory will be seen in it. And I, the Lord Almighty, will bring peace to my people.

The work that they see is not limited to whatever future they can see. God has bigger plans for it. And whether it is as splendid as Solomon's rich temple does not matter. God is the rightful owner of all and can call His resources in whenever He wants too.

The Two Major Encouraging Principles For Us As Leaders Today

The Church Growth Movement swept many of us up. We were greatly encouraged as we studied Church Growth Principles. But subtly, many of us were trapped with the notion of bigger is successful. And so we looked on small works, especially our own, which would not grow, even when we applied church growth principles as failures. And we became discouraged.

Leaders all along the leadership influence continuum[25] have become discouraged at their ministry when it was considered to be smaller than they had hoped for. Discouragement is a normal feeling of leaders involved in small works. Haggai has two perspectives that should encourage us greatly. If we can just get these perspectives in our own personal worldviews we will be different leaders—leaders of the Haggai ilk.

Principle 1. Big or Small?
No work of God is small if God is in it.

> 4... *For I am with you, the Lord Almighty.* 5 ...So don't be afraid nor discouraged.

Principle 2. Not Limited
God is not limited by the smallness of our work. God can accomplish much more through our small work than we can imagine if we will just commit ourselves to faithfully obey God as we minister in this small work.

Haggai's followers must have been astounded to hear these words.

> 9 This new temple shall be better than Solomon's temple for my glory will be seen in it.

Conclusion
As leaders the question we must carefully answer is simply this,

> Is God in this ministry of mine?

If I am sure of this, then the size does not matter. If God is not in it, the size also does not matter.

If the answer to the first question is yes, then we can by faith trust God to accomplish whatever He has in mind with this ministry and bring Glory to Himself.

So be encouraged, dear friend. Be sure God is with you. Let the size of the work not be your criterion for discouragement or encouragement.

---

[25] See **Article**, *Leadership Levels—Looking At A Leadership Continuum*.

Article 15

Haggai—Leadership Coalition

Introduction

In the article on civil leadership I defined several important terms. Several of these definitions are important to the thrust of this article on leadership coalition. To have impact on a society, a broad spectrum is needed which includes civil leadership, mainstream religious leadership, and peripheral religious leadership. Several of these definitions will be used in this article.

Definition   *Civil leadership* refers to people of God, sold out on following God, yet impacting the society via two types of roles often needed—1. Governmental or political roles sanctioned by the society and 2. Military roles sanctioned by the society.

They are not considered religious workers.

Definition   *Mainstream religious* leadership refers to officially recognized religious roles sanctioned by the society and religious structures.

Priest and various ordained ministry roles (e.g. pastor) would be mainstream religious roles.

Definition   *Peripheral religious* leadership refers to those roles, mostly outside the mainstream religious structures, which attempt to speak for God to bring about change in religious groups, structures, and society in general.

These sometimes fringe leaders are frequently needed because mainstream religious leaders go nominal in their pursuit of God. God raises these types of leaders up in an *ad hoc sort of manner*, as and when needed. The oral and writing prophets of the O.T. and those exercising prophetic ministries and some apostolic ministries in the present *Church Leadership* Era typically would be examples of peripheral religious leaders.

Typically, all three of the above types of leadership are needed to accomplish God's work in our world. Table 15.1 lists the six Biblical leadership eras and shows how these roles played out in the various eras.

Coalition is a French word that originated from a Latin participle having to do with growing together. Having crossed over into English its meaning is as follows:

Definition   *Coalition* refers to an alliance, especially a temporary one, of people, factions, parties, or nations.

Haggai—Leadership Coalition

Taking this definition a bit further, we arrive at our Biblical leadership definition,

Definition   A *leadership coalition* in Biblical literature refers to

- a partnership, whether formal or informal,
- which exists between civil leaders, mainstream religious leaders and/or peripheral religious leaders,
- for a temporary period of time

in order to accomplish some God-directed task(s).

The more formal and deliberate is the coalition and the more specifically the task is defined, the more effective is the leadership.

Some Possible Coalitions Throughout The Leadership Eras

Table 15.1 Possible Coalitions in the Leadership Eras

Leadership Era	Partnership	Formal (F) Informal (I)	God-Directed Task	Time Span of Coalition
I. Patriarchal	None seen		None seen	None seen
2. Pre-Kingdom a. Desert	a. Moses, Aaron, Miriam, Joshua	I	Survival in Desert	40 years
2. Pre-Kingdom b. Conquering the Land	Joshua, Eleazar	F	Conquer the Land; Parcel it out to the Tribes	10 years or so???
2. Pre-Kingdom b. Conquered by the Land	Deborah, Barak	I	Military Defense	Very Short (less than a year)
	Samuel, Saul	I	Transition to Kingdom	Relatively Short (year or so??)
3. Kingdom	Frequently you will see some king in a coalition with a military leader and/or some religious priest	I (military part more formal)	Self-preservation	Varied—some for several years
4. Post-Kingdom a. As Kingdom was crumbling	Not clear; except that some kings allied themselves with some priests against the periphereal ministry of prophets	I	Reject God's Corrective Ministry Through Prophets	Relatively short
b. In exile	Mordecai, Esther	I	Preservation of Jewish exiles	Relatively short

| c. Return to Land | Haggai, Zechariah, Joshua and Zerubbabel | I at first but increasingly became more deliberate, F | Rebuilding of Temple | Relatively short |
| | Nehemiah, Ezra | I at first but increasingly became more deliberate, F | Building of Wall Around Jerusalem for Protection | Relatively Short |

Coalitions are dominantly an Old Testament concept having to do with the various leadership needs of the people of God.

Some Observations

The two most effective coalitions were that of Haggai, Zechariah, Joshua and Zerubbabel and that of Ezra and Nehemiah. Some commonalities include:

1. Both of these coalitions were for relatively short times.
2. Both of these collations were very specific, one to rebuild the temple, the other to rebuild the wall around Jerusalem.
3. In both cases, all of the leaders were spiritually alive—civil, formal religious, and peripheral religious.

Some differences include:

1. Ezra operated in the role of formal religious (was a priest) and informal religious leader (calling for reform and renewal). Haggai, the major motivator was a peripheral religious leader. The religious leader, Joshua, was supplementary to Haggai's leadership.
2. Ezra's informal religious ministry was focused on renewal—via the revealed word of God—getting people back to knowing and obeying God's word. Haggai's informal religious ministry was focused on motivating the people to rebuild the temple.
3. Nehemiah was the inspirational leader, though a civil leader. He was the practical, get it done kind of person. Haggai was the inspirational leader, though not in the formal religious structure.
4. Nehemiah, though very practical, was a man of dependence upon God in prayer. Haggai was the practical point person in the rebuilding of the temple. Zechariah was probably the spiritual motivator.
5. The obstacles that Nehemiah and Ezra faced were primarily external (coming from opposition from without though there were some internal obstacles in terms of resources). The obstacles that Haggai, Zechariah, Joshua, and Zerubbabel faced were dominantly internal—in the hearts and minds of the followers.

6. Nehemiah's connections into the power structure provided a source of resources. Zerubbabel had to raise recourses from the people themselves, who were going through major times of depression.

Closure

Coalitions worked because various leadership functions were needed to pull off the accomplishments that God was challenging them to. And leaders who were gifted in the various areas (civil, main stream religious, military, and peripheral religious) were willing to work together and respect the necessary leadership of the others in the coalition. It is the cooperative effort and respect for others leadership that made the two most effective coalitions so successful (Nehemiah's—the building of the wall; Haggai's—the rebuilding of the temple).

Because of the dispersed nature of local churches in various geographical and cultural areas all over the world there is no formal coalition leadership made up of civil political, military, formal religious and peripheral religious leadership. Instead, what is seen in the New Testament expansion of the church into different cultures and geographical areas is the concept of a team, which takes the Gospel into these new regions. It is a diverse gifted team. And the same kind of cooperation and respect are needed for a Gospel expansion team to pull off its ministry.

Probably, several important lessons can be learned from the study of these effective coalitions. (1) God brings together diverse leadership people in order to carry out specific tasks. (2) The more these diverse leaders can recognize the other leaders' functions and respectfully cooperate with them the more effective will be the accomplishment of God's task. (3) For short periods of time—various leaders can contribute their efforts jointly to see something accomplished.

See **Article**, *Leadership Coalition*.

Article 16

Haggai—Lasting Legacies

Introduction

Leadership emergence theory, the study of how God develops leaders over a lifetime, suggests 13 categories of legacies that leaders leave behind as contributions to God's work.[26] In addition, any given leader might have some unique legacies which do not fit the exact 13 categories. This article suggests that Haggai was a leader who left behind 4 legacies. Comparative study shows that leaders usually leave behind 3-6 legacies, of the possible 13. But it does not matter how many are left behind. What is important is doing God's will as a leader in the time God gives one to lead. However, study of legacies serves to inspire present leaders to make their lives count—*The Moses Admonition*.

MOSES' ADVICE

Psa. 90:12
LORD, let us learn to wisely apply ourselves so that our lives might count.

Psa. 90:17
And let the beauty of the Lord our God be upon us. Yes, LORD, establish our life work.

Haggai's life counted. He established something that went on.

Categories of Legacies

Ultimate contributions, another phrase for lasting legacies, identified in the study of leaders who had effective ministries includes the following major categories: *Character*, *Ministry*, *Catalytic*, *Organizational*, and *Ideation*. Each of these major categories has sub-categories as shown below in Table 16.1.

Table 16.1 Ultimate Contribution Categories

Type	Basic Notion
CHARACTER:	
1. Saint	A Model life, not a perfect one, but a life others want to emulate.
2. Stylistic Practitioner	A Model ministry style which sets the pace for others and which other ministries seek to emulate.

---

[26] These 13 categories resulted from comparative study of a number of effective missionary leaders (and a few pastoral leaders).

3. Family	Leaves behind children who follow God and emulate the godliness seen in parents.
MINISTRY:	
4. Mentor	A productive ministry with individuals, small groups, etc.
5. Public Rhetorician	A productive public ministry with large groups.
CATALYTIC:	
6. Pioneer	A person who starts apostolic ministries.
7. Change Person	A person who rights wrongs and injustices in society and in church and mission organizations.
8. Artist	A person who has creative breakthroughs in life and ministry and introduces innovation.
ORGANIZATIONAL:	
9. Founder	A person who starts a new organization to meet a need or capture the essence of some movement or the like.
10. Stabilizer	A person who can help a fledgling organization develop or can help an older organization move toward efficiency and effectiveness. In other words, help solidify an organization.
IDEATION:	
11. Researcher	Develops new ideation by studying various things.
12. Writer	captures ideas and reproduces them in written format to help and inform others.
13. Promoter	Effectively distributes new ideas and/or other ministry related things.

Haggai's Ultimate Contribution Set

Haggai, in this writer's opinion was a public rhetorician and a change agent. His messages impacted and brought about significant change. He was a promoter—of the need to have a place for centralized worship—God's temple rebuilt. He also left behind a written record (whether he wrote it or not) which models inspirational leadership. How do you motivate the people of God to obey God? Haggai modeled this. He may or may not have other ultimate contribution categories (like Saint, Family, Mentor). We simply do not have any record to go by. But he did have a temple finished eventually (Ezr 6:13-15) which was a physical reminder of his ministry—an ongoing legacy. I love the way the book of Ezra records it. Note my bold faced emphasized phrases

> 13 Then Tatnai, governor on this side the river, Shetharboznai, and their companions, according to that which Darius the king had sent, so they did speedily. 14 And the elders of the Jews built, and they **prospered** through the prophesying of Haggai the prophet and Zechariah the son of Iddo. And they built, and **finished [it],** according to the commandment of the God of Israel, and according to the commandment of Cyrus, and Darius, and Artaxerxes king of Persia. 15 And this house **was finished** on the third day of the month Adar, which was in the sixth year of the reign of Darius the king. 16 And the children of Israel, the priests, and the Levites, and the rest of the children of the captivity, **kept the dedication of this house of God with joy,** 17 And offered at the dedication of this house of God an hundred bullocks, two hundred rams, four hundred lambs; and for a sin offering for all Israel, twelve he goats, according to the number of the tribes of Israel. 18 And they set the priests in their divisions, and the Levites in their courses, for the service of God, which [is] at

Jerusalem; as it is written in the book of Moses. 19 And the **children of the captivity kept the passover** upon the fourteenth [day] of the first month. 20 For the priests and the Levites were purified together, all of them [were] pure, and killed the passover for all the children of the captivity, and for their brethren the priests, and for themselves. 21 And the children of Israel, **which were come again out of captivity**, and all such as had separated themselves unto them from the filthiness of the heathen of the land, to seek the LORD God of Israel, did eat, 22 And kept the feast of unleavened bread **seven days with joy**: for the **LORD had made them joyful**, and turned the heart of the king of Assyria unto them, to strengthen their hands in the work of the house of God, the God of Israel.
Ezra 6:13-22

The word *prospered* through the prophesying of Haggai and Zechariah is an interesting word. The word *prospered* (SRN 6744) occurs 4 times in the O.T. It means to cause to be successful. In other words the civil leaders were successful in this temple project because of these prophets' ministry.

The following Venn diagram in Figure 16.1 portrays Haggai's ultimate contributions in a pictorial display.[27]

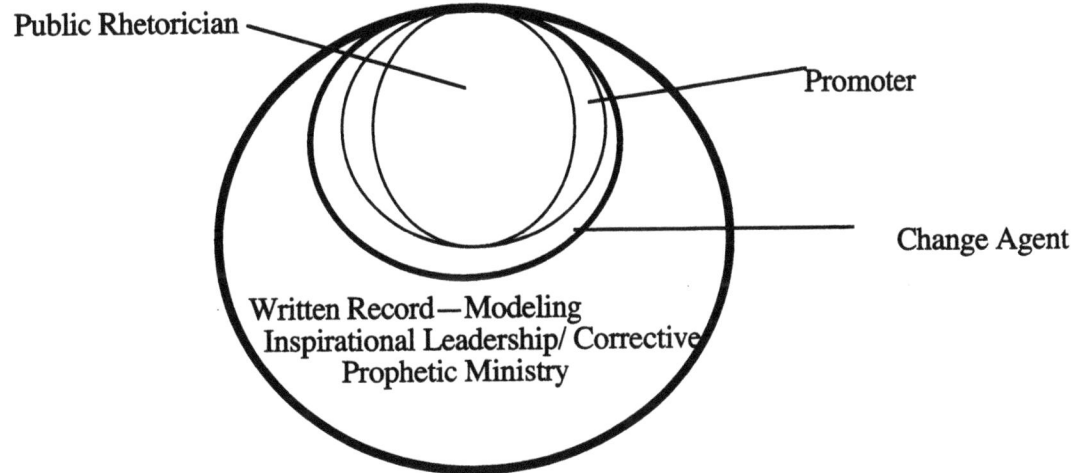

Figure 16.1. Haggai's Ultimate Contribution Set

Closure
Haggai exercised a peripheral religious leadership role and did it effectively. Few prophetic voices in the O.T. were as effective as Haggai. He deserves to be remembered for his contribution to God's drama of redemption.

See **Article**, *Leadership Coalition*; *Civil Leadership—The Missing Ingredient*.

---

[27] A Venn diagram portrays items as symbols. The larger the symbol and more central on a page, the more important is the item. Where there is overlap between symbols it means both items occur at the same time.

Article 17

Haggai—Profiting from the Past

Introduction
Ministry is always challenging, this is especially true when an organization is in a rebuilding phase. Sometimes it seems easier to start from scratch, rather than repair a ministry, which has seen better days. One particular challenge concerns the leader who is working with older members who were present during the ministry's heyday. Long time members provide a wealth of commitment but often deal with the discouraging dynamic of comparing the present state of affairs with the past. This often leads to a longing to return to the good old days, and the belief that the best way forward is to head backwards. The leader is faced with the dual desire to acknowledge and honor God's work in the past, yet accomplish God's work in the present. The two often seem to pull in separate directions. The puzzling situation revolves around this question.

> **Question** – How can a leader respect the past, yet move a ministry project forward.

Why Haggai is Helpful— 4 Helpful Principles from the book of Haggai

In the book of Haggai, God calls the people to rebuild the temple. Among those called to rebuild, are older members who had seen Solomon's Temple before their captivity. When these older workers show up to start, they are confronted with a pile of rubble. They cannot help but compare the present disaster site, with the once beautiful temple. Perhaps some of the older leaders are longing for a return to the "good old days" when the former temple was standing tall in Jerusalem.

In Haggai, God effectively addresses the unique discouragement of those who had seen the temple in its *former glory*. God's approach in Haggai chapter two provides four helpful principles for the leader who wishes to encourage long-time members to press forward with God's purposes.

Principle 1. Recognize and respect the unique discouragement of long-term members.

God does this by asking a three-part question.

> Haggai 2:3 Who of you is left who saw this house in its former glory? How does it look to you now? Does it not seem to you like nothing?

In calling public attention to the matter God recognizes their discouragement as a valid concern. The very fact that He is taking time to address them shows that they are a valuable part of God's plan. God doesn't ignore their hesitancy and move on with a younger group of workers. God takes time to process their reluctance and fully involve them in the project. God deems their involvement worth a prophetic pause in the project as Haggai delivers God's word to this important group of older workers.

What is the implication for the leader facing a rebuilding project? A leader is wise to recognize the unique resource that long-term members embody. These are often people with an unshakeable commitment, demonstrated by the fact they faithfully stayed with the ship, when by all appearances it was sinking. They have weathered the hard times and are now there for the rebuilding.

How do you do it?

Namely—How can a leader recognize and respect the unique discouragement of long term members. God's three-fold question in Haggai 2:3 suggests three practical ways

a. Provide special recognition for these valuable workers – *who of you is left who saw this house in its former glory?* In the book of Haggai God is talking to a larger group of people—both young and old, but in chapter 2, verse 3 He singles out the long time members for special attention. In asking for a show of hands, *who of you is left,* the attention of the entire crowd is directed on the older workers in their midst. These long time members found encouragement realizing that God recognized their presence among the group. While perhaps forgotten by others, God knows them.

> **Implication**—A task-oriented leader may be tempted to move with the *movers*—the younger workers who appear to represent the future of the organization. It's easy for older members to be left aside. Time spent helping older members to feel valued may lead to important involvement in the rebuilding project.

b. Seek out their opinion—*How does it look to you?* God is interested in their opinion on the temple project. In His second question God gives them an opportunity to verbalize their feelings.

> **Implication**—Leaders, especially young leaders, do well to seek out the opinion of long term members. This is an opportunity to establish mutual understanding. When people feel understood, they are more likely to weather transition times.

c. Identify with their discouragement—*Does it not seem to you like nothing?* God agrees that from outward appearances, the temple project doesn't look like much. God lets them know that they are not alone in feeling that the present does not measure up to the past.

> **Implication**—A leader can empathize with the feelings of long time members, even when calling them to press forward.

Principle 2. Help Older Workers Find Personal Encouragement from the Enduring Promises of God (vs 4-5)/

After recognizing their discouragement, God provides personal encouragement with phrases full of promise like, *be strong… I am with you… my Spirit remains among you…Do not fear.* This reminds workers of His presence and rekindling their enthusiasm to continue the work. To meet someone in their discouragement is good, but not enough. A leader can point long time members to something even older than them—the promises found in God's word.[28]

---

[28] See the **Article**, *God the Promise Keeper.*

Principle 3. Use a Ministry's History to Help Long Time Members See God's Power to fulfill His Purposes *This is what I covenanted with you when you came out of Egypt vs. 5.*

If people are oriented to the past, why not take advantage of that? To those who longed for the former temple, God kept them looking in the same direction (backwards), but goes back even further. Instead of looking back to the pre-captivity temple, He draws their attention to the deliverance from Egypt. Why is this important? In the Exodus God shows Himself willing and able to do whatever is necessary to accomplish His purposes for His people. He performed miracles, split seas, defeated armies, rained down manna from heaven, supernaturally sustained people in impossible to survive circumstances.

Frequently, God calls Israel to remember His deeds of old. Recounting His wonders reminded His people of their special part in His plan and His power to accomplish His purposes. When a ministry is in a rebuilding phase, one of the potential millstones it carries is its history. But when used wisely a ministry's history can serve as a resource, instead of a weight.

Value—Use of History
A suggested leadership value is this – During a rebuilding project, the wise leader ought to use history the same way God does.

God reaches back into history, not to point the direction they were to head (backwards) but to gather *spiritual resources* for where they are to go—forward. God points backwards to remind people that He is faithful to His promises. God points backwards to give them hope that what He starts, He will always finish, even in spite of impossible odds.

During a rebuilding project, the leader might ransack the history of the organization looking for the footprints of God's grace along the path of the past. Enduring principles of God's faithfulness can be harvested from a ministry's history to help encourage old and new workers to press forward in spite of overwhelming odds.

A leader can point back to past successes of the current ministry to remind people what God is still capable of doing. God does not change.[29] Jesus Christ is the same yesterday and today and forever (Hebrews. 13:8). This is good news for older members who have experienced God's powerful work in the past: These workers know what is possible with a powerful God. And if God did it before, He can do it again.

Principle 4. Remind People that God's best is still ahead vs. 9 *The glory of this present house will be greater than the glory of the former house.*

In verse 9 God calls them not to focus on what He did, but what He will do, in a *little while*. As long as a leader or the followers are convinced that God's best is behind, energy will always be expended toward an impossible goal—turning back the clock. But there is one person in this discussion who has been around even longer than the old timers—God. God lets them know that He has seen the past and He's seen the future, and in a sense says *trust me – the future is better.*

---

[29] That is the thrust of Hebrews 11. God worked in those lives by faith. He will work in our lives by faith. And the Leadership Mandate of Hebrews 13:7,8 hinges on this kind of faithfulness. *Jesus Christ is the same yesterday and today and forever.* Hebrews. 13:8

In Haggai 2:9 God counteracts the temptation to believe the best is behind by clearly telling them the best is still ahead. *The glory of this present house will be greater than the glory of the former house.* For those that believe God's word, this is a powerful motivator. It's also a needed motivator. When something a person cares about has been destroyed (not just a building, but when hope is destroyed, trust is destroyed, a relationship is destroyed) it is easy to feel like things will never be the same. In this case God says the best is yet to come.

Conclusion

Perhaps God will use you to encourage older workers longing for the past. Perhaps God will use you to call forward those who believe the best is behind. Consider the above four principles to help others believe God for a better tomorrow.

Article 18

Haggai—Prophetic Words

Introduction

Haggai is a prophet. That is a given.

> 1 On the first day of the sixth month in the second year of King Darius, Haggai **the prophet** received a Word from the Lord. Haggai 1:1

Who is Haggai? What is a prophet? And what does a prophet do?

Lets deal with the last two questions first.

Definition — *Prophecy* refers to the genre of Scripture in which the thrust of the passage is an authoritative revelation from God usually through a spokesperson, called a prophet or prophetess, to correct a given historical situation or to warn of a future situation.

Definition — A *prophet* is one who gives revelatory information from God to speak to correct a given situation or to give perspective on the future and frequently to bring hope.

Background on Haggai

Haggai is referred to 11 times in the O.T. All 11 occur in just two books: 2 times in Ezra and 9 times in Haggai (Ezr 5:1; 6:14; Hag 1:1, 3, 12, 13, 2:1, 10, 13, 14, 20). His name means *festive*. We know very little about Haggai. From passages in the book of Ezra we know:

1. (Ezr 5:1ff) he co-ministered prophetically with Zechariah to the returned remnant in Judah and Jerusalem.

2. (Ezra 6:14ff) the two prophets Haggai and Zechariah continued to encourage the returned remnant to rebuild the temple. They did see the completion of the project.

3. (Ezra 6:14) the left hand of God worked mightily through Cyrus, Darius, and Artaxerxes—all rulers of Persia.

From passages in the book of Haggai we know,

1. (Hag 1:1) exactly when he prophesied (the first day of the sixth month in the second year of King Darius—probably about 520B.C.).

Haggai—Prophetic Words

2. (Hag 1:1) to whom his prophecy was given—Zerubbabel (civil leader) and Joshua (religious leader) leaders among the remnant that had returned to Jerusalem.

3. (Hag 1,2)The actual prophetic words he gave. Three of them are corrective and directed toward the rebuilding of the temple. The fourth was to Zerubbabel and was futuristic.

4. (Hag) Haggai had spiritual authority.

5. (Hag) Haggai's prophetic words are practical and straightforward even logically reasoned out. This is contrasted with his partner, Zechariah, who gives symbolic visionary kinds of prophetic words dominantly moving the affect and volition.

6. Haggai first influenced the civil and religious leaders and then the remnant through these two leaders.

Haggai's Prophetic Words

Table 18.1 lists the actual prophetic words and categorizes them in terms of corrective or futuristic.

Table 18.1 Haggai's Prophetic Words

Reference	Summary of Prophecy	Correc-tive	Futur-istic	Observations
1:2-11	God shows the people that their delay in rebuilding the temple directly affects all of their lives and their welfare.	x		To the leaders for the people. This is a pure corrective prophecy given in straightforward words. You have done wrong. I am correcting you. Now respond properly.
1:13	An encouraging word due to the positive reaction of leaders and people. "I will be with you" says the Lord Almighty.	x		To the Leaders. The essential ingredient of any work of God is God's powerful presence.
2:1-9	God recognizes that the work on this small temple is not impressive compared to the former temple. He points out that He can make any work glorify Himself.	x		Given to 2 leaders first but an encouraging word to leaders and followers next. Discouragement in projects done for God usually follow along after an enthusiastic initial response.
2:10-19	God uses questions about the law to teach two main points by analogy. The results of the efforts of the remnant have been tainted because they have not obeyed God. God notes that little has happened yet of His promised blessing but that it will come. This is a benchmark, time wise.	x		To priests, but for the people. Frequently there is a delay in God's blessings happening. Patient faithful obedience is needed. God encourages them to trust Him to fulfill his promises. He is the promise keeper.
2:20-23	God encourages Zerrubabel that He has the power to		x	To Zerubbabel. While this prophecy encouraged Zerubbabel personally,

	protect and pull off this project.			in terms of our present understanding of the Bible this is to be fulfilled in the future, though it probably was fulfilled token wise in Zerubbabel. Zurubbabel was probably a type of Christ.

Note that of the prophetic instances in Haggai most deal with the immediate future. The last prophetic words personally to Zerrubbabel are futuristic.[30]

Conclusion

Haggai uses commonsense language that fits the times. He points out the problems the folks are having in the land and connects their problems to disobedience to God. He does not use visionary language. But his analysis is so on target that it is confirmed in the hearts of the two leaders, Zerrubabel and Joshua, and in the followers' hearts. Zechariah on the other hand uses visionary symbolic prophecies. Both kinds of prophetic words are needed. Haggai is a task-oriented leader. Get the job done! That is what He is about.

See **Article**, *Prophecy Overview*.

---

[30] This final prophecy is probably an illustration of the hermeneutical principle—double fulfillment. The law of double fulfillment means that the prophecy is fulfilled at two different times. Either the fulfillments occur in the day of the prophecy (i.e. fulfilled somehow in Zerubbabel's time) and at the first coming of Christ (who is a greater fulfillment of the Zerubbabel-like figure) or the fulfillments occur at the first coming of Christ and will occur again at the second coming in perhaps some fuller way. But it may sound when the prophecy is given that it will occur once. This comes very close to violating our basic axiom of only one meaning generally to a language communication. Some folks view *desire of all nations* (Hag 2:7) as referring to Christ. I have translated that phrase desire of all nations as "And I will shake all nations and their treasure will be brought here." I think it is referring to the wealth of those nations which will come under the control of this Zerubbabel-like figure.

Article 19

Haggai—Spiritual Warfare

Introduction

Spiritual warfare occurs throughout the Bible, though much more explicitly in the N.T. than the O.T. One of the strange facts is that it is apparently absent altogether in the book of Haggai. There is no mention of satanic involvement at all in Haggai's ministry.[31] What is spiritual warfare?

Definition *Spiritual warfare* refers to the unseen opposition in the spirit world made up of Satan and his demons and their attempts to defeat God's forces including angelic beings and God's people, today called believers. It also involves the response by believers to these attempts.

Is spiritual warfare really absent in Haggai?

Two Major Guidelines

Two major guidelines concerning spiritual warfare deal with two extremes often seen concerning spiritual warfare.

Extreme 1. Overemphasis on Spiritual Warfare[32]

Extreme 2. Under Emphasis on Spiritual Warfare[33]

At first glance it might appear that Haggai observes Extreme 2. And that might well be the case. However, we do know that spiritual warfare was going on during the time of Haggai's ministry. Haggai had a contemporary prophetic colleague, Zechariah. And Zechariah makes it plain that spiritual warfare was going on. In one of his prophetic messages[34] to Joshua, the religious leader, it is clear that Satan is at work trying to discourage Joshua.

---

[31] However, this is not so unusual since most of the prophetic books do not mention Spiritual Warfare.

[32] Our basic understanding of this extreme comes from studying Paul's approach to spiritual warfare in the N.T. Paul does not assign blame for everything that happens on spirit beings, demons, and spiritual warfare. He sees the human side of things as being heavily involved in many of the problems. See **Article**, *Spiritual Warfare—Two Extremes to Avoid; Spiritual Warfare—Two Foundational Axioms*.

[33] Again our basic understanding of this extreme comes from studying Paul's approach to spiritual warfare in the N.T. Paul does recognize that some problems and issues have at their heart spiritual warfare. Demonic influence must be countered. See **Article**, *Spiritual Warfare—Two Extremes to Avoid; Spiritual Warfare—Two Foundational Axioms*.

[34] In fact, this is one of the great Messianic prophecies (see also Haggai's final message to Zerubbabel Hag 2:20-23).

> 1 And he showed me Joshua the high priest standing before the angel of the LORD, and Satan standing at his right hand to resist him.
> 2 And the LORD said unto Satan, The LORD rebuke thee, O Satan; even the LORD that hath chosen Jerusalem rebuke thee: [is] not this a brand plucked out of the fire? 3 Now Joshua was clothed with filthy garments, and stood before the angel. 4 And he answered and spoke unto those that stood before him, saying, Take away the filthy garments from him. And unto him he said, Behold, I have caused your iniquity to pass from you, and I will clothe you with change of raiment.
> 5 And I said, Let them set a fair miter upon his head. So they set a fair miter upon his head, and clothed him with garments. And the angel of the LORD stood by. 6 And the angel of the LORD protested unto Joshua, saying, 7 Thus says the LORD of hosts; If you will walk in my ways, and if you will keep my charge, then you shall also judge my house, and shall also keep my courts, and I will give you places to walk among these that stand by.
> 8 Hear now, O Joshua the high priest, you, and your fellows that sit before you: for they [are] men wondered at: for, behold, I will bring forth my servant the BRANCH. 9 For behold the stone that I have laid before Joshua; upon one stone [shall be] seven eyes: behold, I will engrave the graving thereof, says the LORD of hosts, and I will remove the iniquity of that land in one day. 10 In that day, says the LORD of hosts, shall you call every man his neighbor under the vine and under the fig tree.
>
> Zec 3:1-10

A Possible Explanation

In a given situation, often a coalition of leadership is needed to confront the situation effectively. Not all of the leaders will be able to do all of the leadership functions necessary to influence God's people toward God's purposes. In this case, Zerubbabel was important as a civil leader and influenced that side of the situation. Joshua was a priest, a recognized religious leader with position and standing. He confirmed the informal leadership ministries of Haggai and Zechariah as legitimate and from God. Haggai was the practical minded of the two prophets. He called a spade a spade. He spoke directly and plainly to the situation, explaining in simple language God's message to the people to rebuild the temple. Zechariah's ministry was more mystical. He had visions. His visions were often symbolic. His ministry was much broader than Haggai's and included long-term futuristic prophecies. He also ministered over a longer period of time. His ministry provided the insight into spiritual warfare going on. Apparently Satan was trying to waylay the rebuilding of the temple by discouraging Joshua. Zechariah countered this.

Conclusion

Frequently in situations a range of leadership functions are needed. And one leader cannot provide all of them. Such was the case in the restoration ministry that Haggai, Zechariah, Zerubbabel and Joshua faced. Spiritual warfare is real. But not all leaders are gifted or called to deal with it directly.

See **Article**, *Haggai—Leadership Coalition; Spiritual Warfare—Two Extremes to Avoid; Spiritual Warfare—Two Foundational Axioms*.

Article 20

Holiness – A Motivating Factor for Leaders

Introduction
Consider this call from God recorded in 1 Peter 1:15

> But just as he who called you is holy, so be holy in all you do; 16 for it is written: "Be holy, because I am holy."

This verse contains a powerful motivator for the Christian leader—a call to holiness. The purpose of this article is to consider holiness from a limited perspective—as a source of motivation for the Christian leader.

The possibility of pleasing God and living in a right relationship with Him, is a powerful motivator for the leader with a heart for God. This is so for several reasons.

A Hunger for Holiness is Built into a Christian Leader
The Christian is shipped from the factory (so to speak) with a built in desire to please God and become more like Christ—namely, to be holy. This desire comes from the Holy Spirit's work in the heart of the believer. Not surprisingly, the work of the Holy Spirit, is to make us holy. Holiness is the hunger of a heart indwelt by the Holy Spirit.

It's true that sin works hard to quench that desire, misplaced priorities choke it out, and other desires crowd it out and make it unfruitful. Hardened hearts happen and scripture warns us of the very real consequences of resisting the Spirit of God. Yet as long as the Holy Spirit is present—there is an inner yearning for a life pleasing to God. Holiness is evidence of a leader whose life and ministry is controlled by the Holy Spirit.

The byproduct of Holiness is Spiritual Impact in the Leader's Ministry
Christ is the vine; we are the branches. Any hope for spiritual impact in leadership comes from the promised work of the Holy Spirit in the life and ministry of the leader. The leader with a heart for God desires surrender to the Holy Spirit's work so that sin will not be a blockage to that leader's usefulness to God. When resisting the work of the Holy Spirit, the leader not only cuts off the power source for holiness, but also cuts him/herself off from the empowered use of leadership gifts and abilities. The result is a vine-less branch—disconnected and unable to bear fruit.

A N.T. Example—Holiness as a Motivating factor for Those in Ministry
Paul recognized and used the call to holiness as a motivator for emerging leaders. We see this in Paul's second letter to Timothy. After a strong call for Christians to turn from sinful activity, (2 Timothy 2:19) Paul offers a verse that holds out a promise for the leader who longs to be powerfully used by God.

> 2 Timothy 2:20 In a large house there are articles not only of gold and silver, but also of wood and clay; some are for noble purposes and some for ignoble.

> 21 If a man cleanses himself from the latter, he will be an instrument for noble purposes, made holy, useful to the Master and prepared to do any good work.

Verse 21 presents the promise that if a person cleanses himself/herself from the wood and clay (areas of our lives untransformed by the Holy Spirit's power), that person might expect to be used in ministry in a greater capacity (God's "noble purposes").

Four Results of A Spiritual House-Cleaning

In the above verse the operative condition is "if" a man "cleanses himself." If a leader takes God up on his offer of holiness, consider this four outcomes presented in verse 21.

1) That leader will be an instrument for noble purposes—While not giving further elaboration, this verse refers to a range of purposes, some ignoble, some noble. This passage indicates that in some way the quality of a person's character corresponds with the quality of purpose for which they be used. This is a motivator because a leader with a heart for God desires to be used for God's highest purposes.

2) That Christian will in fact be made holy—Here is both the promise and possibility of holiness for the Christian leader. A leader serving the purposes of God does so most powerfully when serving with the character of God. As one reviews the list of the qualities for leadership selection in passages like Timothy 3 and Titus 1, it is interesting to notice what is included and what is absent. Apart from *able to teach* Paul's leadership list of items all relate to character qualities. Absent is *dynamic personality* and the *ability to delegate*. Leadership skills are important, but can be taught. Godly character, on the other hand, is foundational and non-negotiable.

3) That Leader will become useful to God—The Christian leader with a heart for the Lord longs to be powerfully used in God's purposes. Even newer leaders know the excitement of sensing God working through their lives, and likewise the corresponding struggle when operating on their own strength. A life surrendered to God becomes a vehicle through which God's purposes might flow. A eternal *well done* awaits those who surrender themselves as tools in the hands of the Living God.

4) That leader will be prepared to do any good work—Notice that the leader marked by holiness is prepared to do <u>any</u> good work. Character weaknesses do not limit them to lesser roles in the kingdom of God. A leader with a heart for God would not want character issues to prevent them from being used from any potential "good work" that is in the heart of God.

Haggai—The Important Lesson on Holiness

God uses a series of rhetorical questions in the book of Haggai to get the attention of the listeners—particularly the priestly leaders. His rhetorical questions point out that holiness is important. Sin blocks holiness. He also shows that righteousness is not automatic. Haggai uses the analogies to motivate the followers toward obeying God and completing the work they have started on the temple. God uses the analogies to point out that the financial conditions these followers are facing has been brought on by God. Now while the holiness lesson itself in the book of Haggai does not serve as a motivator for leaders to follow hard after God, it does show that holiness is important to God and that it isn't automatic.

Conclusion

Holiness is a powerful motivator for the Christian leader. Do you have a heart that hungers for holiness? If not, ask for it. If so, take God up on or His offer in 2 Timothy 2:20. Become that person God uses for His noble purposes, ready to be used in any way He may chose.

Article 21

Jesus—Sentness

Introduction

The Pentecostals call it *anointed by God*. Paul uses several phrases—*apostle by commandment of God, putting me in ministry, established as a preacher and apostle, called to be an apostle, apostle by the will of God, an Apostle by Jesus Christ*. Jesus uses the phrase, *Sent By God*. It is this concept of *sentness* that gives a foundational authority to Jesus' ministry. No leader who accomplishes anything for God can do so without a sense of destiny. And it is this notion of *sentness* or calling or *divine appointment* that is the springboard to a sense of destiny. Related concepts include the following:

Definition   A sense of destiny is an inner conviction arising from an experience or a series of experiences in which there is a growing sense of awareness that God has His hand on a leader in a special way for special purposes. See destiny pattern.

Definition   Sentness is a term capturing the divine backing of Jesus' intervention in the world to represent and reveal God to our world. It carries the notion of anointing and appointment by God for a mission, but in Jesus' case—more, since it was the incarnation of God in human form. The closest functional equivalent for leaders today is divine appointment.

Definition   Progressive calling refers to the on-going leadership challenges from God throughout their lifetimes, that leaders will receive, and not just some initial call; such challenges will bring renewal, divine affirmation, ministry affirmation and will continue to give strategic guidance to a leader's ministry.

Definition   Leadership committal is a special shaping activity of God observed in leadership emergence theory which is usually a spiritual benchmark and produces a sense of destiny in a leader. It is the call to leadership by God and the wholehearted response by the leader to accept and abide by that call. Paul's Damascus road experience, the destiny revelation given by Ananias, and Paul's response to it as a life calling provide the New Testament classic example of leadership committal

Sentness

Jesus operated in ministry with a sense of strong divine purpose because he knew he was sent by God. This use of *sentness* permeates the Gospel of John. It is the Gospel equivalent of Paul's apostolic appointment. Paul's repeated claims of apostolic authority all refer essentially to the concept of sentness. Sentness is used: to describe John's ministry of announcing Jesus; when speaking of official representative groups of the Jews; of Jesus ministry; of the Disciples ministry to come; of the Holy Spirit which is to come.

Jesus—Sentness

Two Greek words are used, both translated as *sent* (SRN 3992, SRN 649). Jesus uses these words sent, referring to himself as being sent by God, more than 40 times, each one claiming divine authority behind his ministry. The first occurrence—referring to John the Baptist's official mission to introduce Jesus, is seen in Jn 1:6

> 6 There was a man **sent from God**. His name was John the Baptist. Jn 1:6

This is the first instance of the concept of *sentness* in the Gospel of John. The messengers of the Pharisees ask John later in this chapter what **authority** he has for baptizing. John answers, essentially, in verses 29-34, that **God has sent him**. That is, he has divine authority for his leadership.

The first instance of Jesus using this notion of sentness about himself occurs in John 3:17.

> 17 For God did not **send** His Son into the world to judge it, but to save it. Jn 3:17

Note that this first mention had to do with *what he was sent to do*.

Sent (SRN 3992) is the general term and may even imply accompaniment (as when sent from God). *Sent* (SRN 649) suggests an official or authoritative sending. This last *sent* is a cognate of the word for apostle.

It was clear that Jesus had a strong sense of destiny. He knew he had divine backing. He *was sent by the Father*. At the heart of much of the conflict between Jesus and the religious leaders and others was the notion of sentness—claiming divine authority for his ministry. Jesus claimed to be sent by God and to have a special intimate relationship with God as his Father. The more Jesus claims this divine authority, sentness, and his special relationship with God, as Father, the more the conflict builds.[35] Jesus had a strong sense of destiny as reflected in the more than 40 times in Jn that he refers to being sent by God.

It is this strong sense of destiny, with authoritative backing, that is needed today. Complex leadership situation will force a leader without such an authoritative backing to exit from ministry. Finishing well is difficult in today's leadership world. Without a strong sense of divine backing, sentness, it is impossible.

Implications From the Notion of Sentness

Here are some observations flowing from the notion of sentness.

a. Spiritual authority comes from God. A sense of *sentness* gives an inner confidence and a base of faith to believe in and exercise one's spiritual authority.
b. A leader must have a sense of *sentness* if he/she is to minister with a sense of destiny, authority, and with power in ministry.
c. Conflict in ministry can be faced if a leader has a strong sense of *sentness*.
d. Apostolic leaders must be especially sensitive to the concept of sentness so as to recognize symptoms of it early on. For one apostolic function involves the selection, development, and appointment of leaders.
e. The lifelong leadership selection process really begins with the affirmation of sentness in an emerging leader.

---

[35] See especially the conflict chapters and references to sentness: Jn 5, 5 times mentioned—5:23,24,30,36,37; Jn 6, 5 times mentioned— 6:38,39,40,44,57; Jn 7, 5 times mentioned—7:16,18,28,29,33; Jn 8, 5 times mentioned—8:16,18,26,29,42.

Closure

You should have answers to the following three questions, relating to *sentness*, if you are intend to be a focused leader and a leader who finishes well.

**Who has sent you?
How do you know?
What have you been sent to do?**

If you can not answer these questions with a strong assurance then you probably should not be a leader in ministry.

Jesus was sent by God. He knew it. He knew within. He knew from external confirmation of it. He knew from God manifest power and presence backing up his ministry. He knew what he was sent to do.

See *leadership committal, spiritual authority, destiny processing*, **Glossary**. See **Articles**, *Spiritual Authority; Apostolic Functions*.

Article 22

Leadership Functions—Three High Level Generic Priorities

Introduction

Haggai was an inspirational leader. He was also a highly task focused leaders. So then he portrays better than any other in the O.T. what it means to be an inspirational task oriented leader.

High level Christian leaders[36] perform many leadership functions. In addition to direct ministry functions based on giftedness there are those additional functions that characterize leaders simply because they are people responsible for others.

description   <u>Leadership functions</u> describe general activities that leaders must do and/or be responsible for in their influence responsibilities with followers.

Leadership studies in the mid-50s[37] analyzed the kinds of things leaders did in secular organizations. From a list of over a thousand they reduced them by factor analysis to two major categories. These two categories are roughly equivalent to what we would call today task oriented leadership and relational oriented leadership. In the early 80s and 90s leadership research began to identify another high level function, which I call inspirational leadership.[38]

Figure 22.1 below groups leadership functions into three generic categories: task oriented leadership, relational oriented leadership, and inspirational leadership.

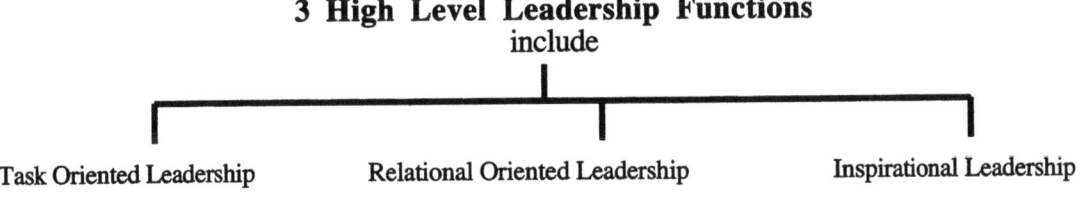

Figure 22.1 3 High Level Leadership Functions

---

[36] I use a five-fold leadership typology adapted from McGavran: Type A—local internal influence in the church or Christian organization; Type B—local external influence in the church or Christian organization; Type C—local/regional influence; Type D—national influence; Type E—international influence. I am speaking mostly about Type C, D, and E leaders when I talk about generic leadership functions for high level leaders. In the O.T., a leader speaking out against a King would be equivalent to a Type D leader.

[37] The Ohio State Leadership Research (1948-1967) reduced the many observed functions of secular leadership by factor analysis to two major generic categories: consideration and initiation of structure.

[38] McGregor and others were doing research on motivation. There was also a growing interest in values underlying why leaders did things.

Leadership Functions, 3 High Level Generic

Task Oriented Leadership

Task oriented leadership (technically called *Initiation of structure* in the Ohio State Research) groups all of those activities which a leader does to accomplish the task or vision for which the structure exists. Task behaviors involve clarifying goals, setting up structures to help reach them, holding people accountable, disciplining where necessary and in short, to act responsibly to accomplish goals. Table 22.1 displays a list of typical task oriented leadership functions.

Table 22.1. Typical Task Oriented Leadership Functions
Christian leaders:
1. must provide structures which facilitate accomplishment of vision;
2. will be involved in crisis resolution related to structural issues;
3. must make decisions involving structures;
4. will do routine problem solving concerning structural issues;
5. will adjust structures where necessary to facilitate leadership transitions;
6. must do direct ministry relating to maintaining and changing structures (extent depends on giftedness).

Relational Oriented Leadership

Relational oriented leadership (technically called *Consideration* in the Ohio State research) groups all of those activities which a leader does to affirm followers, to provide an atmosphere congenial to accomplishing work, to give emotional and spiritual support for followers so that they can mature, in short, to act relationally with followers in order to enable them to develop and be effective in their contribution to the organization. Table 22.2 lists some typical relational oriented leadership functions.

Table 22.2 Typical Relational Oriented Leadership Functions
Christian leaders:
1. must be involved in selection, development and release of emerging leaders;
2. are called upon to solve crises involving relationships between people'
3. will be called upon for decision making focusing on people;
4. must do routine problem solving related to people issues;
5. will coordinate with subordinates, peers, and superiors;
6. must facilitate leadership transition; their own and others;
7. must do direct ministry relating to people (extent depends on giftedness).

Inspirational Leadership

Christian leadership is *externally directed*. That is, goals result from vision from God. Such leadership must move followers toward recognition of, acceptance of and participation in bringing about that God-given vision. Leaders will answer to God for their leadership. Inspirational leadership is needed for this. Some typical inspirational functions are shown in Table 22-3.

Table 22-3 Typical Inspirational Leadership Functions
Christian leaders:
1. must motivate followers toward vision.
2. must encourage perseverance and faith of followers.
3. are responsible for the corporate integrity of the structures and organizations of which they are a part.
4. are responsible for developing and maintaining the welfare of the corporate culture of the organization.
5. are responsible for promoting the public image of the organization.
6. are responsible for the financial welfare of the organization.

7. are responsible for direct ministry along lines of giftedness which relate to inspirational functions.
8. must model (knowing, being, and doing) so as to inspire followers toward the reality of God's intervention in lives.
9. have corporate accountability to God for the organizations or structures in which they operate.

Summarizing Leadership Functions

There are common activities and unique activities for the three categories of leadership functions. A single list helps pinpoint the essential activities of Christian leaders.

1. Utilize giftedness for direct ministry to those in their sphere of influence.
2. Solve crises.
3. Make decisions.
4. Do routine problem solving.
5. Coordinate people, goals, and structures.
6. Select and develop leaders.
7. Facilitate leadership transition at all levels.
8. Facilitate structures to accomplish vision.
9. Motivate followers toward vision. This usually involves changing what is, and providing/ promoting a sense of progress.
10. Must encourage perseverance and faith of followers. This usually involves maintaining what is and creating a sense of stability. This is usually in dynamic tension with activity 9.
11. Accept responsibility for corporate functions of integrity, culture, finances, and accountability.
12. Must model so as to inspire followers toward the reality of God's intervention in lives and history.

Conclusion

These three functions must be carefully tended to if an organization is to go on.[39] Yet, a given leader usually has a predilection toward either task oriented leadership or relational oriented leadership. It is a rare leader who can do both well. But either a task oriented leader or a relational oriented leader can motivate. That is, motivational functions can be done by either a task oriented leader or relational oriented leader. What ever the case, it is up to a high level leader to make sure the functions are done despite his/her own particular bent. To do this a high level leader must be willing to delegate, to depend on and release to others functions that are not his/her own strength.

Haggai exemplifies inspirational task oriented leadership. He demonstrates how a leader with recognized spiritual authority can inspire followers to a task.

See **Article**, *Leadership Levels*.

---

[39] Most task oriented Christian organizations simply assume that these are happening.

Article 23

Leadership Levels—Looking At A Leadership Continuum: Five Types Of Leaders

Introduction

It is helpful to differentiate leaders in terms of some criteria. Several can be constructed. One typical example looks at Christian leadership in a church or denomination or parachurch organization. The primary criterion involves sphere of influence.[40] This typology of leaders along the continuum helps us pinpoint three major problems leaders face as they emerge from low level influence to high levels. These problems will repeatedly be faced around the world as the church emerges: 1. The Experience Gap, 2. The Financial (Logistics) Barrier, 3. The Strategic (Psychological) Barrier

Five Types of Leaders Along An Influence Continuum

Examine Figure 23.1 below which presents a continuum of leaders based on sphere of influence and shows some potential problems along the way.

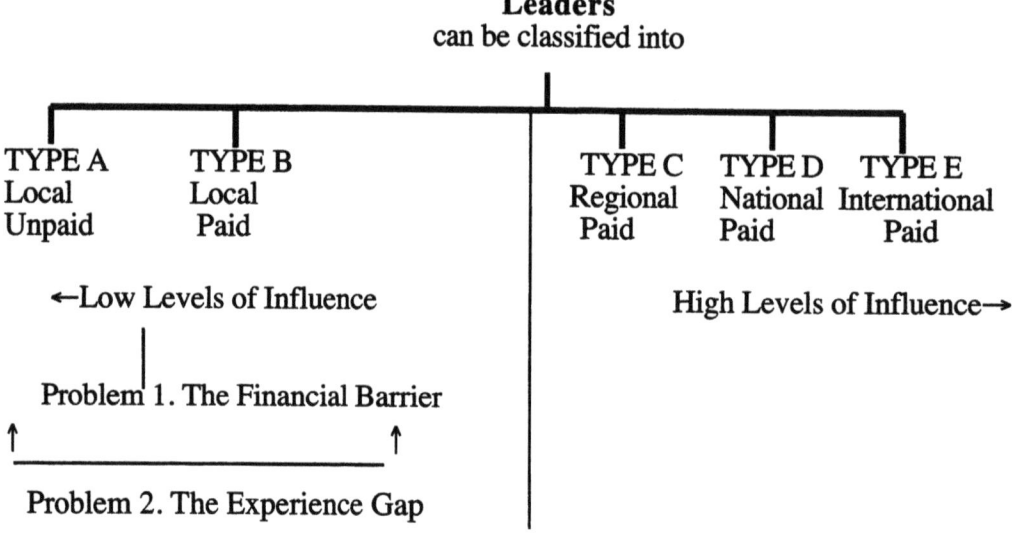

Figure 23.1 Five Types of Leaders—Sphere of Influence Continuum

---

[40] <u>Sphere of influence</u> refers to the totality of people being influenced and for whom a leader will give an account to God. This is subdivided into three domains called direct influence, indirect influence, and organizational influence. Three measures include: 1. Extensiveness—which refers to quantity; 2. Comprehensiveness—which refers to the scope of things being influenced; 3. Intensiveness—the depth to which influence extends to each item within the comprehensive influences. Extensiveness is the easiest to measure and hence is most often used or implied when talking about a leader's sphere of influence.

Table 23.1 further identifies each of the types of leaders.

Table 23.1. Five Types of Leaders Described

Type	Description
A	These are volunteer workers who help local churches get their business done. Low level workers in a Christian organization, who do clerical work or other detailed staff administration work, fit this level of influence also.
B	Paid workers in small churches like pastors of small congregations or pastors of multi-congregations fit here. Sometimes these are bi-vocational workers having to supplement their salaries with outside employment. Associate pastors on staff in a larger church also have this same level of influence. Paid workers doing administrative work in a Christian organizations have the equivalent level of influence from an organizational standpoint.
C	This level of influence includes senior pastors of large churches who influence other churches in a large geographic area (e.g. via Radio/TV ministry, Pastor Conferences, separate organization promoting the pastor's publications, workshops, etc.). It also includes leaders in Christian organizations or denominations who are responsible for workers in a large geographic region.
D	These include senior pastors of large churches who have national influence usually via organizations created by them to promote their ministry. Denominational heads of a country would fit here too. Professors in prestigious seminaries which train high level leaders and are writing the texts which others use would fit here too. Some influential Christian writers might fit here.
E	Heads of international organizations with churches in various countries and or missionaries in many countries fit here. Some influential Christian writers might fit here. Leaders at this level dominantly do strategic thinking. Often Type E leaders will control large resources of people, finances, and facilities. They will have very broad personal networks with other international leaders and national leaders. They will often be on boards of very influential organizations.

It should be explicitly stated here that there is no inherent value attached to any of the types. That is, a Type E leader is not better than a Type A leader. All of the various types are needed in the church and mission organizations. More types A and B are needed than Type E leaders. The type of leader we become depends on capacity that God has given and God's development of us toward roles which use that capacity. To be gifted for Type B leadership and to aspire for Type D is a mismanagement of stewardship. So too, to be gifted for Type E and yet remain at Type C. None of the types are better than any other. All are needed. We need to operate along the continuum so as to responsibly exercise stewardship of our giftedness and God's development of our leadership. Bigger is not better. Appropriate is best.

Problem 1. The Financial Barrier

Problem 1, also called the *Logistics Barrier* or the *Lay/Clergy Dilemma*, deals with finances.[41] In most situations where a church is emerging, a need for workers who can devote their full time and giftedness to accomplish ministry goals will arise. In the Christian

---

[41] Leaders who hold to the major leadership lesson on selection and development, as a value, will face this problem repeatedly as they seek to find ways to move leaders along in development. That lesson (Effective leaders view leadership selection and development as a priority function) carries with it some heavy responsibility.

Leadership Levels

enterprise there are non-professional workers, people doing necessary work in churches. There are para-professional workers, those who give their most energy to church work and have some developed giftedness but who support themselves financially with some sort of secular job. And finally there are semi-professional workers. Some leaders get partial pay for their Christian work. When a worker moves from non-professional, para-professional, or semi-professional status to full time paid Christian worker, that is, workers move from Type A to Type B, he/she will face the financial barrier. How can such workers be financed? [42] Many potential leader stumbles over this barrier and never makes it in to full time ministry (and perhaps because of discouragement, drops out of ministry altogether). Paul was dealing with this problem in 1Co 16 when he exhorts the Corinthians about finances for Christian workers—his own self (subtlety given), Timothy, and Stephanus.

Additional Problems with Problem 1 Moving Across the Financial Barrier

There is a tendency, which I call, *The Projection Tendency,* to seek to pressure effective Type A leaders to *go full time*. The idea involves the subtle implication that full time Christian leaders are more dedicated to God than lay leaders.

There is another minor problem involved in moving from Type A to Type B leadership. I call it *The Expectation Problem*. When leader cross the logistics barrier, it involves a major status change for leaders. Laity perceive full time Christian workers differently than lay leaders. Movement from Type A to Type B leadership means that people will view them differently (perhaps have higher expectations of them) even though their roles may not change.

Problem 2. The Experience Gap

Problem 2, also called the pre-service training problem, basically deals with a modern problem. Where churches have spread in a given geographical area, training institutions like seminaries and Bible colleges have also emerged. Normally, as a church is emerging, leaders are trained on-the-job and take on more responsibility as they are ready for it. But once there is a large number of churches and larger individual churches, people who are untrained on the job and with little or no leadership experience go to these training institutions and in a short period of time are academically trained (sort of) for ministry. They then attempt to enter ministry at Type B or higher level if they can. They don't have the experience for it. So we have people leading at levels they are not experienced to lead. A similar but not identical problem is being dealt with in 1Ti where Paul is seeking to give Timothy, a younger worker, to be accepted by older leaders, the Ephesian elders. The problem is not exactly the same, since Timothy did have experience—but the culture did not respect younger leaders. *The Experience Gap* is a double problem in some cultures since they respect age and experience, and training institutions turn out potential leaders who fit neither requirement.

Problem 3. The Strategic Barrier—Its Two Problems

Problem 3, also called the *ministry focus problem*, deals with a giftedness/responsibility problem seen in leaders who move from Type C ministry to Type D or E ministry. That is, they become leaders who do less direct ministry and more indirect ministry. Heads of organizations with a big sphere of influence face this problem. Direct ministry means dominantly using word gifts to influence people directly. Indirect ministry means leaders who are now helping or directing other leaders in direct ministry but are themselves not primarily doing direct ministry. Usually leaders who rise to these levels do so because they were successful in direct ministry at lower levels of influence. Simply because they were effective at that lower level doing direct ministry depending on their

---

[42] This is a major problem that will be faced around the world as the model which arose in the 19th and 20th centuries in countries with financial resources, that is, at least one full time paid pastor per congregation, go by the by. Bi-vocational workers will most likely dominate in the early part of the next century.

Leadership Levels

word gifts does not insure that they will be successful at a higher level not dominantly using their word gifts. In short, they are not trained for the functions at the higher level. And what is more startling, little or no formal training exists to develop leaders to do these higher level leadership functions.

A second problem arises. It is a psychological one. It has to do with satisfaction in ministry. When one is doing direct ministry and dominantly using word gifts, there is a constant feedback of things happening in lives which gives affirmation and satisfaction. At higher levels most leaders are doing leadership functions like problem solving, crises resolution, structural planning, and strategizing. These functions do not reward one in the same way as direct ministry. They do not receive the same satisfaction in doing these things and getting little affirmation as they did when they effectively did direct ministry.

Two things can help overcome these two problems. One, leaders should be trained for the higher level functions, dominantly by mentoring from leaders who are doing them well, and then transitioned into them. Two, the psychological loss perceived by leaders crossing the strategic barrier can also be addressed in at least the following two ways that I have observed in leaders at high level. One, they can from time to time do forays back into direct ministry which bring satisfaction that was experienced previously. Two, they can learn to see that what is being accomplished has broader potential and more far reaching results than their former direct ministry which had to be sacrificed in accepting the higher level of leadership. This requires strategic thinking and an application of the servant leadership model at a higher capacity level. Paul's later ministry dealt with this strategic barrier problem. Most of his latter ministry was indirect. Note his epistles are largely indirect ministry. He is helping other leaders deal with their issues—problem solving, dealing with crises, etc. He is not out there teaching and preaching directly. Note he got strategic eyes—see 2Co 11:28,Then besides all this, daily, I am burdened with my responsibility for the churches.

Conclusion

Types of leaders, that is, levels of leadership, are distinguished not to imply that bigger is better but to indicate that problems will be faced as leaders develop to higher levels of leadership. Further, leadership issues will vary noticeably with the different types. Types D and E are much more concerned with leadership means/resources, items of organizational structure, culture, dynamics, and power. They are multi-style leaders. They are more concerned with leadership philosophy and with strategic thinking. They know they will have heavy accountability to God in these areas. They are concerned with macro-contextual factors. Because leadership functions vary greatly along the continuum, different training is needed for each type. Informal/non-formal training focusing on skills for direct ministry is needed for Types A/B and should usually be in-service. All three modes (informal, non-formal, and formal) are needed to provide skills and perspectives for Types C, D, and E. In-service and interrupted in-service should dominate for Types C, D, and E.

See *sphere of influence*, **Glossary**.

Article 24

Left Hand of God

Introduction

Vertical verses in a horizontal book like Proverbs demand our attention.[43] Note Proverbs 21:1 in the several translations given below.

>21:1 The king's heart [is] in the hand of the LORD, [as] the rivers of water: he turneth it whithersoever he will. KJV

>21:1 The king's heart is in the hand of Jehovah as the watercourses: He turneth it whithersoever he will. ASV

>2:1 The king's heart is [like] channels of water in the hand of the LORD; He turns it wherever He wishes. NASB

>21:1 The king's heart is in the hand of the LORD; he directs it like a watercourse wherever he pleases. NIV

>21:1 The king's heart [is] in the hand of the LORD, [Like] the rivers of water; He turns it wherever He wishes. NKJV

>21:1 The king's heart is a stream of water in the hand of the LORD; he turns it wherever he will. RSV

>21:1 The Lord controls rulers, just as he determines the course of rivers. CEV

>21:1 The Lord controls the mind of a king as easily as he directs the course of a stream. TEV

>21:1 The king's heart is like a stream of water directed by the Lord; he turns it wherever he pleases. NLT

The terms used—rivers, watercourses, channels, stream, course could refer to a canal or channel of water such as an irrigation ditch. Just as the farmer directs the irrigation ditch so as to bring water where he wants it, so God directs kings and other rulers to do what He wants done.

---

[43] Psalms is a vertical book. That is, most of the Psalms are dealing with humans talking and/or hearing from God (vertical communication). Proverbs is dealing for the most part with humans relating to each other (horizontal relationships or activity). So then in a book dealing with horizontal relationships or activity it behooves us to note those few vertical passages. They demand our attention.

Left Hand of God

Every missionary better learn this verse and its view of God very quickly. For missionaries operate in countries controlled by others. They must abide by decisions made by political rulers—usually not in favor of their being in the country. Missionaries learn to trust God to move in the affairs of these pagan rulers.

Glasser Phrase

Dr. Arthur Glasser uses the phrase, the *Left Hand of God*, to call attention to God's use of non-believers to accomplish His purposes. This *Left Hand of God* is seen numerous times in the Old Testament. Table 24.1 depicts just a few of them.

Table 24.1 Some Occurrences of the Left Hand of God

Passage	Persons Involved	Explanation
Genesis 20, 21	Abraham, Sarah, Abimelech	Abraham lied to Abimelech about Sarah his wife. God protects her while she is with Abimelech and gives Abimelech a dream to let him know who Sarah is.
Genesis	Joseph, Pharaoh	God sends two dreams to Pharaoh, which need to be interpreted. Joseph comes to the forefront by interpreting these dreams and suggesting a wise course of action. Joseph is elevated to high position and is in place to deliver his people when the famine hits hardest.
Daniel	Nebuchadnezzar	Daniel ch 4 is one of the clearest examples of the king's heart being in the hand of Jehovah. God humbles Nebuchadnezzar, a very powerful ruler.
Isa 45	Cyrus; Daniel et al	God predicts He will use Cyrus and He does as noted in Table 24.2 below.
Hag 1:1,2	Darius, Haggai	It is clear that Darius was used by God to help the remnant back in the land.
Ne ch 1 et al	Artaxerxes	Artaxerxes not only wrote decrees allowing the Jews to go back in the land, but he also helped fund their return.

Restoration Leaders

All the restoration leaders were very much aware of the Left Hand of God. They were rebuilding the work of God back in the land. They were there because God had moved in the hearts of pagan rulers, very powerful ones. Those rulers—particularly Cyrus, Darius, Xerxes, Artxerxes—were moved to aid God's people. Esther, Mordecai, Ezra, Nehemiah, Haggai, Zechariah, and Malachi were all aware of the Left Hand of God.

One of the astounding things is God's prediction that He will use these rulers to accomplish His purposes. A beautiful illustration of this is Isaiah's famous passage, Isa 45. Table 24.2 below illustrates just a few of the passages referring to Cyrus.

Table 24.2 God's Left Hand Working Through Cyrus

Passages Predicting	Passages Fulfilling
Isa 44:28 That saith of **Cyrus**, [He is] my shepherd, and shall perform all my pleasure: even saying to Jerusalem, Thou shalt be built; and to the temple, Thy foundation shall be laid.	
Isa 45:1 Thus saith the LORD to his anointed, to **Cyrus**, whose right hand I have holden, to subdue nations before him; and I will loose the loins of kings, to open before him the two leaved gates; and the gates shall not be shut;	
Isa 45:13 I have raised him (Cyrus) up in righteousness, and I will direct all his ways: he shall build my city, and he shall let go my captives, not for price nor reward, saith the LORD of hosts.	
	2Ch 36:22,23 Now in the first year of **Cyrus** king of Persia, that the word of the LORD [spoken] by the mouth of Jeremiah might be accomplished, the LORD stirred up the spirit of **Cyrus** king of Persia, that he made a proclamation throughout all his kingdom, and [put it] also in writing, saying, Thus saith **Cyrus** king of Persia, All the kingdoms of the earth hath the LORD God of heaven given me; and he hath charged me to build him an house in Jerusalem, which [is] in Judah. Who [is there] among you of all his people? The LORD his God [be] with him, and let him go up.
	Ezr 1:2, 7, 8 Thus saith **Cyrus** king of Persia, The LORD God of heaven hath given me all the kingdoms of the earth; and he hath charged me to build him an house at Jerusalem, which [is] in Judah. 7 Also **Cyrus** the king brought forth the vessels of the house of the LORD, which Nebuchadnezzar had brought forth out of Jerusalem, and had put them in the house of his gods; 8 Even those did **Cyrus** king of Persia bring forth by the hand of Mithredath the treasurer, and numbered them unto Sheshbazzar, the prince of Judah.

Closure

Most of us as leaders know something of the *Right Hand of God*. We have experienced God's intervention in our lives and ministries in such a way as to be awed by His power. But can we see His *Left Hand* working today. We need to be aware of this facet of God's power. And we need discernment, maybe even prophetic voices, to point out to us the *Left Hand of God*. It is especially comforting to believe we have a sovereign God in our world controlled by the most part by non-godly political leaders. May we see God turn the heart of the kings to accomplish His purposes.

See *Sovereign Mindset*; **Glossary**.

Article 25

Lord of Hosts

Introduction

Notice the repeated phrase in the following excerpts from Haggai:

Hag 1:2 Thus speaketh the **LORD of hosts**, saying, This people say, The time is not come, the time that the LORD'S house should be built.

Hag 1:5 Now therefore thus saith the **LORD of hosts**; Consider your ways.

Hag 1:7 Thus saith the **LORD of hosts**; Consider your ways.

Hag 1:9 Ye looked for much, and, lo, [it came] to little; and when ye brought [it] home, I did blow upon it. Why? saith the **LORD of hosts**. Because of mine house that [is] waste, and ye run every man unto his own house.

Hag 1:14 And the LORD stirred up the spirit of Zerubbabel the son of Shealtiel, governor of Judah, and the spirit of Joshua the son of Josedech, the high priest, and the spirit of all the remnant of the people; and they came and did work in the house of the **LORD of hosts**, their God,

Hag 2:4 Yet now be strong, O Zerubbabel, saith the LORD; and be strong, O Joshua, son of Josedech, the high priest; and be strong, all ye people of the land, saith the LORD, and work: for I [am] with you, saith the **LORD of hosts**:

Hag 2:6 For thus saith the **LORD of hosts**; Yet once, it [is] a little while, and I will shake the heavens, and the earth, and the sea, and the dry [land];

Hag 2:7 And I will shake all nations, and the desire of all nations shall come: and I will fill this house with glory, saith the **LORD of hosts**.

Hag 2:8 The silver [is] mine, and the gold [is] mine, saith the **LORD of hosts**.

Hag 2:9 The glory of this latter house shall be greater than of the former, saith the **LORD of hosts**: and in this place will I give peace, saith the **LORD of hosts**.
Hag 2:11 Thus saith the **LORD of hosts**; Ask now the priests [concerning] the law, saying,

Hag 2:23 In that day, saith the **LORD of hosts**, will I take thee, O Zerubbabel, my servant, the son of Shealtiel, saith the LORD, and will make thee as a signet: for I have chosen thee, saith the **LORD of hosts**.

This title for God, *LORD of hosts*, clearly dominates Haggai's view of an authoritative God. It occurs 14 times in Haggai's two small chapters. Table 25.1 shows the frequency of this special name for God

Lord of Hosts

Table 25.1 Frequency of Phrase—LORD of hosts

Leadership Era	Frequency of Use
Patriarchal	None
Pre-Kingdom	None
Kingdom	23 times
Post-Kingdom	85 times (14 Haggai; 47 Zechariah; 24 Malachi)
Futuristic Prophetical	147 times (mostly in Isaiah about future and Jeremiah about deterioration of Kingdom in its last days and futuristic). Dominantly used to describe God in the future, including Restoration Era.

The LORD of hosts is dominantly a term showing how God reveals Himself as needed in the Restoration Era. The people of God have been in exile and are controlled by foreign rulers. But God is still overall in charge and will meet His people in these times. This knowledge of God and its required faith acceptance is especially needed by the small remnant who go back into the land. Can God be enough for them? The Restoration Prophets say yes. They see God as the LORD of hosts.

Combination Name—What Does It Tell Us About God?

The LORD of hosts is a combinational name for God. It its made up of *LORD* (SRN 3068) and *hosts* (SRN 6635). LORD, or Jehovah, or Yahweh (as the Message translates it), *the existing One* of the Exodus 3 revelation to Moses is the proper name of the one true God. It is the personal name of God and His most frequent designation in Scripture, occurring some 5000+ times in the OT. The word *hosts* occurs many times also (450+). In combination, LORD of hosts, the phrase occurs 255 times. Hosts carries a military connotation.

Table 25.2 shows how some of the Bible translations render the combination LORD of hosts.

Table 25.2 Bible Translations Rendering of LORD of hosts.

Translation	How Rendered LORD of hosts
KJV	LORD[44] of hosts
ASV	Jehovah of hosts
NIV	LORD of hosts
CEV	Lord All-Powerful
TEV	Lord Almighty
Message	Yahweh of the Angel Armies
RSV	Lord of hosts
NRSV	Lord of hosts
NASB	LORD of hosts
BAS	Lord of Armies
JB	Yahweh Sabaoth

The TEV and the CEV, two semantic translations probably come the closest to the sense of the phrase. When God uses this phrase to describe Himself, as is the case with all the names of God, He is saying something about his character. What does this combined title tell us about God's character.

---

[44] LORD, all capitals, translates Jehovah in the KJV. Lord translates Adonai.

In its fullest sense, the Lord All-Powerful terminology really exalts God. It is associated with His kingship (Isa 6:5; Ps 24:9; 84:3 et al). In the Psalms it exalts a King of Glory. Zechariah expands His kingship beyond just Israel—God is King of the world (cf. Zech 14:16). Isa reinforces this same idea (Isa 37:16). Jeremiah sees this God as the source of all (Jer 10:16). The prophetic implications of both Isa, Jer, and Zech are that His rulership necessitates a time when he will visibly display that lordship here on earth. God will win out over the nations, even though for a while it will appear that the nations that have come against Mount Zion have won. But at that time God will lead a great army (the military connotations of the word are in focus) into battle. God will also control the forces of nature. All will be used to bring all earthly powers (kingdoms and governments) into submission (Dan 2, 7; Isa 13:4; 24:2ff; 29:5-8; 31:4ff, 34:1-12). God will reign universally from Mt. Zion. All earthly powers will acknowledge that He is the Lord All-Powerful.

There is a principle seen here, in the *Restoration Era*, and indeed throughout all Scripture.

Principle
God reveals Himself to His people in their situations in terms of What They Need to Know about Him or What He can Be for His people or What They Need for their Situations.

This King of Glory, this All-Powerful One, this one who will be a final victor, is the God of this remnant back in the land. His commands must be obeyed. He will empower those who obey Him to accomplish His purposes.

What Does Haggai Reveal about the LORD of Hosts?

Haggai uses the phrase, Lord of Hosts—that is, the Lord All-Powerful, 14 times. What are the connotations or implications of his use of that phrase? Table 25.3 suggests some of the implications of Haggai's use of this combined phrase describing God for each of the contexts it is used in.

Table 25.3 Haggai's Use of Lord of hosts—Context By Context

Occurrence	Context/ Flow	Observations
Hag 1:2	Haggai gives his 1st prophetic message as coming from the Lord Almighty.	This is a warning. It is related to the timing of building the temple. Implication is that God knows their excuse about timing and it doesn't hold water.
Hag 1:5	Haggai explains that God is behind their lack of materialistic pursuit.	God is almighty and rules sovereignly over natural forces. Their lack of fruitfulness has God at its source. He is controlling nature so as to bring about failure on their part.
Hag 1:7	Haggai gives the people an option—a response for obedience.	The Lord Almighty promises that He will reveal Himself to them and will be pleased with them, if they obey.
Hag 1:9	Same as in 1:5 but in more detail.	The people respond to the Lord Almighty and are fearful of Him. They recognize His power as being behind their failure.
Hag 1:14	The temple they are working on is recognized as God's temple.	The people know they are building the Lord Almighty's temple.
Hag 2:4	The presence of God as Lord Almighty is promised the people.	God is seen not only as the Lord Almighty but as the one who keeps promises. The people are encouraged that the Lord Almighty will be with them.

Lord of Hosts

Hag 2:6,7	God prophetically promises great power. He is operating on earth to accomplish His purposes. These people are part of His work.	The Almighty part of the phrase is in focus here as God promise to powerfully move (probably futuristic as well as on their behalf).
Hag 2:8	God promises to provide the resources needed.	Here the Lord Almighty as the source of things is seen; the wealth of the world belongs to Him.
Hag 2:9	God encourages the people that even though this temple is not as magnificent as Solomon's He will reveal His glory through it.	The King of Glory thrust of the Lord Almighty is in focus here.
Hag 2:11	God uses analogical insights about the Levitical Law to convince folks of His involvement in their material pursuits.	God is all wise and all knowing and in control of nature.
Hag 2:23	Haggai closes the book with a special futuristic prophecy probably applying to Zerubbabel and the greater Zerubbabel who will come (Messiah)	God as the All Powerful one tells what He will do in the future. He will rule.

Closure

We need to know God in general as to the names He uses to reveal himself to his people. This kind of study will increase our faith to believe who God is and what He will do. We need to know God in terms of our needs and times.

Article 26

Macro Lesson Defined

Introduction

Macro Lessons inform our leadership with potential leadership values that move toward the absolute. We live in a time when most do not believe there are absolutes. In my study of leadership in the Bible, I have defined a leadership truth continuum which recognizes the difficulty in deriving absolutes but does allow for them.[45] Figure 26.1 depicts this.

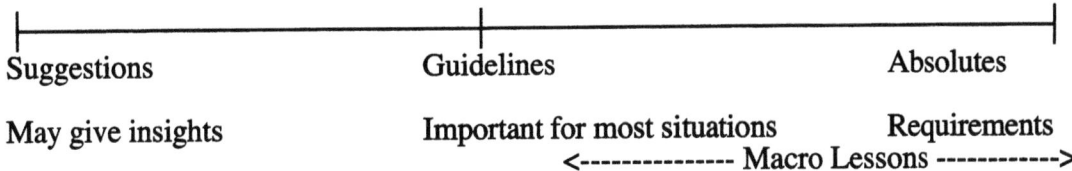

Suggestions   Guidelines   Absolutes

May give insights   Important for most situations   Requirements
                          <--------------- Macro Lessons ------------>

Figure 26.1 Leadership Truth Continuum/ Where Macro Lessons Occur

Introduction to Macro lessons

In the *Complexity Era* in which we now live,[46] the thrust of leadership theory has moved, toward the importance of leadership values. The questions being asked today are not as much what is leadership (the leadership basal elements—leader, followers, and situations) and how does it operate (leadership influence means—corporate and individual) as it is why do we do what we do (leadership value bases). The first three eras (Great Man, Trait, and Ohio State) answered the question, "What is leadership?" The Contingency and early part of the Complexity Era answered the question, "How do we do it?" Now we are grappling with, "Why do we lead? or What ought we to do?" We are looking for leadership values. A leadership value is an underlying assumption which affects how a leader behaves in or perceives leadership situations. They are usually statements that have *ought* or *must* or *should* in them. Macro-Lessons are statements of truth about leadership which have the potential for becoming leadership values. These macro-lessons are observations seen in the various leadership eras in the Bible. Many of these became values for numerous Bible leaders. These macro-lessons move toward the right (requirement, value) of the leadership truth continuum.

What is a macro lesson?

Definition   A <u>macro-lesson</u> is a high level generalization
- of a leadership observation (suggestion, guideline, requirement), stated as a lesson,

---

[45] See Clinton, **Leadership Perspectives** for a more detailed explanation of the continuum and for my approach to deriving principles from the scriptures. See **Article**, *Principles of Truth*.

[46] A study of leadership history in the United States from 1850 to the present uncovered 6 Eras (an era being a period of time in which some major leadership theory held sway): 1. Great Man Era (1840s to 1904); 2. Trait Theory (1904-1948); 3. Ohio State Era (1948-1967); Contingency Era (1967-1980); Complexity Era (1980-present). See Clinton, **A Short History of Leadership Theory**. Altadena, Ca.: Barnabas Publishers.

Macro Lesson Defined

- which repeatedly occurs throughout different leadership eras,
- and thus has potential as a leadership absolute.

Macro lessons even at their weakest provide strong guidelines describing leadership insights. At their strongest they are requirements, or absolutes, that leaders should follow. Leaders ignore them to their detriment.

Examples:

    Prayer Lesson: If God has called you to a ministry then He has called you to pray for that ministry.

    Accountability: Christian leaders minister ought always with a conscious view to ultimate accountability to God for their ministry.

    Bible Centered: An effective leader who finishes well must have a Bible centered ministry.

Macro Lessons are derived from a comparative study of leadership in the Six Leadership Eras. These Six Leadership Eras and number of macro lessons identified are shown in Table 26.1.

Table 26.1 Leadership Eras and Number of Macro Lessons

Leadership Era	Number of Macro Lessons
1. Patriarchal Era	7
2. Pre-Kingdom Era	10
3. Kingdom Era	5
4. Post-Kingdom Era	5
5. Pre-Church Era	9
6. Church Era	5

I have identified 41 macro lessons, roughly 5 to 10 per leadership era. When a macro-lesson is seen to occur in varied situations and times and cultural settings and in several leadership eras it becomes a candidate for an absolute leadership lesson. When that same generalization becomes personal and is embraced by a leader as a driving force for how that leader sees or operates in ministry, it becomes a leadership value.

The top three Macro Lessons for the four O.T. Leadership Eras are listed in Table 26.2.

Table 26.2 Top Three Macro Lessons in O.T. Leadership Eras

Priority	Era	Label	Statement
1	Pre-Kingdom	Presence	The essential ingredient of leadership is the powerful presence of God in the leader's life and ministry. (*Therefore a leader must not minister without the powerful presence of God in his/her life.*)
2	Patriarchal	Character	Integrity is the essential character trait of a spiritual leader. (*Therefore, a leader must maintain integrity and respond to God's shaping of it.*)

Macro Lesson Defined

3	Pre-Kingdom	Intimacy	Leaders develop intimacy with God which in turn overflows into all their ministry since ministry flows out of being. *(Therefore a leader must seek to develop intimacy with God.)*

Table 26.3 gives the top three Macro Lessons for the two N.T. Leadership Eras.

Table 26.3 Top Three Macro Lessons in N.T. Leadership Eras

Priority	Era	Label	Statement
1	Church Centered	Word	*God's Word must be the primary source for equipping leaders and must be a vital part of any leader's ministry.*
2	Pre-Church	Harvest	*Leaders must seek to bring people into relationship with God.*
3	Pre-Church	Shepherd	*Leaders must preserve, protect, and develop those who belong to God's people.*

You will notice that some of these macro lessons are already described in value language (should, must, ought) while others are simply statements of observations. I have put in italics my attempt to give the value associated with the observation.

Comparative study across the six leadership eras for macro lessons makes up one of the seven leadership genres, i.e. sources for leadership findings from the Bible.

Article 27

Macro Lessons Listed

Introduction

Macro Lessons inform our leadership with potential leadership values that move toward the absolute. The following are the 41 lessons I have identified as I comparatively studied the six different leadership eras for leadership observations.

No.	Label	Era	Statement of Macro Lesson
1.	Blessing	Patriarchal	God mediates His blessing to His followers through leaders.
2.	Shaping	Patriarchal	God shapes leader's lives and ministry through critical incidents.
3.	Timing	Patriarchal	God's timing is crucial to accomplishment of God's purposes.
4.	Destiny	Patriarchal	Leaders must have a sense of destiny.
5.	Character	Patriarchal	Integrity is the essential character trait of a spiritual leader.
6.	Faith	Patriarchal	Biblical Leaders must learn to trust in the unseen God, sense His presence, sense His revelation, and follow Him by faith.
7.	Purity	Patriarchal	Leaders must personally learn of and respond to the holiness of God in order to have effective ministry.
8.	Intercession	Pre-Kingdom	Leaders called to a ministry are called to intercede for that ministry.
9.	Presence	Pre-Kingdom	The essential ingredient of leadership is the powerful presence of God in the leader's life and ministry.
10.	Intimacy	Pre-Kingdom	Leaders develop intimacy with God which in turn overflows into all their ministry since ministry flows out of being.
11.	Burden	Pre-Kingdom	Leaders feel a responsibility to God for their ministry.
12.	Hope	Pre-Kingdom	A primary function of all leadership is to inspire followers with hope in God and in what God is doing.
13.	Challenge	Pre-Kingdom	Leaders receive vision from God which sets before them challenges that inspire their leadership.
14.	Spiritual Authority	Pre-Kingdom	Spiritual authority is the dominant power base of a spiritual leader and comes through experiences with God, knowledge of God, godly character and gifted power.
15.	Transition	Pre-Kingdom	Leaders must transition other leaders into their work in order to maintain continuity and effectiveness.
16.	Weakness	Pre-Kingdom	God can work through weak spiritual leaders if they are available to Him.
17.	Continuity	Pre-Kingdom	Leaders must provide for continuity to new leadership in order to preserve their leadership legacy.
18.	Unity	Kingdom	Unity of the people of God is a value that leaders must preserve.

Macro Lessons Listed

#	Lesson	Era	Description
19.	Stability	Kingdom	Preserving a ministry of God with life and vigor over time is as much if not more of a challenge to leadership than creating one.
20.	Spiritual Leadership	Kingdom	Spiritual leadership can make a difference even in the midst of difficult times.
21.	Recrudescence	Kingdom	God will attempt to bring renewal to His people until they no longer respond to Him.
22.	By-pass	Kingdom	God will by-pass leadership and structures that do not respond to Him and will institute new leadership and structures.
23.	Future Perfect	Post-Kingdom	A primary function of all leadership is to walk by faith with a future perfect paradigm so as to inspire followers with certainty of God's accomplishment of ultimate purposes.
24.	Perspective	Post-Kingdom	Leaders must know the value of perspective and interpret present happenings in terms of God's broader purposes.
25.	Modeling	Post-Kingdom	Leaders can most powerfully influence by modeling godly lives, the sufficiency and sovereignty of God at all times, and gifted power.
26.	Ultimate	Post-Kingdom	Leaders must remember that the ultimate goal of their lives and ministry is to manifest the glory of God.
27.	Perseverance	Post-Kingdom	Once known, leaders must persevere with the vision God has given.
28.	Selection	Pre-Church	The key to good leadership is the selection of good potential leaders which should be a priority of all leaders.
29.	Training	Pre-Church	Leaders should deliberately train potential leaders in their ministry by available and appropriate means.
30.	Focus	Pre-Church	Leaders should increasingly move toward a focus in their ministry which moves toward fulfillment of their calling and their ultimate contribution to God's purposes for them.
31.	Spirituality	Pre-Church	Leaders must develop interiority, spirit sensitivity, and fruitfulness in accord with their uniqueness since ministry flows out of being.
32.	Servant	Pre-Church	Leaders must maintain a dynamic tension as they lead by serving and serve by leading.
33.	Steward	Pre-Church	Leaders are endowed by God with natural abilities, acquired skills, spiritual gifts, opportunities, experiences, and privileges which must be developed and used for God.
34.	Harvest	Pre-Church	Leaders must seek to bring people into relationship with God.
35.	Shepherd	Pre-Church	Leaders must preserve, protect, and develop God's people.
36.	Movement	Pre-Church	Leaders recognize that movements are the way to penetrate society though they must be preserved via appropriate ongoing institutions.
37.	Structure	Church	Leaders must vary structures to fit the needs of the times if they are to conserve gains and continue with renewed effort.

38.	Universal	Church	The church structure is inherently universal and can be made to fit various cultural situations if functions and not forms are in view.
39.	Giftedness	Church	Leaders are responsible to help God's people identify, develop, and use their resources for God.
40.	Word Centered	Church	God's Word is the primary source for equipping leaders and must be a vital part of any leaders ministry.
41.	Complexity	All eras	Leadership is complex, problematic, difficult and fraught with risk—which is why leadership is needed.

See Also **Article** *Macro Lessons—Defined*.

Article 28

Principles of Truth

Introduction

Leaders who finish well are described by six characteristics.[47] Two of these claim that,

> **They maintain a learning posture and can learn from various kinds of sources—life especially.**
>
> **Truth is lived out in their lives so that convictions and promises of God are seen to be real.**

How does a leader get truth from the scriptures—one of the sources for learning? How does a leader get truth, form convictions, and arrive at promises from God?

Further, this leadership commentary has described a Bible centered leader.

> A <u>Bible Centered leader</u> refers to a leader whose leadership is being informed by the Bible and who personally has been shaped by Biblical values, has grasped the intent of Scriptural books and their content in such a way as to apply them to current situations and who uses the Bible in ministry so as to impact followers.

How does one get informed by the Bible on leadership? How does a leader get values which shape him/her?

This article suggests perspectives that help answer these questions. It details my own framework—the perspectives that have guided me as I comment on the Scriptures, suggest observations, guidelines, values, principles of truth, macro lessons, etc.

Principles

Observations of truth provide one useful result of leadership studies. These truths help us understand other leadership situations and predict what ought to be. They also help us in the selection and training of leaders since they give guidelines that have successfully been applied in past leadership situations. These truths are usually seen first as specific statements concerning one leader in his/her situation. They are then generalized to cover other leaders and like situations. The question of how generally they can be applied to

---

[47] Six characteristics of a good finish include the following. Leaders ho finish well have: (1) a vibrant personal relationship with God; (2) a learning posture; (3) Christ-likeness in character; (4) lived by Biblical convictions; (5) left behind ultimate contributions; (6) and fulfilled a sense of destiny.

Principles of Truth

others is a genuine one. The certainty continuum and screening questions provide cautions about this.

Definition *Principles* refer to generalized statements of truth which reflect observations drawn from specific instances of leadership acts or other leadership sources.

God's processing of leaders includes shaping toward spiritual formation, ministerial formation, and/or strategic formation. Analyzing formational shaping, serves as an important stimulus for deriving principles.

A few examples will help clarify. Analysis of God's use of the integrity check, word check, and obedience check to develop spiritual formation in numerous young leader's lives led to the following three principles.

> **Integrity is foundational for leadership; it must be instilled early in a leader's character.**

> **Obedience is first learned by a leader and then taught to others.**

> **Leadership gifts primarily involve word gifts which initially emerge through word checks**

Analysis of Samuel's final public leadership act in 1 Sa 12 (see especially vs 23) led to the following truth.

> **When God calls a leader to a leadership situation he calls him/her to pray for followers in that situation.**

The Certainty Continuum and Related Definitions

Attempts to derive statements of truth from leadership studies meet with varied success. Some people seem to intuitively have a sense of generalizing from a specific situation a statement, which apparently fits other situations. Others are not so good at this skill. This part of leadership theory is in is infancy stage. In the future we hope to delineate more structured approaches for deriving statements and for validating them. But for now we need to recognize that these statements often can not be proved as truth (in the sense that physical science can prove truth) hence we, as researchers, need to be careful of what we say is truth. Below is given the certainty continuum and the major generalization concerning the derivation of *truth* statements. These are an attempt to make us as researchers cautious about applying our findings.

Principles of truth are attempts to generalize specific truths for wider applicability and will vary in their usefulness with others and the authoritative degree to which they can be asserted for others.

description The *certainty continuum* is a horizontal line moving from suggestions on one extreme to requirements on the other extreme which attempts to provide a grid for locating a given statement of truth in terms of its potential use with others and the degree of authority with which it can be asserted.

Principles of Truth

The basic ideas are that:
1. Principles are observations along a continuum.
2. We can teach and use with increasing authority those principles further to the right on the continuum.

```
Suggestions                    Guidelines                    Requirements
|------------------------------------------------------------|

Tentative Observations                                        Absolutes
                                   Certain                   Very Certain

More certain of truth     ─────────────────────────────>
Little Authority          <─────────────────────────────     Great Authority
```

Figure 28-1 The Certainty Continuum

I am identifying principles as a broad category of statements of truth which were true at some instant of history and may have relevance for others at other times.

There is little difference between *Suggestions* and *Guidelines* on the continuum. In fact, there is probably overlap between the two. Some *Guidelines* approach *Requirements*. But there is a major difference from going from *Suggestions* to *Requirements*—the difference being *Suggestions* are optional but *Requirements* are not. They must be adhered to.

Definition   *Suggestions* refers to truth observed in some situations and which may be helpful to others but they are optional and can be used or not with no loss of conscience.

Definition   *Guidelines* are truths that are replicated in most leadership situations and should only be rejected for good reasons though their will be no loss of conscience.

Definition   *Absolutes* refer to replicated truth in leadership situations across cultures without restrictions. Failure to follow or use will normally result in some stirrings of conscience.

Absolutes are principles which evince God's authoritative backing. All leaders everywhere should heed them.

Suggestions are the most tentative. They are not enjoined upon people. They may be very helpful though.

Remember that a *Suggestion* or *Guideline* may move to the right or left if more evidence is found in the Bible to support such a move. If a *suggestion* or *guideline* identified in one place in the Scriptures is found to be abrogated, modified or somehow restricted at a later time in the progressive flow of revelation then it will move most likely to the left. However, if later revelation gives evidence of its more widespread usage or identifies it more certainly for everyone then it will move to the right.

Principles of Truth

Six Assumptions Underlying Derivation Of Principles

Principles are derived from Biblical leadership situations as well as from life situations. Several assumptions underlie my approach to deriving principles of truth. The following six assumptions underlie my approach to getting truth.

1. **Truth Assumption**: All truth has its source in God.

I need not fear the study of secular material (social science materials, leadership theory, present day situations, etc.). If there is any truth in it I can be certain it is of God. For there is no truth apart from God. I don't have to limit truth to the Bible. The Bible itself shows how God has revealed truth by many different means. These means were certainly not just limited to ancient written revelation. The problem then lies in how to discern if something is truth.

2. **Source Assumption:** All of life can be a source of truth for those who are discerning.

The central thrust of Proverbs 1:20-33 and in fact the whole book of Proverbs is that God reveals wisdom in life situations. The book of Proverbs is more than just content for us to use; it is a modeling of how that content was derived over time and in a given society. We can trust God to reveal wisdom in the life situations we study (whether from the Bible or today). Truth that evolved in Israeli history came to take on at least guideline status and much of it became absolutes.

3. **Applicability Assumption.** Just because a statement of truth was true for a specific given situation does not mean the statement has applicability for other leaders at other times. Wider application must be determined via comparative means.

A statement of truth is an assertion of fact drawn from a specific situation. The dynamics of the situation may well condition the statement. That is, the truth itself may apply only in situations which contain the same dynamics. The fact that the truth did happen means it is at least worthy of study for potential wider use. Because of the consistency of God's character we know that the truth can not violate His nature. But its happening is not sufficient justification for its use anywhere at anytime by any leader.

4. **Dogmatic Assumption.** We must exercise caution in asserting all truth statements as if they were absolutes.

Fewer truths will be seen as absolutes if screened with applicability criteria. The use of applicability criteria, especially that of comparative study, will force one to identify a higher level function behind a given principle. Thus a statement of truth at some lower level when compared with other situations and similar statements of truth might lead to a higher order generic statement of truth. These higher level statements of truth, though more general in nature, preserve the function intended rather than the form of the truth. Such statements will allow more freedom of application. Statements which do not carry wide applicability or have attached to them dynamics of situations which can not be fully assessed will most likely have to be asserted with less dogmatism.

5. **Dependence Assumption.** We are forced more than ever to depend upon the Holy Spirit's present ministry to confirm truth we are deriving.

Because of the sources (life as well as Biblical) from which we are drawing truth, we will need more dependence upon the ministry of the Holy Spirit. That is, we will be forced to situationally rely on and become more sensitive to the Holy Spirit's leading and voice. We will need to recognize giftedness in the body and learn to trust those who have spiritual

Principles of Truth

gifts which expose, clarify, and confirm truth (discernings of spirits, word of knowledge, word of wisdom, teaching, exhortation, etc.).

6. **Trust Assumption.** Because we are following Biblical admonitions (Heb 13:7,8; 1 Co10:6,11, Ro 15:4) in our attempts to derive truth we can expect God to enable us to see much truth.

God does not command us to do things that are impossible. God's commands contain within them the promise of enablement. Because there are great needs for more and better leadership and because we need leadership truth to develop that leadership and because God has told us to study leaders to learn from their lives, we can expect God to lead us to truth that will greatly affect our lives. By faith we can trust Him to do this.

Conclusion

For each of the Key Leadership Insight sections for individual books, of my commentary series, I have listed statements called observations, principles, values, lessons. Each of these will need to be assessed on the certainty continuum to determine their level of applicability.

See *integrity check, word check, and obedience check, spiritual formation, ministerial formation, strategic formation,* **Glossary**.

Article 29

Promises of God

Introduction
Paul makes the following wonderful statement in the midst of a challenge to the Corinthians to give to a relief fund to help out Jerusalem Christians.

> 8 And God is able to provide more than you need. You will have what you need with some left over for giving. 2Co 9:8

I believe this to be a **promise** from God that is broader than just the Corinthians. When believers give cheerfully and generously and to meet God-directed needs, I believe they can expect God to enrich them to give. The right kind of attitude is crucial however. They don't give to get. They give because God gives them grace to give and gives them liberal and joyous hearts to give. And they surrender themselves to God for this giving ministry through them. When this is done, I believe this promise is as good as gold.

I also believe the equalizing principle is in effect.

> 13 I don't intend that you should give so much that you suffer for it. But there is an equalizing principle here. Right now you have more than you need and can help them out. Later you may have need and they may help you out.

If they give out of their surplus they can expect help when they have need. A Pauline leadership value occurs here.

> **Financial Equality Principle: Christian leadership must teach that Christian giving is a reciprocal balancing between needs and surplus.**

This equalizing principle, giving when we have abundance and others have need, and in turn receiving when we have needs and others have abundance, must be recognized, embraced, and then applied very carefully so as to not create dependencies.[48]

What I have just done is introduce you to the notion of a promise from God, but one that has conditions. God will supply. But we must generously give. We can give out of our surplus. Later there will be times when we don't have enough. Others will give to us.

---

[48] This principle is difficult for western Christians to see. For the most part western Christians don't realize just how wealthy they are when in comparison with many other non-western Christians. With no exposure to missions and churches around the world, Christians will rarely ever really embrace this principle. Leaders must raise awareness levels about needs around the world as well as teach this principle (and model it in their own lives).

Promises of God

Some promises are unconditional and are for all who want to appropriate them. Others promises are for a special group or person. Other promises have conditions. A leader must be able to discern promises of God, both for himself/herself, for the leadership situation, and for followers within his/her influence. This article defines a promise and gives some general guidelines about promises and introduces the image of God as *The Promise Keeper*.

Promises of God

When I was a little boy my friends and I would often say, "I promise." And the other person would say, "Cross your heart and hope to die?" The meaning was, "Do you really mean it?" Now little boys make and break promises about as fast as can be. But with God it is not so. One, He does not promise helter skelter like. And when He does promise He can be trusted. Our problem is learning to hear Him promise and being sure what we heard was a promise from Him, for us.

Definition — A *promise from God* is an assertion from God, specific or general or a truth in harmony with God's character, which is perceived in one's heart or mind concerning what He will do or not do for that one and which is sealed in our inner most being by a quickening action of the Holy Spirit and on which that one then counts.

There are three parts to the promise:

1. the cognitive part which refers to the assertion and its understanding, and
2. the affective part which is the inner most testimony to the promise, and
3. the volitional act of faith on our part which believes the assertion and feelings and thereafter counts upon it.

A leader can err in three ways, concerning promises. One, the leader may misread the assertion. That is, misinterpret what he/she thinks God will do or not do. Or two, the leader may wrongly apply some assertion to himself/herself which is does not apply. It may even be a true assertion but not for that leader or that time. Or the leader may misread the inner witness. It may not be God's Spirit quickening of the leader.

Sometimes the assertion comes from a command, or a principle, or even a direct statement of a promise God makes. The promise may be made generally to all who follow God or specifically to some. It may be for all time or for a limited time. Commands or principles are not in themselves promises. But it is when the Holy Spirit brings some truth out of them that He wants to apply to our lives that they may become promises. Such truths almost always bear on the character of God.

One thing we can know for certain, if indeed we do have a promise from God, then He will fulfill it. For Titus 1:2 asserts an important truth about God.

God can not lie.

He is the promise keeper. This is an image of God that all leaders need.

Examples of God As The Promise Keeper

God keeps his promises. He is the Promise Keeper. Table 29.1 gives some examples to shore up our faith in **The Promise Keeper**. I could have chosen 100s of promises.[49]

---

[49] Over the years I have kept a listing of promises I felt God has made to me and my wife. Many of these have been fulfilled. In December of 1997 I reviewed all of these—an encouraging faith building exercise.

Table 29.1 God The Promise Keeper—Examples

To Whom	Vs	Basic Promise/ Results
Abraham	Gen 12:1,2	Bless the world through Abraham. Give descendants. Spawn nations. Give a land. / This has happened and continues to happen.
Nahum	Whole book	Judgment on Nineveh/ Assyria. Promises fulfilled.
Obadiah	Whole book	Judgment on Edom. Promises fulfilled.
Habakkuk	Ch 2	Judgment on Babylon. Promises fulfilled. See Da 5.
Zechariah	Lk 1:13	Birth of John the Baptist. Promise fulfilled.
Mary	Lk 1:35	Birth of Jesus. Promise fulfilled.
Hezekiah	Isa 39:1ff, especially vs 5-7	Babylonian captivity. Royal hostages taken (Daniel was one of these). Promise fulfilled.
Daniel	Ch 2	The broad outlines of history/ nations and God's purposes. Promise fulfilled in part with more to come.
Daniel	Ch 9	Messiah and work of cross. Promise fulfilled.
Daniel	Ch 10-11:35	Again the broad outline of history particularly with reference to Israel. Everything up to 11:35 has taken place in detail as promises. The rest is yet to come.

Conclusion

The dictionary defines a promise as giving a pledge, committing oneself to do something, to make a declaration assuring that something will or will not be done or to afford a basis for expectation. Synonyms for promise include: covenant, engage, pledge, plight, swear, vow. The central meaning shared by these verbs is *to declare solemnly that one will perform or refrain from a particular course of action*. God is **The Promise Keeper**. As children of His we should learn to hear His promises and to receive them for our lives. As a leader you most likely will not make it over the long haul if you do not know God **as The Promise Keeper**.

One of the six characteristics[50] of a leader who finishes well is described as,

> **Truth is lived out in their lives so that convictions and promises of God are seen to be real.**

---

[50] The six characteristics include: 1. They maintain a personal vibrant relationship with God right up to the end. 2. They maintain a learning posture and can learn from various kinds of sources—life especially. 3. They manifest Christ-likeness in character as evidenced by the fruit of the Spirit in their lives. 4. Truth is lived out in their lives so that convictions and promises of God are seen to be real. 5. They leave behind one or more ultimate contributions. 6. They walk with a growing awareness of a sense of destiny and see some or all of it fulfilled.

Promises of God

A leader who has God's promises and lives by them will exemplify this characteristic. Paul did. Paul, the model N.T. church leader knew God as **The Promise Keeper**. Do you?

See *cognitive; affect; volitional*; **Glossary**. See **Article**, *Principles of Truth*.

Article 30

Prophecy Overview

Introduction

Much of the Bible has prophetic overtones. Prophecy is very important for a Bible student who would grasp the whole Bible. The N.T. comments on why prophecy is so important. It gives two main reasons none of which is to satisfy our curiosity about things to come:

Reason 1. According to John 13:19, the study of fulfilled prophecy should confirm our faith.

Reason 2. According to Revelation 15:15 and 1 John 3:3 the study of unfulfilled prophecy should influence our conduct. It should exhort us and encourage us to get ready, be ready and always be looking for the return of Christ.

Excluding the book of Revelation, which is entirely prophetic, in the N.T., there are 164 prophetic passages. Of these, 141 are directly related to conduct and apparently given to affect conduct not merely to increase our knowledge. There are many O.T. passages.

Definition   *Prophecy* refers to the genre of Scripture in which the thrust of the passage is an authoritative revelation from God usually through a spokesperson, called a prophet or prophetess, to correct a given historical situation or to warn of a future situation.

Example
Genesis 3:15 predicts a long-term conflict between Satan and God's people, which will be culminated by the defeat of Satan by Christ.

Example
Many corrective prophetic passages occur in the book of Amos. For example: Amos 1:3-5; 6-8; 9-10; 11-12; 13-15.

Example
Jeremiah contains both warnings to the present situation and future predictions of the fall of the southern kingdom.

Example
Ezekiel contains both warnings of the on-coming fall of the southern kingdom. Once it fell the remainder of his book contains encouraging prophecies of the future in which God will again bring hope and restoration to His people.

Corrective Prophecy

Usually corrective prophecy is straightforward and can be directly applied to the situation. However, futuristic prophecy is more difficult and has the following four characteristics. And occasionally corrective prophecy will also show these characteristics.

Prophecy Overview page 130

4 Characteristics of Futuristic Prophecy

1. Prophecy whenever given was contemporary in nature. Its form was conditioned by the views and ideas at the time of utterance. The prophets felt compelled to speak with a view toward their listeners (true of both corrective and futuristic).

2. Prophecy was often partial in nature. Individual prophetical utterance is often of a partial nature dealing with only one side of the coin (it is written; Yes, but it is written again; e.g. Isa 11:14 and Zec 9:13 Kingdom of God taken by arms or force. But this picture must be balanced by others. Isa 9:6 and Zec 9:9 show that these warlike expressions are to be understood figuratively since the Messiah king is more than all others a Prince of Peace (true especially of futuristic).

3. Jammed perspective. Often the prophet sees together and at once upon the surface of the picture things which are to be fulfilled only successively and gradually. Isa 40-66 shows the near future of the return from captivity and glorification of the City of God—return was near but glorification was to take place in the future (true mainly of futuristic).

4. Progressive. Prophecy is progressive in the following senses.

   a. Later revelation is based upon earlier revelation.
   b. Later revelation is climactic.
   c. Later revelation is more full—it discloses elements omitted from earlier revelation.

Eight Guidelines for Interpreting Prophecy

Prophecy, like Hebrew Poetry, covers a great mass of material. There is a lot of prophetic Scripture both in the Old Testament and New Testaments. It is deeply imbedded in New Testament literature. It is also a subject that is fascinating everyone today. And for that reason, we as Bible teachers should be aware of our need to teach prophetic literature in order to build up faith and get people to change their lives in preparation for Christ's return. Our goal should not be to satisfy curiosity. And we must remember that prophecy is perhaps the least understood Biblical genre. Table 30.1 gives some guidelines, which I am using in my study of prophetic literature.

Table 30.1 Eight Guidelines for Interpreting Prophecy—Basic Hermeneutics

Guideline	Statement/ Explanation
1.	Apply the rules of general hermeneutics.
2.	State to whom and about whom the prophecy is given.
3.	Interpret all figures of speech and all symbols.
4.	Apply the procedure for cultural equivalents where necessary.
5.	State concisely the central idea of the prophecy to which the smaller details relate. Here is a good place to observe whether a passage is predictive or didactic and corrective. If it is predictive, note any conditions. If the prediction was fulfilled, study all the materials that illuminate the fulfillment. If unfulfilled, seek to determine the time and nature of the fulfillment.

Prophecy Overview page 131

6.	Where fulfillment of prophecy is found in the New Testament, differentiate between (for the sake of clarity) **direct** and **typological prediction**. (Direct prediction consists of Old Testament prophetical statements which refer to nothing prior to New Testament times—e.g. Birth of Christ at Bethlehem—Micah 5:2 and Matthew 2:5,6)(A typological prediction is an Old Testament prophetic statement that does refer to something prior to New Testament times, although it finds its highest application of meaning in the events, people, or message of the New Testament).
7.	Apply the laws of time element and double fulfillment where the prophecy fits the conditions of these special language prophecy laws.
8.	Let the finality of God's revelation in Christ color all earlier revelations (see Hebrews 1:1ff).

O.T. Prophecy About Christ

One function of prophecy in the O.T. is to predict truth about Jesus Christ. Christ speaks of himself in the New Testament as being seen in the Old Testament. Three such ways that this occurs are shown in Figure 30.1.

3 Types of Prophecy About Christ

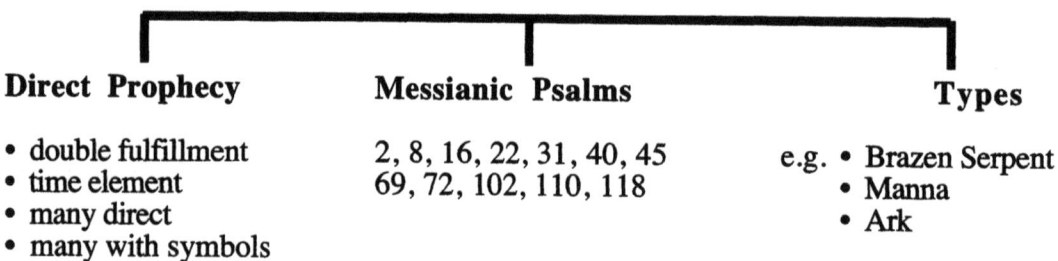

Direct Prophecy
- double fulfillment
- time element
- many direct
- many with symbols

Messianic Psalms
2, 8, 16, 22, 31, 40, 45
69, 72, 102, 110, 118

Types
e.g.
- Brazen Serpent
- Manna
- Ark

Figure 30.1 3 Types of Prophetic Genre Concerning Jesus Christ

Commentary on Prophecy—4 Warnings

Prophecy is a very complex genre. Some practical warnings are needed. Here are four such warnings.

1. Be God-centered, not event centered in your study of prophecy.
2. Remember, in prophecy, the total picture is incomplete. Old Testament people sure thought some of these prophecies different than they turned out.
3. Prophecy does not always have to be fulfilled.
4. It is not necessarily wrong not to know and to seek out for understanding. The Old Testament prophets sure did this (2 Peter 1:10).

4 Descriptions of Prophecy

We learn what something is when we contrast it—by showing what it is not as well as what it is. Two things prophecy is not include the first two descriptions below.

1. What it is not! Prophecy is not a more vivid way of writing history.

The entire predictive aspect of prophecy came under attack when naturalistic rationalism argued that real prediction is impossible in a universe governed wholly by cause and effect...The rationalists had to do something with the Biblical claims to predictive prophecy, and with the large amount of material which appears to the average prudent person to be predictive prophecy. This was their answer. Most of

Prophecy Overview

the apparently predictive materials were written after the events that they predict. Since history is rather dull to many readers, the prophetic style livens up the narrative and makes it more readable. Earlier interpreters who did not perceive the method were either naive or *unenlightened*. If a certain passage could not be dismissed by this strategy, its message was generalized and called brilliant insight by one whose mind refused to be shut up within the confines of Hebrew daily life. (Mickelsen 1963:289)

2. What it is not! Prophecy is not history written beforehand.
Prophecy never gives a complete picture of an event, as does a historian's account. The historian must provide some account of the antecedents to an event, of the event itself, and of its consequences. He must, in other words, supply many particulars...Prophecy cannot be history written beforehand because God does not disclose major and minor elements that are essential for even an incomplete historical picture. What God makes known as well as what he withholds are both a part of the total plan of redemption. As history moves on, the full-orbed picture emerges.

3. What it does!
Earlier intimations of what is to come serve to remind the people that the totality of history is in God's sovereign control.

4. What it is!
Prophecy, simply speaking, is that which someone moving in a prophetic gifting writes or says. The prophet is a spokesperson for God who declares God's will to the people. In declaring God's will to the people, the prophet may touch upon the past, present, or future.

3 Possible Approaches
The following different approaches to the particular language used in prophecy have been noted in the literature.

1. **Literalistic View**—This view expects a literal fulfillment of all details. If the prophet mentions horses and bridles, there will be horses and bridles. If the prophet mentions shields, bucklers, bows and arrows, handstaves, spears (Eze 39:9) these exact weapons will be utilized.

2. **Entire Symbolical View**—in contrast to the literalist, this view may insist on the symbolic meaning of an entire prophecy. Finding elements that belong to a past epoch, the interpreter proceeds to make every aspect of the prophecy simply a picture of ideal hopes, etc. or He/she may apply it as a prophetic picture of the present Christian church (this view is sometimes called *spiritualizing*.)

3. **Analogical Equivalents**—A third way of approaching prophecy is in terms of equivalents, analogy, or correspondence. The transportation (chariot—for example) of the prophet's day will have a corresponding equivalence in the time of its fulfillment (like an armored car). Likewise the weapons mentioned by the prophet will have the counter parts at the time of the fulfillment. The enemies of the people of God in one period will be replaced by later enemies. The details of worship of God's people at an earlier period will be replaced by the means laid down by God during the period of fulfillment (see Mickelsen p. 296 for Eze 40-48 for example).

Two Important Observations

From observation of prophecy both in the Old and New Testaments and comparative study two basic guidelines have emerged. These are the law of double fulfillment and the law of the time element. Table 30.2 gives these observations.

Table 30.2 Two Special Observations on Prophecy—Relating to Fulfillment

Law	Explanation
Double Fulfillment	The law of double fulfillment means that the prophecy is fulfilled at two different times. Either the fulfillments occur in the day of the prophecy and at the first coming of Christ or the fulfillments occur at the first coming of Christ and will occur again at the second coming in perhaps some fuller way. But it may sound when the prophecy is given that it will occur once. This comes very close to violating our basic axiom of only one meaning generally to a language communication.
Time Element	The law of the time element means that although the prophet states two things apparently as if the were to occur together yet the New Testament shows that they will be fulfilled a different times. It is as if the prophet is looking telescopically at two mountains way down in front of him. They appear together. But as you near the mountains you can see that there is actually much distance between them.

Conclusion

In the Biblical leadership commentaries, O.T. books of Deuteronomy, Daniel, Jonah, Habakkuk, Haggai, Micah, and Malachi all contain various prophetical passages. The information in this article gives a general overview of prophecy. These prophetic passages of these books should first be studied to identify the intent as to corrective, futuristic, or both. Then they should be interpreted using the general hermeneutical guidelines. Of special help is the notion of double fulfillment and the telescoping time element. At the conclusion of this article I give a study sheet for prophecy passages that flows from the information given in this article.

Bibliography

Mickelsen, A. Berkley
    1963   **Interpreting The Bible**. Grand Rapids: Eerdmans Publishing Company.

Prophecy Study Sheet

John 13:19...that when it comes to pass our faith will be strengthened.
1 John 3:3...Everyone that has this future expectation will change his behavior.

Name _____ Passage _____ Date _____

A. The Passage in Its Historical Setting

1. What is the occasion for this prophetic passage? State what you believe to be the intent of the one giving the prophetic utterance to the hearers of his day.

2. State explicitly to whom or to what the statement or passage refers. Is the passage addressed to the hearers or readers while also being about them? Or is it proclaimed to them about someone else?

3. Put yourself in the place of the first hearers or readers of the passage. What would it have meant to you in that day?

B. Analyzing the Prophecy

1. Identify any imagery or figurative language involved in the passage. If unidentifiable, state that also. Use the general rules for symbols where apocalyptic imagery is involved.

2. Is the passage primarily predictive or didactic? Identify the didactic purpose. Identify the predictive element.

3. What conditions if any are attached to the predictive prophecy? Has this prophecy been fulfilled? If so, describe its fulfillment. Does the law of double fulfillment apply? Does the law of the time element apply?

4. Are there parallel passages which limit, reveal, or explain further this passage?

C. Drawing Conclusions

1. See if you can rewrite the passage in your own words using modern equivalents, analogies, or correspondences existing in the time of the fulfillment.

2. Since prophecy is given to confirm our faith and to change our conduct you should derive some practical help from this study. List here any practical applications seen in this study.

Helpful Statements in the study of prophecy:

1. Be God centered not event centered or time centered as you study prophecy. God is longing to change lives not to satisfy the curious.
2. Remember the total picture is incomplete.
3. A fulfillment of any prophecy is application not interpretation.
4. The law of double fulfillment means that the prophecy is fulfilled at two different times. Either the fulfillments occur in the day of the prophecy and at the first coming of Christ or the fulfillments occur at the first and second coming.
5. The law of the time element means that although the prophet states two things apparently as if the were to occur together yet the New Testament shows that they will be fulfilled a different times.

Article 31

Prophetic Authority

Introduction
Often in scripture God will speak powerfully and authoritatively through a prophet to bring a needed message into a ministry situation. A prophetic word may be just what is required to catalyze an important ministry project or to launch people into the purposes of God. This word-based demonstration of God's presence captures and convicts the hearts of the hearers and provides the spiritual fuel needed to get things moving.

What is Prophetic Authority?

Definition
Prophetic authority is a form of spiritual authority expressed via a revelatory power base—the gift of prophecy.

Prophetic authority occurs when a prophetically gifted person delivers an authoritative and accurate word of God into a situation. The prophetic message has authority because as a spokesperson for God, the word is backed by the full authority of God himself.

Why prophetic authority is a powerful leadership tool.

The purpose of this article is to consider the role of prophetic authority from a leadership perspective. To start out, let's look at a few Biblical examples of ways God uses prophetic authority as a powerful leadership tool. God uses prophetic authority to:

- Mobilize people for large scale works of God—Moses
- Appoint new leadership—Samuel (both Saul and David)
- Provide for leadership transitions—Samuel
- Correct leaders who sin—Nathan (David after sinning with Bathesheba).
- Confront leaders who begin trusting more in ministry resources than God for success—Gad (When Satan incited David to count the fighting men) 1Chronicles 21.
- Call to account leaders who forget that leadership involves caring for people—Ezekiel (to the shepherds who cared for themselves but not the sheep)
- Help leaders understand God's hand in history—Daniel
- Jumpstart a stalled out ministry project—Haggai (rebuilding the temple).
- Bolster morale during difficult ministry tasks – Zechariah, Haggai (to those rebuilding the temple)
- Call leaders to account when compromising God's standards—Malachi (to the priests who accepted blemished sacrifices)
- Prepare people for the coming of the Messiah—John the Baptist.
- Remind leaders of the cost of following Christ—Agabus (to Paul before arriving in Jerusalem)

The Nature of Prophetic Authority
The authority resides primarily in the message, and secondarily in the messenger. The prophetic message carries authority because it comes from God, and prophetic messenger, as the bearer of the message and one sent by God, by association shares in this authority.

Prophetic Authority

The Constraint of Prophetic Authority
Because the authority resides first in the message and not the messenger, prophetic authority comes with some constraints. The prophet's authority is limited by the desire of God to communicate through him or her. Some prophets had long careers and were consistently used by God over a long period of time – like Samuel, Jeremiah. Some prophets appear once, are used powerfully, and then are not heard from again – such as the man of God from Judah who delivered a confrontative message against Jeroboam as he stood ready to offer a sacrifice on the altar. (1Kings 13) In that case we do not even know the prophet's name.

Similarity With Other forms of Spiritual Authority
Three ways prophetic authority is similar to other forms of spiritual authority[51] include:

1) **Response to Prophetic Authority is Response to God Himself.**
   In a sense, the prophet is a middleman, simply delivering the message. Like other forms of spiritual authority, the accountability ultimately occurs between the source of the message, God, and the recipient of the message, the listener

2) **Confirmed and Defended by God**
   And like other forms of spiritual authority, the leader, in this case the prophet, doesn't need to defend the prophetic message. God will confirm the message and do any defending that needs to happen.

3) **Extrinsic and Intrinsic Components**
   Prophetic authority, like spiritual authority, has both an internal (ISA – Intrinsic Spiritual Authority) and an extrinsic component (ESA external spiritual authority). Ultimately, spiritual authority is conferred by God on a leader, but it is also something that can, and should, be recognized by followers.

Example: Samuel
Samuel is a good example of someone who operated with prophetic authority. His prophetic authority was both internal and external.

1) **Intrinsic Spiritual Authority – Confirmed by God**
   "The Lord was with Samuel as he grew up, and he let none of his words fall to the ground." 1 Samuel 3:19

2) **Extrinsic Spiritual Authority – Recognized by the People**
   " And all Israel from Dan to Beersheba recognized that Samuel was attested as a prophet of the Lord." 1Samuel 3:20

Speaking Truth to Power Holders – The interaction between Prophetic Authority and Positional Authority
Often God sent prophets to confront leaders who had gone astray. Prophets were the ones who boldly spoke truth to power holders. This is likely due to the reality that the prophets were the only ones with enough authority to confront powerful leaders – like the kings of Israel. The reason they had authority was because they came to that earthly king, in the name and authority of the Great King, God Himself. God would often accompany their words by a demonstration of power – e.g. hands that shriveled, shadows that went backwards, altars that split, leprosy, fire from heaven, drought. Some kings repented and

---

[51] See *spiritual authority*; *intrinsic spiritual authority*; *extrinsic spiritual authority*; **Glossary**. See **Article**, *Spiritual Authority*.

responded. David did at Nathan's prophetic word to him about Bathsheba and Uriah. Others refused to respond, like one king of Israel who acknowledged,

> "There is still one man through whom we can inquire of the Lord, but I hate him because he never prophesies anything good about me, but always bad." 2 Chronicles 18:7.

Implications for Today's Leaders

It's not unusual for strong leaders, especially task oriented leaders, to find themselves in the same place as many of the Old Testament kings, with little functional accountability. For the leader with a heart for God, prophetic correctives can curb abuses of power and bring the leader in line with God's purposes. Leaders should welcome those willing to speak the truth, even when it's hard to hear.[52]

Sometimes Prophetic Authority is welcomed and sometimes it isn't. Not all people willingly recognize or favorable respond to prophetic authority. This is equally true in the case of both leaders and followers. In the O.T. many, in fact, not only disobeyed the message, but persecuted the messenger. The Bible has plenty examples of prophets who faced rejection when speaking to the people they were sent to serve. O.T. examples abound, including both Joseph and Jeremiah who share the honor of being thrown in a pit for their prophecies. The most obvious N.T. example is Christ who was crucified by leaders who have "no room" for His words (John 8:37). Note the negative reception of the O.T. prophets who are certainly among those mentioned in Hebrews 11 who

> "...faced jeers and flogging, while still others were chained and put in prison. They were stoned; they were sawed in two; they were put to death by the sword. They went about in sheepskins and goatskins, destitute, persecuted and mistreated- the world was not worthy of them. They wandered in deserts and mountains, and in caves and holes in the ground." Hebrews 11:36-38

Why Do People Respond Positively To Prophetic Authority?

In any given case, a number of factors likely contribute. But at it's root the reason for a positive response might be simply stated as this. *Due to either the prior or present work of the Holy Spirit, the heart of the hearer is obediently sensitized to respond favorably to God's message through the prophet.*

Why Do People Not Respond Positively To Prophetic Authority?

Likewise, when a negative response occurs, a combination of factors might be pointed to. But ultimately the problem could be summarized as this. *The heart of the hearer has been hardened against the work of the Holy Spirit and in such a state does not respond positively to the grace of God extended through that prophetic message.*

God's Promise Of Prophetic Authority For The God-Sent Prophet

Biblical prophets faced many challenges. Some were external—from listeners who did not want to hear from God. Some were internal—from their own fears and insecurities. In speaking for God, a leader often finds himself/herself in a mismatched and awkward spot. In one combined moment of ministry such a leader has a powerful and authoritative message—the prophecy, presented by a very human and often vulnerable person—the

---

[52] In the N.T., the prophetic role corresponds to the gift of prophecy. A person gifted in prophecy may operate at a local church level, regional level, or some sort of roving ministry. Such was the case in the N.T. Church people were warned not to ignore prophetic words, nor to accept them without careful testing. See 1 Th 5:19-22.

Prophetic Authority

prophet. Many of the listeners in the Bible only saw the prophet at the moment of delivering the message—which often appeared to be done with great confidence. But the Bible gives us a behind the scenes look at the human side of the prophets. We see that prophets ran from God—like Jonah, and become discouraged or even suicidal—like Elijah.

Considering the emotional and physical risk when speaking for God, it's no wonder that from time to time, God provides promises to prophetic spokespeople to assure them that they can expect God's authoritative backing when delivering the message.

Table 31.1 Examples of God's Full Backing—Promise of His Presence

Person Involved	Scripture	Scriptural Promise
Moses	Ex 4:15	"... I will help both of you speak and will teach you what to do."
Isaiah	Isa 58:1	"Shout it aloud, do not hold back. Raise your voice like a trumpet. Declare to my people their rebellion and to the house of Jacob their sins.
Jeremiah	Jer 1:19	They will fight against you but will not overcome you, for I am with you and will rescue you," declares the Lord.
Jesus' Disciples	Luke 12:11	"When you are brought before synagogues, rulers and authorities, do not worry about how you will defend yourselves or what you will say, 12 for the Holy Spirit will teach you at that time what you should say."

Conclusion

Prophetic authority plays an important leadership role in the Bible. Leaders and followers alike need to hear clearly from God. When the prophetic spokesman sounds the trumpet clearly, the result is often mobilization for ministry.

Prophetic authority still occurs today. The functional equivalent of prophetic authority occurs in the N.T. when leaders who have the gift of prophecy hear from God and speak into situations. This prophetic function occurs both in itinerant and church-based ministries. The qualities describing O.T. prophetic authority occur almost identically with the leaders use of the gift of prophecy in the N.T.

Article 32

Prophetic Crises—Three Major Biblical Times

Introduction
Years ago, when I took the class on prophets by James (Buck) Hatch, each of us was assigned a major project—do a chart on the prophets. Professor Hatch knew that the historical background was crucial to understanding the writing prophets. I still have that chart today and use it whenever I introduce any of the prophetic books. I am thankful to Professor Hatch for that project and his course that introduced me to each of the prophetic books. Getting perspective, on the times these books address, was a great leap forward in understanding them. Most of the writing prophets cluster around three major crises in the life of God's people. It is these prophetic crises, which prompted the rise of the prophetic ministry as reflected in the writing prophets.

1. The Assyrian Crisis
2. The Babylonian Crisis
3. The Restoration Crisis

Let me briefly describe each of these and identify the books, which speak to them.

General Background And Some Basic Definitions
Samuel's leadership ministry transitioned the commonwealth into a kingdom that Saul ruled over. This was followed by David's rule and then his son Solomon's rule. This sets the stage for God's disciplinary work among His people.

The Assyrian and the Babylonian Crises
The story line leading to the Assyrian crisis and the Babylonian crisis hinges around the following major events:
1. Solomon goes away from the Lord providing a great warning to all leaders—He had the best start of any king yet did not finish well. A good start does not insure a good finish.
2. Rehoboam (1 Kings 12) makes an unwise decision to increase taxes and demands on people—kingdom splits as prophecy said. 10 tribes go with the northern kingdom, Judah with the southern. A poor start might not be overcome.
3. The northern kingdom under Jereboam quickly departs from God. Jereboam is used as the model of an evil king to whom all evil kings are likened; He had a good start also—God would have blessed him. Abuse of power is a major barrier to finishing well.
4. The southern kingdom generally is bad with occasional good Kings and partially good kings: Asa, Jehoshaphat, Joash, Amaziah, Uzziah, Jotham, Hezekiah, Josiah. But the trend was always downward. The extended length

of life of the southern kingdom more than the northern kingdom is directly attributed to the spiritual life of the better kings. Spiritual leadership does make a difference. Lack of spiritual leadership speeds up deterioration and leads to God's bypassing of the leadership structures and even destruction of the wayward people.

5. During both the northern and southern kingdoms God sent prophets to try and correct them—first the oral prophets (many—but the two most noted were Elijah and Elisha) and then the prophets who wrote.

Now in order to understand this long period of history you should know several things:
1. The History books that give background information about the times.
2. The Bible Time-Line, need to know when the books were written.
3. Need to know the writing prophets: northern or southern kingdom, which crisis, direct or special.

The History Books

The history books covering the time of the destruction of a nation include 1, 2 Samuel, 1,2 Kings, and 1,2 Chronicles. The following chart helps identify the focus of each of these books as to major content.

Chart 32.1 The History Books—Major Content

1 Samuel	2 Samuel 1 Chronicles	1,2 Kings 2 Chronicles
Samuel, Saul, David	David	1,2 Kings: Solomon to Zedekiah (gives time oriented details on northern and southern kingdoms) 2 Chronicles exclusively on line of Judah (southern kingdom)

There are four categories of prophetical books. Prophetical books deal with three major crises: the Assyrian crisis which wiped out the northern kingdom; the Bablonian crisis which wiped out the southern kingdom; the return to the land after being exiled. There are also prophetical books not specifically dealing with these crises but associated with the time of them. The prophetical books dealing with these issues are:

Category 1. Northern—Assyrian Crisis
Jonah, Amos, Hosea, Nahum, Micah

Category 2. Southern—Babylonian Crisis
Joel, Isaiah, Micah, Zephaniah, Jeremiah, Lamentations, Habakkuk, Obadiah

Category 3. In Exile
Ezekiel, Daniel, Esther

Category 4. Return From Exile—The Restoration Crisis
Nehemiah, Ezra, Haggai, Zechariah, Malachi

In addition, to knowing the crises you must know the prophets that wrote:

A. Direct to the Issue of the Crisis either Assyrian, Babylonian, or Return To The Land—The Restoration Crisis. These were:
    Amos, Hosea, Joel, Micah, Isaiah, Jeremiah, Ezekiel, Haggai, Zechariah, Malachi

B. Special-These were:
    Jonah, Nahum, Habakkuk, Obadiah, Zephaniah, Daniel.

The special prophets, though usually associated with one of the crisis times, wrote to deal with unique issues not necessarily related directly to the crisis. The following list gives the special prophets and their main thrust.

1. Jonah—a paradigm shift, pointing out God's desire for the nation to be missionary minded and reach out to surrounding nations.
2. Nahum—vindicate God, judgment on Assyria.
3. Habakkuk—faith crisis for Habakkuk, vindicate God, judgment on Babylon.
4. Obadiah—vindicate God, judgment on Edom for treatment of Judah.
5. Zephaniah—show about judgment, the Day of the Lord.
6. Daniel—give hope, show that God is indeed ruling even in the times of the exile and beyond, gives God's plan for the ages.

Having overviewed the story line that threads through the *Assyrian Crisis* and the *Babylonian Crisis* and briefly listed the Biblical books (both history and prophetical) that apply to these crises, we can move on to the *Restoration Crisis*.

The Restoration Crisis Overviewed

Several Bible books are associated with the return to the land from the exile. After a period of about 70 years (during which time Daniel ministered) Cyrus made a decree, which allowed some Jews (those that wanted to) to return to the land. Some went back under Zerubbabel, a political ruler like a governor. A priest, Joshua, also provided religious leadership to the first group that went back. This group of people started to rebuild the temple but became discouraged due to opposition and lack of resources. They stopped building the temple. Two prophets, after several years, 10-15, addressed the situation. These two, Haggai and Zechariah, were able to encourage the leadership and the people to finish the temple.

Another thirty or forty years goes by and then we have the events of the book of Esther, back in the land. Her book describes the attempt to eradicate the Jewish exiles—a plot which failed due to God's sovereign intervention via Esther, the queen of the land and a Jewish descendant going incognito, and her relative Mordecai.

Still another period of time passes, 20 or so years and a priest, Ezra, directs another group to return to the land. The spiritual situation has deteriorated. He brings renewal.

Another kind of leader arrives on the scene some 10-15 years later. Nehemiah, a lay leader, and one adept at organizing and moving to accomplish a task, rebuilds the wall around Jerusalem. He too has to instigate renewal.

Finally, after another period of 30 or so years we have the book of Malachi which again speaks to renewal of the people. The Old Testament closes with this final book.

A recurring emphasis occurs during the period of the return. People are motivated to accomplish a task for God. They start out, become discouraged, and stop. They must be renewed. God raises up leadership to bring renewal.

Prophetic Crises, three Major

Let me now introduce some important definitions before giving further detail on the *Restoration Crisis*.

Some Definitions

In my leadership literature I define two restoration terms that are important. They have some overlap but also need to be seen as distinct.

Definition   *Restoration* (individual leader) is the process whereby a fallen leader is transitioned back into leadership. It usually involves repentance, restitution where appropriate, correction of the aberrant leadership dysfunctionalities, and recognition by other leaders of the restoration process and their stamp of approval for the leader to renew ministry.

Definition   *Corporate restoration* refers to God's attempts to restore the people of God as a viable channel through whom He can work to carry out His Biblical purposes.

It is this latter definition that is important to the third major crisis—the *Restoration Crisis*.

Description   The *restoration crisis* refers to the period of time from 539 B.C. to 430 B.C. and which covers the activity of God in bringing His people back into the land and establishing a testimony there. His providential care of His people (both in the land and outside it) is also shown.

The Restoration Crisis—Further Details

While it is true that God attempts restoration efforts throughout almost all the leadership eras in both the O.T. and N.T., I define the *Restoration Crisis* as the time specifically dealing with the return of the exiles to the land and the aftermath activities that occurred. This means the time from 539 B.C. when Daniel initiated the time with his great intercessory prayer in Daniel 9 to around 430 B.C. when Malachi made a major thrust at restoration. Table 32.1 gives a brief overview of this time. The major Biblical books dealing with the *Restoration Crisis* include: Ezra, Haggai, Zechariah, Ezra, Nehemiah, Esther, and Malachi.

Table 32.1 The Restoration Era Crises And Related Biblical Material

Item	539 B.C.	536 B.C.	520-516 B.C.	486-465 B.C.	465-424 B.C.	430 B.C.
Restoration Activity	Daniel Prays	Work on Temple Begun	Work on Temple begun again and Completed	Israelites Preserved due to Esther and Mordecai's activities	Wall is constructed around Jerusalem—Ezra and Nehemiah bring about restoration movement	Malachi again engenders restoration movement
Biblical Material	Daniel 9	Ez 3:12	Ez 6:13-15 Haggai Zechariah	Esther	Nehemiah; latter part of Ezra	Malachi
Crises	1. God's Timing and Faith	2. Public Testimony Needed Back in the Land	3. Public Testimony Needed—Work Stopped	4. People of God Outside of Land—Danger of being Destroyed	5. Protection of Jerusalem/ Public Testimony of People	6. Leadership Nominality; follower nominality

Prophetic Crises, three Major

The themes of each of the biblical books dealing with the restoration crises should be seen in terms of the crises given above in Table 31.1.

Table 32.2 gives the theme of the relevant books along with the crisis that most likely prompted the activity of the book.

Table 32.2 The Restoration Era Crises And Related Biblical Material

Crisis	Book	Theme/ Brief Explanation Relating to Corporate Restoration
1. God's Timing and Faith	Daniel	**THE MOST HIGH** (sovereign God) **RULES** in the affairs of individuals, nations, and history. **Brief Explanation:** Daniel shows how God is sovereignly working out his purposes and lays out a time table for God's future work. Included in that book is the crucial identification of the 70 years in captivity and the time to begin the restoration effort in Jerusalem.
2. Public Testimony Needed Back in the Land	Ezra	See below for explanation of Ezra theme.
3. Public Testimony Needed—Work Stopped	Ezra	See below for Ezra Theme
	Haggai	**God's Work in Rebuilding the Temple** (Under Haggai's Prophetic Impact) began when His people back in the land were renewed and reprioritized their lives in response to God's Word, initially brought discouragement and was counteracted by God's promise of His presence and blessing as the rebuilders obeyed God's Word, continued to be fueled by a God-given vision of what it could be, not what it was, and carried with it God affirmation and promise of power to the leadership inspiring this work, in an overwhelming time.
	Zechariah	**THE WORKING OF THE LORD ALMIGHTY** involves encouragement in the present to leaders, brings correction and hope to sincere followers, and reveals His future plans so as to cause anticipation and encouragement. **Brief Explanation:** Corporate restoration is an on-going process. Hope along with restoration comes when we get perspective on what God is doing and will do in the future.
4. People of God Outside of Land—Danger of being Destroyed	Esther	**THE PROVIDENTIAL WORKING OF GOD** involves foresight which includes His use of apparently natural events and responses behind the scenes in *anticipation* of later events, will test leadership in the crisis, will have timely intervention in unusual yet natural events to protect, and will accomplish His purposes in the end. **Brief Explanation:** This shows that God is still working both outside the land as well as in the land. The left hand of God is seen in the affairs of preservation that Mordecai and Esther take part in. The Left Hand of God is an important concept in the whole restoration era.
5. Protection of Jerusalem/ Public Testimony of People	Ezra	**EFFECTIVE LEADERSHIP IN JERUSALEM UNDER EZRA** built on a foundation of that done by Haggai, Zechariah, Zerubbabel, and Joshua, and involved a call back to Biblical standards for the people in Jerusalem. **Brief Explanation:** The heart of corporate restoration is to have people understand God's revelation for them and to obey it. Ezra's ministry did this.

	Nehemiah	**NEHEMIAH'S ORGANIZATIONAL LEADERSHIP** made itself felt in the face of obstacles to rebuild the wall, was inspirational in bringing about reform and a covenant in Jerusalem, and included drastic steps of separation in order to insure an on-going meaningful religious atmosphere. **Brief Explanation:** This book emphasizes the importance of civil leadership working with religious leadership in bringing about corporate restoration.
6. Leadership Nominality; follower nominality	Malachi	**NOMINALITY**, religious form without power and meaning, reflects a lack of understanding of God's love, is manifested by half-hearted obedience which hinders God's purposes, is perpetuated by nominal leadership, and ultimately will be corrected by God. **Brief Explanation:** The heart of corporate restoration is to have people understand God's revelation for them and to obey it. Malachi, like Ezra's ministry, did this. Both Ezra and Malachi's ministries show that the people of God will tend toward nominality over time and need intervention ministries that will call them back to God.

The important macro lessons that are illustrated in the restoration crisis era include the following (numbers refer to a list of 41 macro lessons seen in the Bible):

19. Stability — Preserving a ministry of God with life and vigor over time is as much if not more of a challenge to leadership than creating one.

20. Spiritual Leadership — Spiritual leadership can make a difference even in the midst of difficult times.

21. **Recrudescence** — **Kingdom God will attempt to bring renewal to His people until they no longer respond to Him.**

22. By-pass — God will by-pass leadership and structures that do not respond to Him and will institute new leadership and structures.

23. Future Perfect — A primary function of all leadership is to walk by faith with a future perfect paradigm so as to inspire followers with certainty of God's accomplishment of ultimate purposes.

24. Perspective — Leaders must know the value of perspective and interpret present happenings in terms of God's broader purposes.

25. Modeling — Leaders can most powerfully influence by modeling godly lives, the sufficiency and sovereignty of God at all times, and gifted power.

26. Ultimate — Leaders must remember that the ultimate goal of their lives and ministry is to manifest the glory of God.

27. **Perseverance** — **Once known, leaders must persevere with the vision God has given.**

Of these, macro lessons 19, 20, 21, and 24 directly relate to corporate restoration.

General Lessons Learned From Perspective on The There Major Crises

In observing the length of time of the northern kingdom leading to the Assyrian Crisis as compared to the length of time of the southern kingdom leading to the Babylonian Crisis, a much longer time, one can emphasize strongly the spiritual leadership macro lesson.

20. Spiritual Leadership
Spiritual leadership can make a difference even in the midst of difficult times.

In observing the intervention times in all three prophetic crises, one cannot but help notice the crucial sense of timing involved in God's activity through the prophets.

3. Timing Macro-Lesson
God's Timing Is Crucial To Accomplishment Of God's Purposes.

We should also be warned. God has by-passed leadership and structures in the past, which did not respond to His warnings. This can happen again to us in our church leadership eras. We should be warned.

22. By-pass
God will by-pass leadership and structures that do not respond to Him and will institute new leadership and structures.

In general, we note that if we are to be Bible Centered leaders who apply O.T. scriptures appropriately in our N.T. Church leadership era, we must study carefully the details of the historical background surrounding these O.T. writing. We must adhere carefully to the General Hermeneutical principle involved with historical background.

Historical Background Hermeneutical Principle
In The Spirit, Prayerfully Study The Historical Background Of The Book Which Includes Such Information As:
  a. the author of the book and the *historical perspective* from which he/she wrote.
  b. the *occasion* for the book
  c. the *purpose* for the book including where pertinent the people for whom it was intended and their situation.
  d. any geographical or cultural factors bearing on the communication of the material.

Closure
Perspective makes a difference. The difference between leaders and followers is perspective. The difference between leaders and more effective leaders is better perspective. Leaders today need perspective on how God has worked. To understand the writing prophets, the three major crises detailed in this article become very significant. Bible centered leaders who want to apply concepts from the writing prophets to today's ministry must understand the historical background associated with these major crises.

See **Article**, *Haggai—Calendar and Dating; Restoration Leaders; Civil Leadership, The Missing Ingredient; Left Hand of God; Redemptive Drama, The Biblical Framework; Six Biblical Leadership Eras—Seeing the Bible With Leadership Eyes; Macro Lesson, Defined; Macro Lessons, List of 41 Across Six Leadership Eras.*

Article 33

Redemptive Drama, The Biblical Framework

Introduction

In each of the overviews on the various individual books in the leadership commentary series I have a section called **Where It Fits**. In that section, I try to deal with the application of my first general hermeneutical principle,[53]

Language Principle 1 Book and Books
In The Spirit, Prayerfully Study The Book As A Whole In Terms Of Its Relationship To Other Books In The Bible (i.e. the Bible as a whole) **TO INCLUDE:**
  a. its place in the progress of redemption (both as to the progress of revelation, what God has said, and also the notion of what God has done in redemptive history)
  b. its overall contribution to the whole or Bible literature (i.e. *its purposes — why is it in the Bible?*) and
  c. its abiding contribution to present time.

I seek to find **Where It Fits** using two basic overall frameworks:

1. *The Unfolding Drama of Redemption* — that is, telling the story of what God has said and done in the Bible.[54]

2. *The Leadership Framework.* Since this is a leadership commentary series, I want to trace the contribution of a book to leadership. The leadership era it fits in helps inform us as to how to interpret its leadership findings.

This article is concerned with the first of these two frameworks: *The Unfolding Drama of Redemption.* I have previously dealt with the second framework in several articles.[55]

I will first introduce the overall framework with a diagram. Then I will give a brief synopsis for each chapter of the redemptive drama. Finally, I will list the Bible books in terms of the chapters of the redemptive drama.

---

[53] See Appendix G in **Having A Ministry That Lasts** for the whole hermeneutical system I use.
[54] I am deeply indebted to a teaching mentor of mine, James M. (Buck) hatch who introduced me to this framework in his course, Progress of Redemption, given at Columbia Bible College. I have used his teaching and adapted it in my own study of each book in the Bible in terms of the Bible story as a whole. I have also written in depth on this in my handbook, **The Bible and Leadership Values**. This article is a condensed version of that larger explanation.
[55] See **Articles**, *Six Biblical Leadership Eras--Overviewed; Macro Lesson Defined; Macro Lessons--List of 41 Across Six Leadership Eras.*

Redemptive Drama, The Biblical Framework page 147

Overall Framework—Redemptive Drama Pictured

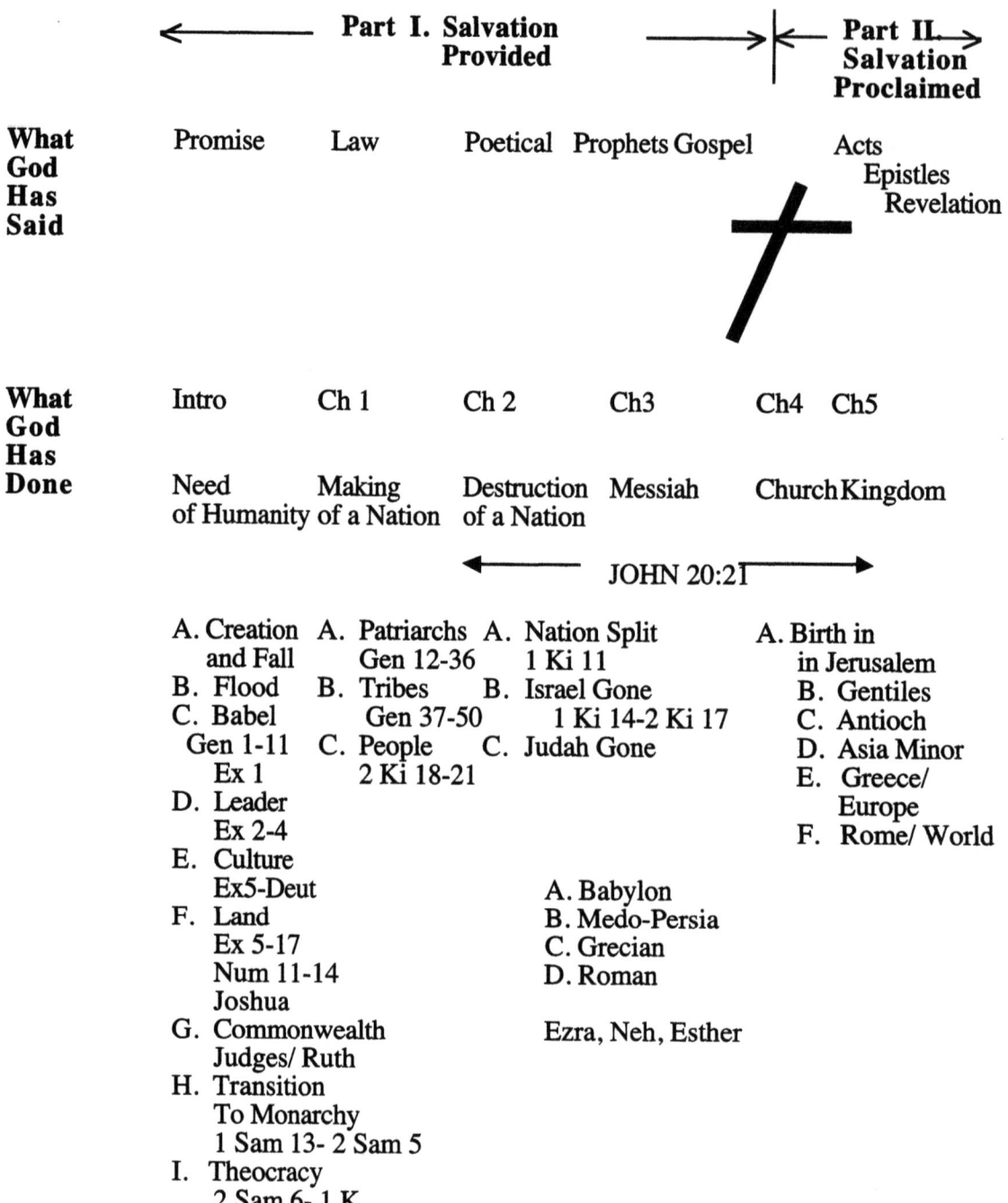

Figure 33.1 Overview of Redemptive Drama Time Line

The **Time-Line of the Redemptive Story** contains six sections,

> Introduction,
> Chapter 1. The Making of A Nation,
> Chapter 2. The Destruction of A Nation,
> Chapter 3. Messiah,
> Chapter 4. The Church, and
> Chapter 5. The Kingdom.

This story is briefly explained in a Running Capsule of the Redemptive Story. The story traces **what God does** and **what He says** throughout the Bible. And it shows that there is a progressive revelation of God throughout the whole drama. The Bible is unified around this salvation history. Once this is recognized then the notion of intentional selection becomes important. Each book in the Bible is there for a purpose and contributes something to this salvation story.

It is this framework which provides the macro context for studying each book of the Bible. Where is the book in the progress of redemption time-line? What does it contribute to it? Why is it there? What would we miss if it were left out? Understanding each book in terms of its own purpose is a preliminary first step that must be done before we can interpret it for leadership findings.

The Running Capsule for the Redemptive Story
I will first give an overview and then give more detail from each part of the redemptive drama.

Overall
At the center of the Biblical revelation is the concept of a God who has intervened in human history. He created the human race. He has revealed himself to that race. That race rebelled against His desires. In its fallen state it continually rebels against His wishes and desires and for the potential that it could accomplish.

So He started again and selected specifically a people through whom He could reveal Himself to the world. God moves unswervingly toward His purpose which is to redeem people and relate to them. He moves toward His purposes whether or not the people He has chosen follow them or not. They can willingly be a part in which they enjoy the blessings of God or they can be by-passed and He will find other ways to accomplish His purposes. He patiently works with them to include them in His purposes. But when all is said and done He moves on with or without them.

All the time He is increasingly revealing more of Himself and His purposes to His people. They come to know Him as a mighty God, all powerful and controlling, yet allowing human beings their choices. He is a holy God, that is, a being of perfection. He reveals His purposes as that of having a Holy people following Him. People who are becoming Holy as He is holy. They learn that to fall short of His demands or standards is to sin against Him and is deserving of retribution if justice is to be satisfied.

Part I of the redemption drama, **SALVATION PROVIDED**, is His selection of a people, which will prove foundational to accomplishing His purposes. Out of that people will come one who is central in the decrees of God. Not an afterthought but mysteriously beyond our thinking, known to God. Look at Revelation 13:8, the Lamb slain before the foundation of the world. In terms of what we know of God today, we see this Part I as revealing to us, God the Father, that is, the God who is source of all that we are and to whom we relate, infinite, eternal, powerful, a spirit.

God protects that line through which He will come over a period of many years and in times of failure on their part to know Him and obey Him as they should.

His incarnation into the world begins Part II of the Redemptive Drama, **SALVATION PROCLAIMED**. Galatians 4:4, in God's time. That incarnate God, manifest in the flesh, to communicate directly with the human race, to be a part of it, to share in its joys and sorrows, finally pays the supreme price of rejection, by a world who wanted to call its own shots, the death of the Cross, perfection paying the perfect price to satisfy God's Holy just demands. The great dilemma was solved, how God could be absolutely just and yet lovingly receive to Himself, those for whom justice demanded the harsh penalty of death. That time in which Jesus lived and walked and taught and did so many things to reveal God to us is the time, as we now know it of God the Son, God revealed to a human race as one of that race. Having accomplished the first portion of His work, the Cross, He ascended to heaven and will yet come again. Having ascended, He sent the Holy Spirit into the world, the intimation of what is to come, the Spirit who indwells those people He has chosen.

In the meantime while we wait we are involved in Part II **Salvation Proclaimed**, which shows that this message was more than just for the Jews but for a whole world. And that is what we are about today, the proclamation of that reconciling message, that God has provided a way in which sinful human beings can be rightly related to Him and progress to live a satisfying and fruitful life, in harmony with His purposes. And as they live this purposeful life, demonstrating the power and presence of God in their time on earth, they know that God is going to make all things right someday—there is a justice coming; the Lord Jesus, now a risen Savior, a life-giving Spirit will return to claim His own. There will be a time of His reigning on earth and then there will be eternity. And we who have been called out, as a people to His name, will reign with Him for all eternity. In terms of what we know today, this is the Age of God, the Spirit.

<u>Introduction</u>
Genesis tells us of many beginnings. It tells of the beginning of the creation, the human race, of sin in the world, of the spread of the race, of judgment on the race and a new beginning for the race. It does not satisfy all our questions. We would ask more and want more. But it does give us the backdrop for the salvation story. Humanity is in need. It can not get along with itself. It has alienated itself from God. Left to itself it will be destructive at best. There is a need. And the salvation story which begins in Genesis chapter 12 will give God's response to meet that need.

<u>Chapter 1. The Making of a Nation</u>
God's basic plan is to choose a people and to reveal Himself and His plans for reconciling the world to Himself through that nation. Chapter 1 tells of the story of God's building of the nation.

If I were to pick out the most important events in the making of a nation, Chapter 1 of the redemptive drama I would say the following would certainly be a part of it.
1. The call of Abraham—the Abrahamic Promise
2. The renewal of the covenant with Isaac
3. The renewal of the covenant with Jacob
4. The deliverance of Jacob and sons through Joseph
5. The call of Moses
6. The power encounters in Egypt and the Exodus
7. The Red Sea deliverance
8. The Spies in the Land/corporate failure of a faith check
9. The Giving of the 10 Commandments/covenant

10. Moses' failure—striking the rock
11. Moses' outstanding leadership in the desert years with a rebellious followership and his transition of Joshua into leadership
12. Crossing of Jordan
13. Circumcision at Gilgal
14. Joshua meets the Captain of the Hosts
15. Capture of Jericho
16. Failure at Ai
17. Success at Ai
18. Gibeonite deception
19. Capture of Land (lack of total obedience)
20. Repetitive Failure—moving from dependence to independence. The Cycle of the Judges (need for centralized influence)
21. Samuel's unifying influence
22. Saul's anointing and failure
23. David's anointing and success
24. David's failure and discipline
25. David's preparation for building the temple

Lets examine some of the Bible books which present these events.

From Genesis

From the introduction we know that humanity is not in good shape and is in need of intervention by God. And God has a plan thought out in eternity past.

God chooses one man, Abraham, and Promises (*The First Great Revelation—The Promise*) to make of him a great nation and to give them land and to bless the world through his offspring. (Gen 12:1-3, 7; 15:4,18, et al) Now God plans to use the nation He will bring forth to be a channel of redemption and revelation of Himself. So He begins to build a nation. For a nation you need people (including numbers) a coherent culture, a land, and a leader.

God begins to work on these things—the people first (the land has people on it who will be judged eventually when they are too evil to be redeemed). From this one man, who exemplifies faith in God's promise, comes a son, Isaac. Isaac has two sons, one of whom, Jacob, becomes the successor of the family line through which God will work—the 12 heads of the tribes: Reuben, Simeon, Levi, Judah, Zebulun, Issachar, Dan, Gad, Asher, Naphtali, Joseph, Benjamin.

Joseph, a son of Jacob's old age and his favorite, is sold into slavery by his jealous brothers (Acts 7:9). Because the patriarchs were jealous of Joseph they sold him as a slave into Egypt. But God was with him and rescued him from all his troubles. He gave Joseph wisdom and enabled him to gain the goodwill of Pharaoh king of Egypt; so he made him ruler over Egypt and all his palace.) Joseph, a person of proven integrity, rises to power through a series of providential appointments in which he shows wisdom from God upon several occasions. God gives some dreams to Pharaoh, the ruler of Egypt, which predict some good years followed by famine years. Joseph gives a wise plan to Pharaoh on how to prepare for it. He is put in charge and is right on target to protect his own family when the famine hits. The family comes to Egypt and rides through the famine years. It stays and expands in the land. Joseph, never losing sight of God's promise, exacts a promise from his brothers and fellow Israelites that they will take him back into the land when God takes them back. That is how Genesis ends.

From Exodus

Exodus opens many years later. There are many Israelite descendants, so many in fact, that the Egyptian King is fearful of them so he subjugates them. They are slaves and being ill-treated. Persecution takes the form of enforced labor and attempts to cut down the population (executing the boy babies).

God, having fulfilled the first part of his plan, getting a people, now works on the second part—getting a leader. Moses, an Israelite baby is preserved providentially and taken into the palace and educated as an Egyptian royal class person. As he reaches adulthood he recognizes that his people by blood relationship are in great bondage. So he wants to free them. His first attempt to help them is a disaster. He kills an Egyptian and has to flee Egypt. He goes to Midian, settles down, marries a Midianite woman, and has a family. After forty years, God selects him via a miraculous revelation, to go back to Egypt to lead God's people out of Egypt and into the promised land. Moses goes back and after 10 major confrontations with the Egyptian ruler (in which God-given power is seen—Moses certainly has spiritual authority) the people are freed to leave. But on the way the Egyptian ruler has second thoughts and pursues with his military. The military should overtake the Israelites who will be trapped by the Red Sea. God miraculously intervenes and they escape across the Red Sea on dry ground. The sea moves back as the military forces start to cross and they are wiped out. This is the heart of *the Exodus*.

From Exodus and Leviticus

God next begins to build the people culturally into what He will need. He gives them the LAW, the second great revelation and reveals more of Himself, His standards, and His purposes. The tabernacle which He gives the plans for reveals more of who God is in terms of access and revelation. The rest of EXODUS is given to that, revealing who God is as is the whole of LEVITICUS. It is especially in Leviticus that the holiness of God is developed—an understanding of sin and its implications; what atonement is (that is, being made right with God by making up for wrong against Him).

From Numbers

After disobedience and a lack of faith prevent the people from going in to the land (see NUMBERS) they wander for 40 years in the Sinai desert until the older rebellious people die off. During the desert years they learn to trust in God's provision. God reveals Himself primarily through his leader Moses. Near the end of the 40 years they are again ready to go into the land. God has a people, a culture, a leader, Moses, and a leader to take his place, Joshua. Moses prepares them for that push into the land by giving them a series of addresses (DEUTERONOMY—second law). These messages, his final words to them, reflect warnings drawn from their desert experience, remind them of standards of obedience which reflects what they have learned of God, and gives encouragement in the form of expectations as they enter the land. He closes his final words to them with songs of warning and blessing that portend the future. And thus we are ready for the third part of God's plan to build Himself a people—getting them into the land.

From Joshua

Joshua transitions into leadership with some sterling miraculous interventions by God which give him the spiritual authority he will need to follow Moses (a hard act to follow) as leader. Joshua seizes Jericho, after following a supernaturally revealed plan for its capture. He proceeds after an unexpected failure, which teaches an important corporate lesson on obedience, to the people, to split the land in two militarily and then begins to mop up in the north and south. The land is allotted. Each tribe has a portion, just as Moses had planned. They decentralize and begin to settle into their spots—with much trouble. After having been so long in a centralized authoritarian mode, they enjoy being decentralized and having autonomy. But this decentralization eventually leads to spiritual deterioration. This brings us up into the times of the judges.

From Judges

For a long period of time, longer than we in the United States have been a nation, the twelve tribes live scattered. There is frequent civil war in specific locales and much fighting with various surrounding nations and peoples who were not totally destroyed when the land was taken.

In short there is an oft repeated cycle: the people deteriorate spiritually getting far from God, God brings judgment upon them, they finally recognize that their problem is relationship with God—they repent and cry out for God's help. He sends along leaders, very charismatic who usually lead a volunteer army to defeat their enemies. There are at least 13 of these including: Othniel, Ehud, Shamgar, Deborah (Barak), Gideon, Abimelech, Tola, Jair, Jephthah, Ibzan, Elon, Abdon, and Samson. Some of these are more well known than others. Gideon and Samson for example. These are evil times and few there are who follow God.

In a section of the Judges (Judges 2:7) the writer sums it up well, "After Joshua had dismissed the Israelites, they went to take possession of the land, each to his own inheritance. The people served the Lord through out the lifetime of Joshua and of the elders who outlived him and who had seen all the great things the Lord had done for Israel." And then again in the closing portion a repeated phrase haunts us—Judges 21:25, "In those days Israel had no king; everyone did as he saw fit." These are the pre-kingdom years. Corporately the people are negatively prepared for the kingdom which will come.

From Ruth

There is a spark of life during those dreadful times. Ruth introduces us to that life by showing that there were some people of integrity who honored the Lord. This little romantic book shows how God provides and also allows us to see how the line through which the redeemer will later arise progresses.

The Judges and Ruth are pre-kingdom times. They prepared the Israelites to want a centralized structure after so much independence and autonomy. The Israelites were dependent upon voluntary armies raised up in times of crisis. Many times, other of the tribes than the one threatened, were not interested in their local squabbles and would not fight for them. Thus the entire commonwealth of tribes comes to the place where it needs, wants, and will accept a kingdom. Again God steps in and provides a transition leader—Samuel.

From 1 Samuel

The first thirteen chapters show how Samuel was providentially raised up as a leader. His ministry as judge was not just a momentary deliverance but a continual one. He visited the different tribes and judged them—that is, established law and justice for them. Samuel paves the way for a centralized kingdom. Crises around the people spur the need; Samuel's own sons are not able to replace him. The people demand a king—showing their need for one but also showing that they basically did not trust the unseen King. God gives them one king, Saul, who outwardly is what they would expect. But he fails repeatedly to follow God. His kingdom is spiritually bankrupt. God replaces him with David, whom God describes as *a man after my own heart*. The last part of 1 Samuel describes Saul's fall and David's early pre-kingdom years, in which David is gaining military expertise as a guerrilla warfare leader with a para-military band.

Redemptive Drama, The Biblical Framework

From 2 Samuel and 1 Chronicles and the Psalms

2 Samuel and 1 Chronicles give David's story—one written earlier to it and one written later. David is a long time in getting the kingdom as Saul's descendants try to hold on to the kingdom. After seven years of civil war, David is ruling a smaller part of Israel, the kingdom is united. God gives a covenant to David concerning his descendants. The poetical literature, particularly the Psalms, emerge more solidly from this era. David is an artistic person who spends time alone with God in worship. Many of the Psalms come out of those times alone with God, many spurred on by crises in David's kingdom. The kingdom is established under David and expands. In mid-life David has a major sin which tarnishes his lifetime. He has one of his military leaders killed in order that he might take his wife for himself. It and failure to manage his family well lead to a rebellion by one of his sons Absalom. David is deposed briefly but comes back winning a strategic battle. He is reinstated. Most of the rest of his kingdom is downhill. David's son, Solomon, after some manipulation and political intrigue succeeds David.

A number of the Psalms are ascribed to David. They reveal something of the personal touch—what that great leader was feeling during some of the more important times of his kingdom. They particularly show his need for God and why God calls him a "man after my own heart."

From Proverbs and Ecclesiastes

Solomon has the best start of any king in all the history of Israel. There is peace in the land. The borders have expanded almost to the full extent of God's promise. There is money and resources in the kingdom as well as a good military. Times are stable. Solomon builds the temple for God—a symbol of the centralized importance of religious worship in the capital. Solomon's early years are characterized by splendor. Most likely during the early and middle part of his reign many of the Proverbs were collected. These sayings embody truth that has been learned over the years (times of the Judges, times of the kingdom) about how to live harmoniously with others. Toward the end of his reign, he slips and falls away from following God. In this latter part of his reign, he writes Ecclesiastes which sums up much that he has learned over his lifetime. Its cynical tone shows need for an intimate relationship with God that is missing.

The nation is there. There are people. They know of God and his desires for them. There is a land. But they continually fail to live up to what God wants. During the reigns of David and Solomon the kingdom reaches its zenith. And thus ends Chapter 1, the making of a nation. In it all, God is seen to weave His purpose all around a people who frequently rebel against Him. They freely choose to live as they do, whether following after God or not. But even so He manages to move unswervingly forward to His purposes.

Chapter 2. The Destruction of a Nation

The story-line of chapter 2 hinges around the following major events:

1. Solomon goes away from the Lord, great warning—had the best start of any king yet did not finish well.
2. Rehoboam (1 Kings 12) makes unwise decision to increase taxes and demands on people—kingdom splits as prophecy said. 10 tribes go with the northern kingdom, Judah with the southern.
3. The northern kingdom under Jereboam quickly departs from God. Jereboam is used as the model of an evil king to whom all evil kings are likened; He had a good start also—God would have blessed him.
4. The southern kingdom generally is bad with an occasional good Kings and partially good kings: Asa, Jehoshaphat, Joash, Amaziah, Uzziah, Jotham, Hezekiah, Josiah. But the trend was always downward. The extended length

of life of the southern kingdom, more than the northern kingdom, is directly attributed to the spiritual life of the better kings. Spiritual leadership does make a difference.
5. During both the northern and southern kingdoms God sent prophets to try and correct them—first the oral prophets (many—but the two most noted were Elijah and Elisha) and then the prophets who wrote.

Now in order to understand this long period of history you should know several things:
1. The History books that give background information about the times.
2. The Bible Time-Line, need to know when the books were written.
3. Need to know the writing prophets: northern or southern kingdom, which crisis, direct or special.

The History Books

The history books covering the time of the destruction of a nation include 1, 2 Samuel, 1,2 Kings, and 1,2 Chronicles. The following chart helps identify the focus of each of these books as to major content.

Chart 33.1 The History Books—Major Content

1 Samuel	2 Samuel 1 Chronicles	1,2 Kings 2 Chronicles
Samuel, Saul, David	David	1,2 Kings: Solomon to Zedekiah 2 Chronicles exclusively on line of Judah

There are four categories of prophetical books. Prophetical books deal with three major crises: the Assyrian crisis which wiped out the northern kingdom; the Bablonian crisis which wiped out the southern kingdom; the return to the land after being exiled. There are also prophetical books not specifically dealing with these crises but associated with the time of them. The prophetical books dealing with these issues are:

A. Northern—Assyrian Crisis
   Jonah, Amos, Hosea, Nahum, Micah
B. Southern—Babylonian Crisis
   Joel, Isaiah, Micah, Zephaniah, Jeremiah, Lamentations, Habakkuk, Obadiah
C. In Exile
   Ezekiel, Daniel, Esther
D. Return From Exile
   Nehemiah, Ezra, Haggai, Zechariah, Malachi

In addition, to knowing the crises you must know that prophets wrote:

A. Direct to the Issue of the Crisis either Assyrian, Babylonian, or Return To The Land
   Amos, Hosea, Joel, Micah, Isaiah, Jeremiah, Ezekiel, Haggai, Zechariah, Malachi
B. Special
   Jonah, Nahum, Habakkuk, Obadiah, Zephaniah, Daniel.

Redemptive Drama, The Biblical Framework page 155

The special prophets, though usually associated with one of the crisis times, wrote to deal with unique issues not necessarily related directly to the crisis. The following list gives the special prophets and their main thrust.

1. Jonah—a paradigm shift, pointing out God's desire for the nation to be missionary minded and reach out to surrounding nations.
2. Nahum—vindicate God, judgment on Assyria.
3. Habakkuk—faith crisis for Habakkuk, vindicate God, judgment on Babylon.
4. Obadiah—vindicate God, judgment on Edom for treatment of Judah.
5. Zephaniah—show about judgment, the Day of the Lord.
6. Daniel—give hope, show that God is indeed ruling even in the times of the exile and beyond, gives God's plan for the ages.

<u>The Destruction of A Nation—The Return From Exile</u> (see page 32)

Several Bible books are associated with the return to the land from the exile. After a period of about 70 years (during which time Daniel ministered) Cyrus made a decree which allowed some Jews (those that wanted to) to return to the land. Some went back under Zerrubabel, a political ruler like a governor. A priest, Joshua, also provided religious leadership to the first group that went back. This group of people started to rebuild the temple but became discouraged due to opposition and lack of resources. They stopped building the temple. Two prophets, after several years, 10-15, addressed the situation. These two, Haggai and Zechariah, were able to encourage the leadership and the people to finish the temple.

Another thirty or forty years goes by and then we have the events of the book of Esther, back in the land. Her book describes the attempt to eradicate the Jewish exiles—a plot which failed due to God's sovereign intervention via Esther, the queen of the land and a Jewish descendant going incognito, and her relative Mordecai.

Still another period of time passes, 20 or so years and a priest, Ezra, directs another group to return to the land. The spiritual situation has deteriorated. He brings renewal.

Another kind of leader arrives on the scene some 10-15 years later. Nehemiah, a lay leader, and one adept at organizing and moving to accomplish a task, rebuilds the wall around Jerusalem. He too has to instigate renewal.

Finally, after another period of 30 or so years we have the book of Malachi which again speaks to renewal of the people. The Old Testament closes with this final book.

A recurring emphasis occurs during the period of the return. People are motivated to accomplish a task for God. They start out, become discouraged, and stop. They must be renewed. God raises up leadership to bring renewal.

<u>Preparation for the Coming of Messiah—The Inter-Testamental Period</u>

I do not deal with this in detail, that is in terms of the various historical eras.[56] Some 400+ years elapse between the close of the Old Testament and the Beginning of the New Testament. There are significant differences in the Promised Land. The following chart highlights these differences.[57]

---

[56] In **Leadership Perspectives**, I do deal more in a detailed way with the various historical sub-phases of this period of history. A number of books in the Catholic canon occur during this period of time.
[57] These notes are adapted from material studied with Frank Sells at Columbia Bible College in his Old Testament survey course.

Chart 33.2 Differences in Palestine—Close of O.T., Beginning of N.T.

The End of the Old Testament	The Beginning of the New Testament
1. Palestine was part of a Persian satrapy, since Persian, an eastern nation was the greatest governmental power in the world at the time.	1. Palestine was a Roman province, since the entire world had come under the sway of the western Nation of Rome.
2. The population was sparse.	2. One of the most dense parts of the Roman empire.
3. The cities of Palestine as a whole were heaps of rubbish.	3. There was general prosperity throughout Palestine.
4. The temple of Zerubbabel was a significant structure.	4. The temple of Herod the Great was a magnificent building.
5. There were no Pharisees or Sadducees, although the tendencies from which they developed were present.	5. The Pharisees and Sadducees were much in evidence and strong in power.
6. There were no synagogues in Palestine.	6. Synagogues were located everywhere in the Holy Land. There was no hamlet or village so small or destitute as to lack a synagogue.
7. There was little extra-biblical tradition among the Jews.	7. There was a great mass of tradition, among both the Jews of Palestine and those of the dispersion.
8. The Jews were guilty of much intermarriage with the surrounding nations.	8. There was almost no intermarriage between Jews and non-Jews.
9. Palestine was under the rule of a Hebrew.	9. Palestine was under the rule of an Edomite vice-king, Herod the Great.
10. The Hebrew governor was regarded by the Jews as their spiritual leader.	10. The scribes and priest were regarded by the Jews as their spiritual leaders.

In addition to differences, there were some similarities between end of O.T. times and beginning of N.T. times.

1. **Freedom from idolatry**. God had used the Babylonian Captivity to free His people from their oft-repeated tendency to idolatry.
2. **Israel in two great divisions**, the Jews of the Homeland (Isolation) and the Jews of the Dispersion (who were scattered throughout the world). In the time of Malachi a relatively small proportion of God's chosen people was located in Palestine, while by far the larger part was still in exile. Although Palestine was much more thickly populated in the time of Christ than in the time of Malachi, the same general situation prevailed as to the two-fold division of Israel into Palestinian Jews and Jews of the Diaspora (Dispersion), with a far greater number in exile than in the land of Canaan.
3. **Externalism and dead orthodoxy**. A comparison of Malachi (the last prophetical book of the Old Testament) and Nehemiah (the last historical book of the Old Testament) with the Gospels indicates that the outward conformity of the Pharisees to the law which they inwardly revolted from, was but an advanced step of the hypocritical conformity which had marked many Israelites at the end of Old Testament days.

Redemptive Drama, The Biblical Framework

It was during the inter-testamental period that these changes occurred. Daniel had foretold of the various empires that would emerge after Babylon: the Medo-Persian, the Grecian, and the Roman. Each of these were used by God to prepare the way for the coming of Messiah, the next chapter in the redemptive drama.

Galatians 4:4 states that Messiah came at the "fullness of time." That is, the time was ready. Some have suggested a fivefold preparation for Christ's Coming.

1. Religious Preparation—both negative and positive
2. Political Preparation—world at peace
3. Cultural Preparation—lack of meaning; cultural vehicle through which to spread the Gospel
4. The Social Preparation—great needs; life under bondage
5. The Moral Preparation

Chapter 3. Messiah

At the right moment in time—Jesus was born. His miraculous birth attested to his uniqueness.

He was the fulfillment of the Old Testament as to many of its prophecies, types, symbols. He was the seed of the woman who dealt a fatal blow to the seed of the serpent (Genesis 3:15); he was the tabernacle who lived among us (Exodus 25-40); he was the arch type of the brazen serpent, lifted up that people might look, see and be healed (Numbers 21); he was the arch types of the Levitical offerings, the perfect sacrifice (Leviticus 1-5); he was that prophet like unto Moses (Deuteronomy 18); he was the ultimate fulfillment of the Davidic covenant (2 Samuel 7); he was the Messianic Sufferer (Psalm 22); he was the one who was anointed to preach good news to the poor, to proclaim freedom for the captives, and release from darkness those who are prisoners, to proclaim the year of the Lord's favor (Isaiah 61:1ff) and the Suffering Servant (Isaiah 53); he was the righteous branch from David's line (Jeremiah 23); he was the one shepherd, the servant David, the prince of Ezekiel (Ezekiel 37); he was the one greater than Jonah, the sign after three days he arose (Jonah 21); he was the proper leader coming out of obscure Bethlehem (Micah 5:2); and we could go on.

Matthew showed he was the Messiah King, rejected. Mark showed him to be vested with divine power, a person of action and authority. Luke showed him to be the perfect representative of the human race: one of courage, ability, social interests, sympathy, broad acceptance. And John showed him to be Immanuel, God with us, revealing God to us and acting to demonstrate grace and truth, the heartbeat of the divine ministry philosophy.

The bottom line of the story line is given in a quote taken from John, "He was in the world, and though the world was made through him, the world did not recognize him. He came unto his own, but his own did not receive him. Yet to all who received him, to those who believed in his name, he gave the right to become children of God, children born not of natural descent, nor of human source but born of God. The Word became flesh and made his dwelling among us. We have seen his glory, the glory of the One and Only, who came from the Father, full of grace and truth." (John 1:10-14).

The story of this chapter of the redemptive drama ends abruptly. But there is a postscript. Each of the Gospel stories and the Acts tell us of Jesus Christ's resurrection. After His death He arose and was seen for a period of about 40 days upon various occasions. During those days He gave the marching orders for the movement He had begun. The great commissions repeated five times, Matthew 28:19,20, Luke 24:46,47,

Mark 16:15, John 20:21, and Acts 1:8. Each of these carry the main thrust which is to go into the world and tell the Good News of salvation, that people can be reconciled to God. Each also carries some special connotation. It is these marching orders which set the stage for Chapter 4, The Church, in the redemptive story.

Chapter 4. The Church

The essence of the story line of chapter 4, is contained in the book of Acts. Its central thematic message is the essence of the story line.

Theme: **The Growth Of The Church**
- which spreads from Jerusalem to Judea to Samaria and the uttermost parts of the earth,
- is seen to be of God,
- takes place as Spirit directed people present a salvation centered in Jesus Christ, and
- occurs among all peoples, Jews and Gentiles.

This basic phenomenon reoccurs as the Gospel spreads across cultural barriers throughout the world. Though the message of the book of Acts covers only up through the first two thirds of the first century its basic essence reoccurs throughout the church age until the present time in which we live.

About half of the book of Acts tells of the formation of the church in Jerusalem and its early expansion to Jews, Samaritans, and finally to Gentiles. The latter half of the book traces the breakout of the Gospel to Gentiles in Asia and Europe. The structure of the book highlighted by the linguistic discourse markers (the Word of the Lord grew) carries the notion of a God-given church expanding.

Structure: There are seven divisions in Acts each concluding with a summary verse. The summary verses: 2:47b, 6:7, 9:31, 12:24, 16:5, 19:20, 28:30,31

I.	(ch 1-2:47)	The Birth of the Church in Jerusalem
II.	(ch 3-6:7)	The Infancy of the Church in Jerusalem
III.	(ch 6:8-9:31)	The Spread of the Church into Judea, Galilee, Samaria
IV.	(ch 9:32-12:24)	The Church Doors Open to the Gentiles
V.	(ch 13-16:5)	The Church Spreads to Asia Minor
VI.	(ch 16:6-19:20)	The Church Gains a Foothold in Europe
VII.	(ch 19:21-28)	The Travels of the Church's First Missionary To Rome (The Church on Trial in its Representative Paul)

As to details there are many important pivotal events in the Acts, many of which have similarly reoccurred in the expansion of the Gospel around the world and throughout church history. Acts begins with Jesus' post resurrection ministry to the disciples and his Ascension to heaven. Then the disciples are gathered at Jerusalem praying when the Pentecost event, the giving of the Holy Spirit to the church, as promised in Luke's version of the Great Commission, happens and Peter gives a great public sermon which launches the church.

Early church life is described. Peter and John imbued with power heal a lame man at the temple gate and are put in prison. They are threatened and released. An incident with Ananias and Sapphira shows the power and presence of the Holy Spirit.

Stephen an early church servant has a strong witness and is martyred for it. General persecution on the church breaks out. The believers are scattered and preach the gospel where ever they go. Phillip, another early church servant leads an Ethiopian palace administrator to Christ and has ministry in Samaria.

Saul, the persecutor of Christians, is saved on the road to Damascus. Peter demonstrates Godly power in several miraculous events. Peter is divinely chosen to preach the Gospel to a Gentile, Cornelius. Herod kills James and imprisons Peter. Peter is miraculously delivered.

The story line now switches to follow the missionary efforts of Barnabas and Paul (formerly Saul) to Cyprus and Asian minor. It then goes on to follow Paul's efforts which go further into Asia minor and Greece. Paul makes a return visit to Jerusalem where he is accused by the Jewish opposition in Jerusalem. Eventually after several delays and hearings he is ordered to Rome. The book ends with the exciting journey to Rome, including a shipwreck.

The books of the New Testament were written to various groups during the church chapter. Many were written by Paul. These generally were letters to the various churches which had resulted from his missionary efforts. Each was contextually specific—written at a certain time, written at a certain stage of Paul's own development as a leader, and dealing with a specific situation—either an individual in a church or to a corporate group, some church at a location or in a general region.

Other New Testament books were not written by Paul. The book of Hebrews, author uncertain, John's three letters, Jude's one letter and Peter's two letters all are of a general nature. With the exception of possibly 2nd and 3rd John, these letters were written to believer's in general in scattered regions—probably Asia minor.

All of these, Paul's letters, and the general books, deal with the church. They give us insights into church problems, church situations at that time, and the essence of what the church is and how Christians ought to live. These New Testament books are filled with leadership information. Each of them represents a major leadership act of a leader seeking to influence followers of Christ. Many of them have actual details that reflect leadership values, leadership problem solving, and leadership issues. All of them have important modeling data.

We would have an unfinished story if we were left only with *just these* New Testament books. We would have a task. And men and women would be out and about the world attempting to fulfill that task. But where is it leading. What about those Old Testament prophecies yet to be fulfilled about *that day*. Our story is incomplete. We need to know how this redemptive drama is going to end. And so the Revelation.

Chapter 5. The Kingdom

The final book of the Bible is aptly named. The Revelation (unveiling, revealing, making clear) of Jesus Christ (the unveiling of Jesus Christ) brings closure to the redemptive drama. This final book in the Bible has among others these purposes:

1. to reveal future purposes of Jesus Christ and graphically show the power He will unleash in accomplishing His purposes, which include bringing about justice and bringing in His reign,
2. to show those purposes and power to be in harmony with His divine attributes, and
3. to bring a fitting climax to the redemptive story developed throughout Scripture.

The theme statement of the book of Revelation highlights the fitting climax of the redemptive drama.

Theme: **God's Ultimate Purposes For His Redemptive Program**
- center in the Person of His Son,
- involve His churches,
- will take place in a context of persecution and struggle—as described cryptically by many visions,
- will focus on the triumph of Jesus and his judgment of all things in harmony with his divine attributes, and
- will be realized in final victory for His people and ultimate justice accomplished in the world.

God's intent from the first of Genesis on has been to bless His people with His eternal presence. Ezekiel closes his book with that thought in mind. Numerous of the prophets point to a future day in which things would be made right and God would dwell with His people. The plan has had many twists and turns but through it all God has sovereignly moved on to His purpose.

Some have followed hard after God and were included in His purposes. Others refused to follow God. They were cast aside. God moved on.

In the New Testament God prepares a way where He can reveal Himself in justice and love and reconcile all people unto Himself. The Cross climaxes all of God's preparation to bless the world. The message of the Cross is seen to be for all. The church goes out into all the world. It has its problems. But always it seeks to be part of God's future purposes looking forward to Christ's return. Were there no Revelation, the Redemptive Story would be incomplete. The Revelation brings to a fitting climax all of God's working to bless the world. There is an ultimate purpose in history! Justice is meted out! And then a final blessing—God's eternal presence of with His people.

Suggested Chronological Writing of New Testament Books

When we study a given book of the bible we should know where it occurs in the redemptive drama. We should be familiar with what God has revealed to that point in time and what God has done redemptively up to that time. Table 33.1 below list each book of the Bible in terms of the Chapter in the redemptive story in which it falls. I have attempted to list each book in chronological order though there is not scholarly consensus on when some of these books were written.

Table 33.1 Bible Books Related To Chapters of the Redemptive Drama

The Bible Books: Chapter 1. The Making of a Nation

Exodus	Joshua	2 Samuel	Ecclesiastes
Leviticus	Judges	1 Chronicles	Song of Songs
Numbers	Ruth	Psalms	
Deuteronomy	1 Samuel	Proverbs	

The Bible Books: Chapter 2. The Destruction of a Nation

1,2 Kings	Hosea	Zephaniah	Daniel	Nehemiah
2 Chronicles	Micah	Jeremiah	Haggai	Malachi
Jonah	Isaiah	Lamentations	Zechariah	
Joel	Nahum	Obadiah	Esther	
Amos	Habakkuk	Ezekiel	Ezra	

The Bible Books: Chapter 3. Messiah
Matthew   Mark   Luke   John

The Bible Books: Chapter 4. The Church
James	2 Corinthians	Colossians	Titus	2 John
Acts	Galatians	Philemon	2 Timothy	3 John
1 Thessalonians	Romans	1 Peter	Hebrews	
2 Thessalonians	Ephesians	2 Peter	Jude	
1 Corinthians	Philippians	1 Timothy	1 John	

The Bible BOOK Chapter 5. Kingdom
Revelation

Article 34

Restoration Leaders

Introduction

In my leadership literature I define two restoration terms that are important. They have some overlap but also need to be seen as distinct.

Definition   *Restoration* (individual leader) is the process whereby a fallen leader is transitioned back into leadership. It usually involves repentance, restitution where appropriate, correction of the aberrant leadership dysfunctionalities, and recognition by other leaders of the restoration process and their stamp of approval for the leader to renew ministry.

Definition   *Corporate restoration* refers to God's attempts to restore the people of God as a viable channel through whom He can work to carry out His Biblical purposes.

It is this latter definition that is important to the third major crisis—the *Restoration Crisis*, which has to do with our notion of restoration leaders.

Description   The *restoration crisis* refers to the period of time from 539 B.C. to 430 B.C. and which covers the activity of God in bringing His people back into the land and establishing a testimony there. His providential care of His people (both in the land and outside it) is also shown.

Definition   *Restoration leaders* refer to the important leaders—civil, religious, and prophetical—who worked during the restoration crisis years to bring some kind of recrudescence to God's people.

This article will list several of these leaders and give an overall evaluation of their restoration leadership.

The Restoration Crisis Overviewed

Several Bible books are associated with the return to the land from the exile. After a period of about 70 years (during which time Daniel ministered) Cyrus made a decree, which allowed some Jews (those that wanted to) to return to the land. Some went back under **Zerubbabel**, a political ruler like a governor. A priest, **Joshua**, also provided religious leadership to the first group that went back. This group of people started to rebuild the temple but became discouraged due to opposition and lack of resources. They stopped building the temple. Then two prophets, after several years, 10-15, addressed the situation. These two, **Haggai** and **Zechariah**, were able to encourage the leadership and the people to finish the temple.

Restoration Leaders

Another thirty or forty years go by and then we have the events of the book of Esther, back in the land. Her book describes the attempt to eradicate the Jewish exiles—a plot which failed due to God's sovereign intervention via **Esther**, the queen of the land and a Jewish descendant going incognito, and her relative **Mordecai**.

Still another period of time passes, 20 or so years and a priest, **Ezra**, directs another group to return to the land. The spiritual situation has deteriorated. He brings renewal.

Another kind of leader arrives on the scene some 10-15 years later. **Nehemiah**, a lay leader, actually a civil leader, and one adept at organizing and moving to accomplish a task, rebuilds the wall around Jerusalem. He too has to instigate renewal.

Finally, after another period of 30 or so years we have the book of **Malachi**, which again speaks to renewal of the people. The Old Testament closes with this final book.

A recurring emphasis occurs during the period of the return. People are motivated to accomplish a task for God. They start out, become discouraged, and stop. They must be renewed. God raises up leadership to bring renewal.

Restoration Leaders

Restoration leaders are listed along with times and the basic restoration activity and crisis involved.

Table 34.1 The Restoration Era Crises And Related Biblical Material

Item	539 B.C.	536 B.C.	520-516 B.C.	486-465 B.C.	465-424 B.C.	430 B.C.
Restoration Activity	Daniel Prays	Work on Temple Begun	Work on Temple begun again and Completed	Israelites Preserved due to Esther and Mordecai's activities	Wall is constructed around Jerusalem—Ezra and Nehemiah bring about restoration movement	Malachi again engenders restoration movement
Restoration Leader	Daniel	Joshua Zerubbabel	Haggai Zechariah	Esther Mordecai	Nehemiah; Ezra	Malachi
Crises	1. God's Timing and Faith	2. Public Testimony Needed Back in the Land	3. Public Testimony Needed—Work Stopped	4. People of God Outside of Land—Danger of being Destroyed	5. Protection of Jerusalem/Public Testimony of People	6. Leadership Nominality; follower nominality
Results	Cyrus gives decree; God's Restoration activity begins.	People go back to the land; they establish homes and lay the foundation for the temple	People start again on building God's temple; eventually it is completed.	Jewish people in exile are preserved.	Nehemiah sees walls rebuilt; Ezra sees revival and folks following God's word.	Not sure; but people are certainly made aware of God's desires for them.

Restoration Leaders

Macro Lessons Emphasized By Restoration Ministry

The important macro lessons that are strongly illustrated in the ministry of these restoration leaders include the following (numbers refer to a list of 41 macro lessons seen in the Bible):

19.	Stability	Preserving a ministry of God with life and vigor over time is as much if not more of a challenge to leadership than creating one.

All of the restoration leaders (probably apart from Esther and Mordecai) illustrate this.

21.	**Recrudescence**	**Kingdom God will attempt to bring renewal to His people until they no longer respond to Him.**

This is certainly a conviction of Ezra, Haggai, and Zechariah who ministered to bring spiritual renewal.

22.	By-pass	God will by-pass leadership and structures that do not respond to Him and will institute new leadership and structures.

The inclusion of civil leaders like Zerubbabel and Nehemiah, along with priests like Ezra and Joshua and prophetic leaders like Haggai, Zechariah and Malachi, certainly demonstrate this macro lesson. The kingdom structure was bypassed. What the new structures will be is not clear from this part of Biblical history. But leaders and leader functions necessary are seen.

27.	**Perseverance**	**Once known, leaders must persevere with the vision God has given.**

Haggai and Nehemiah particularly emphasize this macro lesson.

Closure

Leaders attentive to God and who want to see vital relationships renewed between God and His people can be used to see this happen, no matter how bleak the situation around them. God is still the Lord Almighty. Further, no work of God is small if God is in it. The general restoration activity back in the land took part with a small remnant. Compared to the earlier days of the kingdom, the work seemed very small. But God was in it and used it as a foundation later for Messiah to come. Restoration leaders are needed especially in our Church Leadership Era where so many Christian groups have become nominal. We need to study these restoration leaders in the O.T. to be inspired by what they did and to know the Lord Almighty they knew.

See **Article**, Haggai—*Calendar and Dating; Restoration Leaders; Civil Leadership, The Missing Ingredient; Left Hand of God; Redemptive Drama, The Biblical Framework; Six Biblical Leadership Eras—Seeing the Bible With Leadership Eyes; Macro Lesson, Defined; Macro Lessons, List of 41 Across Six Leadership Eras.*

Article 35

Six Biblical Leadership Eras
Approaching the Bible with Leadership Eyes

Introduction

In my opinion, the Bible provides one of the richest resources that Christian leaders have on leadership. The Bible is full of leadership insights, lessons, values and principles about leaders and leadership. It is filled with influential people and the results of their influence... both good and bad.

Three assumptions undergird what I will say in this article.

1. I have a strong **conviction** that the Bible can give valuable leadership insights.
2. I have made a **willful decision** to study the Bible and use it as a source of leadership insights.[58]
3. To study the Bible for leadership insights, you need **leadership eyes** to see leadership findings in the Bible. That is, there are many leadership perspectives, i.e. paradigms, that help stimulate one to see leadership findings. I have been discovering and using these in my own study.

I want to do three things in this keynote overview. I want to introduce two most helpful perspectives for studying the Bible for leadership findings: 1. Seeing Leadership Eras; 2. Recognizing Leadership Genre. I will give more space to *the Six Leadership Eras*. These two concepts will help give one *leadership eyes*. And then I want to talk about the impact of the two most important boundary times between leadership eras, Moses desert leadership and Jesus' foundational work instigating a major movement. Both of these were fundamental and foundational times of Biblical leadership. They introduced radical macro lessons that deeply impact our own leadership today.

The Six Leadership Eras

A first step toward having *leadership eyes*, for recognizing leadership findings in the Bible involves seeing the various leadership eras in the Bible. These time periods share common leadership assumptions and expectations. These assumptions and expectations differ markedly from one leadership time period to the next. Though, of course, there are commonalties that bridge across the eras.

Definition   A *leadership era* is a period of time, usually several hundred years long,[59] in which the major focus of leadership, the influence means, basic leadership

---

[58] I have been doing this deliberately for ten years at this writing.

[59] There is one exception. Though technically, the N.T. Pre-Church Era includes the inter-testamental time, I only really focus on Jesus' ministry which lasted a short period of time. But it is so unique and so radically different from what preceded and followed it that I treat it as the essential time in this era.

Six Biblical Leadership Eras—Overviewed

functions, and followership have much in common and which basically differ with time periods before or after it.

Table 35.1 contains the outline of the six eras I have identified.

Table 35.1 Six Leadership Eras Outlined

Era	Label/ Details
I.	**Patriarchal Era** (Leadership Roots)—Family Base
II.	**Pre-Kingdom Leadership Era**—Tribal Base A. The Desert Years B. The War Years—Conquering the Land, C. The Tribal Years/ Chaotic Years/ Decentralized Years—Conquered by the Land
III.	**Kingdom Leadership Era**—Nation Based A. The United Kingdom B. The Divided Kingdom C. The Single Kingdom—Southern Kingdom Only
IV.	**Post-Kingdom Leadership Era**—Individual/ Remnant Based A. Exile—Individual Leadership Out of the Land B. Post Exilic—Leadership Back in the Land C. Interim—Between Testaments
V.	**New Testament Pre-Church Leadership**—Spiritually Based in the Land A. Pre-Messianic B. Messianic
VI.	**New Testament Church Leadership**—Decentralized Spiritually Based A. Jewish Era B. Gentile Era

The three overarching elements of leadership include: the *leadership basal elements* (leader, follower, situation which make up the **What** of leadership); *leadership influence means* (individual and corporate leadership styles which make up the **How** of leadership); and *leadership value bases* (theological and cultural values which make up the **Why** of leadership).[60] It was this taxonomy which suggested questions that helped me see for the first time the six leadership eras of the Bible. It is these categories that allow comparison of different leadership periods in the Bible. Later I will apply the taxonomy to each of the eras and give my preliminary findings.

Using these leadership characteristics I studied leadership across the Bible and inductively generated the six leadership eras as given above. Table 35.2 adds some descriptive elements of the eras.

Table 35.2 Six Leadership Eras in the Bible—Definitive Characteristics

Leadership Era	Example(s) Leader(s)	Definitive Characteristics
1. Foundational	Abraham,	Family Leadership/ formally male dominated/ expanding into tribes and

---

[60] See the **Article**, *Leadership Tree Diagram* which explains in details these three elements of leadership.

	(also called Patriarchal)	Joseph	clans as families grew/ moves along kinship lines.
2.	Pre-Kingdom	Moses, Joshua, Judges	Tribal Leadership/ Moving to National/ Military/ Spiritual Authority/ outside the land moving toward a centralized national leadership.
3.	Kingdom	David, Hezekiah	National Leadership/ Kingdom Structure/ Civil, Military/ Spiritual/ a national leadership—Prophetic call for renewal/ inside the land/ breakup of nation.
4.	Post-Kingdom	Ezekiel, Daniel, Ezra, Nehemiah	Individual leadership/ Modeling/ Spiritual Authority.
5.	Pre-Church	Jesus/ Disciples	Selection/ Training/ spiritual leadership/ preparation for decentralization of Spiritual Authority/ initiation of a movement.
6.	Church	Peter/ Paul/ John	decentralized leadership/ cross-cultural structures led by leaders with spiritual authority which institutionalize the movement and spread it around the world.

When we study a leader or a particular leadership issue in the Scripture, we must always do so in light of the leadership context in which it was taking place. We cannot judge past leadership by our present leadership standards. Yet, we will find that major leadership lessons learned by these leaders will usually have broad implications for our leadership.

Second Major Perspective for Getting Leadership Eyes—The Seven Leadership Genre

Further study of each of these leadership eras resulted in the identification of seven leadership genre which served as sources for leadership findings. I then worked out in detail approaches for studying each of these genre.[61] These seven leadership genre are shown in Table 35-3.

Table 35.3 Seven Leadership Genre—Sources for Leadership Findings

Type	General Description/ Example	Approach
1. Biographical	Information about leaders; this is the single largest genre giving leadership information in the Bible/ **Joseph**	Use biographical analysis based on leadership emergence theory concepts.
2. Direct Leadership Contexts[62]	Blocks of Scripture which are giving information directly applicable to leaders/ leadership; relatively few of these in Scripture/ **1 Peter 5:1-4**	Use standard exegetical techniques.
3. Leadership Acts[63]	Mostly narrative vignettes describing a leader influencing followers, usually in some crisis situation; quite a few of these in the Bible/ **Acts 15 Jerusalem Council**	Use three-fold leadership tree diagram as basic source for suggesting what areas of leadership to look for.
4. Parabolic	Parables focusing on leadership perspectives: e.g. stewardship parables,	Use standard parable exegetical techniques but then use leadership perspectives to draw out

---

[61] See **Leadership Perspectives—How To Study the Bible for Leadership Findings**. Altadena: Barnabas Publishers.
[62] I have identified many of the direct leadership texts and exegetically analyzed the important ones.
[63] Many leadership acts have been identified and more than 20 have been analyzed. There is much work to do on analyzing leadership acts.

Six Biblical Leadership Eras—Overviewed

Passages[64]	futuristic parables; quite a few of these in Matthew and Luke./ **Luke 19 The Pounds**	applicational findings; especially recognize the leadership intent of Jesus in giving these. Most such parables were given with a view to training disciples.
5. Books as a Whole	Each book in the Bible[65]; end result of this is a list of leadership observations or lessons or implications for leadership/ **Deuteronomy**	Consider each of the Bible books in terms of the leadership era in which they occur and for what they contribute to leadership findings; will have to use whatever other leadership genre source occurs in a given book; also use overall synthesis thinking.
6. Indirect Passages	Passages in the Scripture dealing with Biblical values applicable to all; more so to leaders who must model Biblical values/ **Proverbs; Sermon on the Mount**	Use standard exegetical procedures for the type of Scripture containing the applicable Biblical ethical findings or values.
7. Macro Lessons[66]	Generalized high level leadership observations seen in an era and which have potential for leadership absolutes/ **Presence Macro**	Use synthesis techniques utilizing various leadership perspectives to stimulate observations.

The Criteria For Evaluating An Era

What Are the Distinguishing Characteristics We Are Looking For? I have used the following categories:

1. Major Focus—

Here we are looking at the overall purposes of leadership for the period in question. What was God doing or attempting to do through the leader? Sense of destiny? Leadership mandate?

2. Influence means—

Here we are describing any of the power means available and used by the leaders in their leadership. We can use any of Wrong's categories or any of the leadership style categories I define. Note particularly in the Old Testament the use of force and manipulation as power means.

3. Basic leadership functions—

We list here the various achievement responsibilities expected of the leaders: from God's standpoint, from the leader's own perception of leadership, from the followers. Usually they can all be categorized under the three major leadership functions of task, relational, and inspirational functions. But here we are after the specific functions.

4. Followers—

---

[64] I have studied every parable, exegetically, in Matthew, Mark and Luke for its central truth and applicable leadership lessons.

[65] I have done this for each book in the Bible over the past 10 years. My findings are included in **The Bible and Leadership Values** (and in this **Handbook**). Though I have made a good start, there is much more to be done here. I am intending other Handbooks which include all of the top 25 Bible books on leadership.

[66] This area needs the most research. Several PhD research projects are now focused on this.

Six Biblical Leadership Eras—Overviewed

Here we are after sphere of influence. Who are the followers? What are their relationship to leaders? Which of the 10 Commandments of followership are valid for these followers? What other things are helpful in describing followers?

5. Local Leadership—
In the surrounding culture: Biblical leaders will be very much like the leaders in the cultures around them. Leadership styles will flow out of this cultural press. Here we are trying to identify leadership roles in the cultures in contact with our Biblical leaders.

6. Other:
Miscellaneous catch all; such things as centralization or decentralization or hierarchical systems of leadership; joint (civil, political, military, religious) or separate roles.

Thought Questions—
In addition to the above categories, I try to synthesize the questions that I would like answered about leaders and leadership if I could get those answers. With these thought questions I am considering such things as the essence of a leader (being or doing), leadership itself, leadership selection and training, authority (centralized or decentralized), etc.

My preliminary findings for these categories for each leadership era follows.

1st Leadership Era: Patriarchal Leadership

1. **Major Focus**—Pass on the promise and heritage of the Most High God to the family; priestly role (regularity)—intercede, sacrifice, and worship the Most High God;
2. **Influence means**—apostolic style, father-initiator, father-guardian, full range of Wrong's typology: force, manipulation, authority (coercive, inducive, positional—fatherly head, competence, personal), spiritual authority
3. **Five basic leadership functions**—(1) Godly/ priestly functions:- demonstrate absolute loyalty to God; - demonstrate reality of the unseen God; - pass on heritage of what is known (revelatory) of God and His ways and desires, very little revelation, animistic; - pass on sense of destiny; —God's prophetic promises; (2) Primarily performing the inspirational function—largely through modeling; the relational function consisted primarily of keeping the family together and obedience to the patriarch. Inspirational function -Creating hope in God - Creating sense of God's intervention in life; (3) Mediate Blessing of God: - contagious blessing; - heritage blessing; (4) Military head—protection of family; (5) Civil—judge/ justice
4. **Followers**—family members: (1) Age/masculine-oriented; (2) Almost all of 10 Followership Laws in force; (3) Oldest to receive blessing and birthright; (4) The one receiving blessing and birthright passes it on to next generation
5. **Local Leadership**—in the culture around the Patriarchs: - tribal heads; - City States / Regional heads (called kings);
   - local priests (practitioners/ animistic); - local military
6. **Other:** Highly Decentralized; each given family responsible to God

Thought Questions—1. How did other families relate to God (Melchezidek's, Labin's, etc.)? 2. What were expectations of Patriarchs as leaders? by followers? by God? by surrounding culture? 3. What was the foundational aspect of character? What was integrity to the Patriarchs? 4. What was the birthright? What was the blessing? 5. If modeling was the primary training methodology, what were the most important positive leadership qualities modeled by Abraham? by Isaac? by Jacob? by Joseph? by Job? 6. Using a modified form of the six characteristics of finishing well, how did the Patriarchs finish? Abraham? Isaac? Jacob? Joseph? Job?

2nd Leadership Era: Pre-Kingdom Leadership

Six Biblical Leadership Eras—Overviewed

1. **Major Focus**—Uniting of a people, preparing them to follow God, preparing them to invade the promised land, settling them in the land. The Desert leadership is one of discipline, a heavy time of revelation, and supernatural events backing leadership. The Challenge Era is one of stretching of faith to overcome the many obstacles involved in capturing the land. The Judges Era has the major challenge of how to unite disparate peoples, survive attacks, and degeneration of relationship to God. In each there is Charismatic Leadership: You lead because of spiritual authority, personal authority or competence not because of nepotism or birth; a formal priestly role is secondary—there is an inheritance with this role—and this leadership is weak, probably because of that.
2. **Influence means**—apostolic style, father-initiator, father-guardian, full range of Wrong's typology: force, manipulation, authority (coercive, inducive, positional—fatherly head, competence, personal), spiritual authority
3. **7 basic leadership functions** seen include: (1) Centralize Authority/ Develop Authority Structures:- military, political, religious;- tribal/ trans-tribal (elders); (2) Primarily performing the inspirational function: -Creating hope in God; -Creating sense of God's intervention in life. (3) Revelatory (Desert)/Inscribe and pass on the basic revelation of God as given in the law/how to live separated lives; (4) Military head—protection/ mobilize an on-call army distributed over the tribes; (5) Civil—judge/ justice/ set up legal system for interpreting and applying the law; (6) Fulfill Promise of Taking the Land; settling it; (7) Call to renewal; recrudescence; see God work anew.
4. **Followers**—12 large tribes:(1) Age/ masculine-oriented leadership; (2) Almost all of 10 Followership Laws in force; centralization out of balance; leadership more nepotistic than functional; reciprocal commands a legalistic thing carried by enforcement of law.
5. **Local Leadership**—in the surrounding culture:- tribal heads; - City State / Regional heads (called kings); - local priests (practitioners/ animistic); - local military
6. **Other**: Highly centralized during desert and capturing of land; highly decentralized during Judges era/ continuity of leadership a major problem except for the first transition from Moses to Joshua

Thought Questions:
1. How were leaders selected and developed? 2. What did they do at the different levels? 3. What is missing from the Judges Era that was the driving force of the Warfare Era? 4. What has happened to the Abrahamic mandate? Which of the eras, if any, are concerned with that mandate? 5. How does this era compare with the Patriarchal, spiritually?

3rd Leadership Era: Kingdom Leadership

1. **Major Focus**—The Kingdom united the dispersed tribal groups into a more cohesive nation which could provide government and military protection. The Davidic covenant was part of an on-going means to bring about Abraham's promise and to manifest the concept of God's rule on earth as well as provide resources to bring others into relationship with God. It never lived up to its ideals.
2. **Influence means**—the full range of Wrong's typology : **force, manipulation, authority** (coercive, inducive, positional)—fatherly head; competence, personal, spiritual authority.
3. **6 basic leadership functions** seen include:(1) Centralize Authority/ Develop Authority Structures:- military, political, religious; - tribal/ trans-tribal (elders); (2) Revelatory (Particularly in the Divided Kingdom and the Single Kingdom)/ Much of the corrective revelation done by the prophets was oral. But there was also the Prophetic revelation which was inscribed. Often these writings were a call to repentance, renewal, and a return to kingdom ideals; (3) Military head—protection/ have a standing army that could defend against the attacks that were coming more frequently from the expanding empires or ambitious kings. They would also mobilize an on-call army distributed over the tribes to go along with the standing army in big crises. (4) Civil—judge/justice/set up legal system for interpreting and applying the law; (5) Call to renewal; recrudescence; see God work anew (prophetic function); (6) Persevere as a people of God; maintain a base from which God could work. Major Problems: communication and control; followership scattered over large area; -large empires on the rise
4. **Followers**—a. United Kingdom-12 large tribes, also the many surrounding small kingdoms that were conquered
b. Divided Kingdom—Northern-10 1/2 Large Tribes c. Southern—About 1 1/2 tribes—mostly Judah; Leadership (1) Age/ masculine oriented; (2) Almost all of 10 Followership Laws in force; centralization out of balance; leadership more nepotistic than functional;

Six Biblical Leadership Eras—Overviewed

5. Local Leadership—in the surrounding cultures: - tribal heads; - kings of territories with a number of cities; usually one dominated and was walled; - local priests (practitioners/ animistic); - military.

6. Other: Large Empires are vying for world dominion or at least for large influence: Assyria, Egypt, Babylon

Thought Questions: 1. Why were the prophets raised up? 2. According to Deuteronomy what was the place of the law for the Kings? Was it followed? 3. Was the central religious function (the three yearly treks) carried out? 4. Why was the nepotistic approach to leadership selection used? Was it successful? 5. How does this era compare spiritually with the Pre-Kingdom era?

4th Leadership Era: Post-Kingdom Leadership

1. Major Focus—The nation no longer exists. It has been disciplined by God. Leadership during this time must do several things: analyze what happened and why; bring hope during this time; demonstrate the importance of godliness under oppressive conditions; demonstrate the importance of God's sovereignty; point to the future in which God is going to work.

2. Influence means—largely by modeling, spiritual authority, toward latter time in the time of the return, Jewish leaders again take up roles: political, religious, quasi-military for the Jewish people.

3. Basic leadership functions seen include: The inspirational function is dominant. The need for community in little pockets brings out the need for the relational function of leadership. The rise of the synagogues—small communities upholding their Jewish origins and religion bring about the need for scribes, and those who interpret the written scriptures.

4. Followers—Pockets of scattered Jewish people

5. Local Leadership—in the surrounding cultures: - tribal heads; - City States / Regional heads (called kings); - local priests (practitioners/ animistic); - local military; - emperors/ kings/ heads of powerful international groups formed by conquering vast territories and kingdoms/ various administrative leaders under these

6. Other: ?

Thought Questions: 1. Why did Jewish leaders prosper during these oppressive days? 2. What kinds of leadership did they participate in? 3. What has happened to the Abrahamic promise? How did the Jewish people feel about it in these days? 4. How were religious leaders selected (e.g. for the synagogues)?

5th Leadership Era: Pre-Church Leadership

1. Major Focus—Galatians 4:4. This is the acme of charismatic leadership. Jesus models servant leadership and ideal spiritual authority—all aspects of it. The end result of this leadership is revelation, redemption, and a movement to universalize the redemption to all humankind.

2. Influence Means—the entire range of Pauline leadership styles are demonstrated. The whole range of Wrong's Typology is seen.

3. Leadership Functions: (1) Provide the redemptive base reconciling God and humankind and its major ramifications, the revelation and enabling power for human beings to realize their idealized human potential.
(2) Provide a leadership mandate that will utilize all three major leadership functions in its fulfillment. Task, relational, and inspirational functions are essential to the accomplishment of the mandate. (3) Create a movement that will institutionalize the leadership functions for on-going effective leadership. (4) Provide a call for renewal to Israel. (5) Present the Kingdom of God in concept and power. (6) Provide a revelatory base, model, and standards for future revelation.

4. Followers—In the land there were remnants of the tribes, mixed ethnic groups (like Samaritans), religious leadership like the Pharisees, Saducees, and the political leaders of the Roman empire along with garrisons of Roman Military to give authority as well as the Jewish Religious leaders the Sanhedrin.

5. Local Leaders: Sanhedrin, Saducees, Pharisees, Lawyers, Roman Military, Synagogues/ elders, Rabbis.

6. Other: This is a mixed era of centralized and decentralized means and authority. Jerusalem provided some means of religious centralization. There was political centralization in a number of centers. But Jesus leadership was not centralized.
Thought Questions: 1. What renewal aims did Christ specifically focus on? 2. What were the leadership selection and development processes in existence in the culture? 3. What were Jesus' leadership selection and development processes? How different? 4. How does Christ leadership compare or contrast with essential characteristics of each of the previous eras?

6th Leadership Era: Church Leadership

1. Major Focus—When Barnabas and Paul give their report to the elders back in Jerusalem at the Jerusalem conference described in Acts 15, there is much discussion. Finally, James summarizes the essence of the major focus of the Church leadership era, "Simon has declared how God at the first did visit the Gentiles, to take out of them a people for his name (Acts 15;14)." The central message of the book of Acts emphasizes this thrust in more detail. THE GROWTH OF THE CHURCH which spreads from Jerusalem to Judea to Samaria and the uttermost parts of the earth is seen to be of God, takes place as Spirit directed people present a salvation centered in Jesus Christ, and occurs among all peoples, Jews and Gentiles. During this leadership era, God is developing an institution that will carry His salvation to all cultures and all peoples. The development of this decentralized institution which can be fitted to any culture and people, the church, with its nature its leadership and its purposes for existing will be at the heart of this leadership era. Paul is a major architect of this leadership era. The book of 2 Corinthians is especially helpful to give us insights into early church leadership.

2. Influence Means—My past leadership studies have identified a number of leadership styles. In particular, I have categorized ten Pauline leadership styles. The entire range of Pauline leadership styles are demonstrated during the Church Leadership Era. The whole range of Wrong's Typology is seen including force, manipulation, authority, and persuasion power forms.

3. Leadership Functions—All three of the generic leadership functions are prominent: task oriented leadership, relationship oriented leadership and inspirational leadership. The major models for this era include Peter, John, and Paul with much more information given about Paul. Paul is dominantly a task-oriented leader with a powerful inspirational focus. He sees the necessity of relationship oriented leadership but that is not his strength. John is more of a relationship-oriented leader who also has a powerful inspirational thrust. Peter is dominantly a task oriented leader with inspirational thrust. As each matures they become more gentle—that is, relational leadership begins to come to the front. But always they are dominantly inspirational. God is creating new forms through which to reveal Himself to the world and followers must be inspired to participate and carry it all over the world in the face of persecution and obstacles.

4. Followers—The beauty of the church lies in its ability as an institutional form to fit into any culture. Since leadership in a given culture is defined in part by the followers expectations of what a leader is, we will have distinctive differences in various cultures as to leadership and followership. Each cultural situation will be different and hence have its unique demands. But there are commonalties in Biblical church leadership across cultures. This is seen especially in the values which determine why leaders operate and the standards by which they are judged. The book of 2 Corinthians helps us understand key leadership values.

5. Local Leaders—Various kinds of models of leadership existed in the various cultures. Paul, the main architect of local church leadership, gives us various descriptions of qualitative characteristics of leaders in his various epistles. The essential trait that flows throughout all of them is integrity. But Paul having described key character traits recognizes that these will manifest themselves differently in different cultures and situations.

6. Other—The church leadership era is a highly decentralized period of time. Churches are to exist in all cultures and peoples. They will be spread far and wide. Because of the decentralized nature of the church it is especially important to ask what unites it? What is common? Particularly is this important for leadership. And one of the answers is leadership values. 2 Corinthians helps us see some of the values that Paul modeled.

Six Biblical Leadership Eras—Overviewed

The Findings—The Best of Each Era

Table 35.4 summarizes the more important aspects of each of the leadership eras.

Table 35.4 Six Leadership Eras in the Bible—On-Going Impact Items/ Follow-Up Study

Era	On-Going Impact Items And Areas For Follow-Up Study
1. Patri-archal	Destiny leadership; Introduction of biographical study of leadership (Abraham, Isaac, Jacob, Joseph, Job); God's shaping processes introduced; intercession macro lesson introduced; character strength highlighted (Abraham, Jacob, Joseph); leadership responsibility to God instigated (accountability); leadership responsibility to followers introduced (blessing); leadership intimacy with God introduced (Abraham—friend of God, Job—trusting in deep processing). **Key Macro Lesson**: Destiny—Leaders must have a sense of destiny.
2. Pre-Kingdom	Seven Macro lessons from Moses' desert leadership (Timing; Intimacy; Intercession; Burden; Presence; Hope; Transition); Spiritual authority highlighted in Moses' and Joshua's ministries; pitfalls of centralized leadership seen; pitfalls of decentralized leadership seen; roots of inspirational leadership seen (Moses, Joshua, Caleb, Deborah, Jephthah, Samuel, David); outstanding biographical genre material. **Key Macro Lesson**: Presence—The essential ingredient of leadership is the powerful presence of God in the leader's life and ministry.
3. Kingdom	Five macros carry a warning for all future leadership (Unity; Stability; Spiritual Leadership; Recrudescence; By-Pass). Excellent biographical material both positive and negative examples (Saul, David, Asa, Josiah, Uzziah, Hezekiah, Elijah, Elisha, Jonah, Habakkuk, Ezekiel, Jeremiah and many others). **Key Macro Lesson**: Spiritual leadership can make a difference in the midst of difficult times.
4. Post-Kingdom	All five macros stress revelational perspective (Future Perfect; Perspective; Modeling; Ultimate, Perseverance). Excellent biographical genre available (Ezekiel, Daniel, Ezra, Nehemiah). **Key Macro Lesson**: Future Perfect—A primary function of all leadership is to walk by faith with a future perfect paradigm so as to inspire followers with certainty of God's accomplishment of ultimate purposes.
5. Pre-Church	Selection/ Training/ spiritual leadership/ preparation for decentralization of Spiritual Authority/ initiation of a movement. Major Biographical— Jesus' and his movement leadership. **Key Macro Lesson**: Focus—Leaders must increasingly move toward a focus in their ministry which moves toward fulfillment of their calling and their ultimate contribution to God's purposes for them.
6. Church	Decentralized leadership/ cross-cultural structures led by leaders with spiritual authority, which institutionalize the movement and spread it around the world. Excellent biographical (Peter, Barnabas—a bridge leader, Paul, John); numerous leadership acts. **Key Macro Lesson**: Universal—The church structure is universal and can fit any culture. It must be propagated to all peoples.

Six Biblical Leadership Eras—Overviewed page 174

The Foundational Transitions—Moses' And Jesus' Leadership Eras

Three figures give perspectives on Biblical leadership. Figure 34.1 illustrates the relative time involved in the six leadership eras. Figure 34.2 pinpoints distinctive features of leadership across the time-line. Figure 34.3 focuses on the two major transitions—Moses' Desert Leadership; Jesus' Movement Leadership.

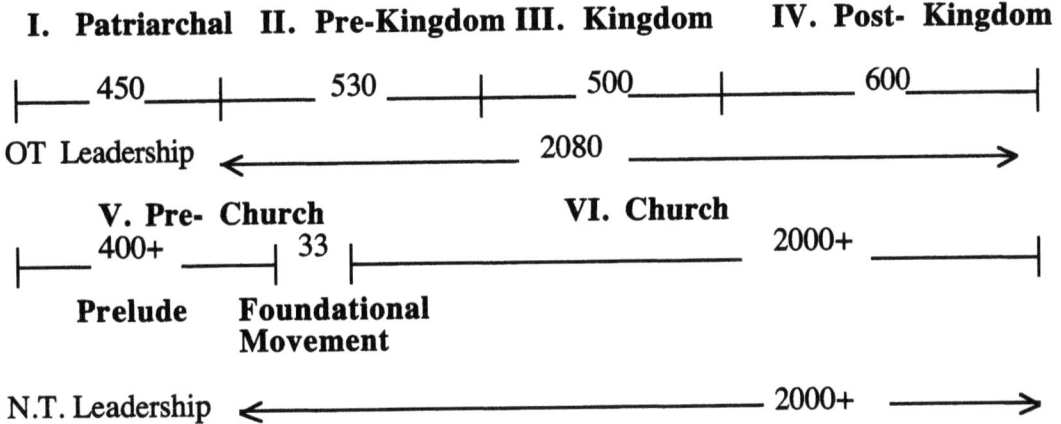

Figure 35.1 Leadership Eras—Approximate Chronological Length In Years

I. Patriarchal Leadership Roots	II. Pre-Kingdom Leadership	III. Kingdom Leadership	IV. Post-Kingdom	V. N.T. Pre-Church Leadership	VI. Church Leadership
A. Abraham B. Isaac C. Jacob D. Joseph E. Job	A. Desert B. Conquering The Land C. Conquered By the Land	A. United B. Divided C. Single	A. Exile B. Post Exile C. Interim	A. Pre-Messianic B. Messianic	A. Jewish B. Gentile
Family	Revelatory Task Inspirational	Political Corrective	Modeling Renewal	Cultic Spiritual Movement	Spiritual Institutional
Blessing Shaping Timing Destiny Character Faith Purity	(Timing) Presence Intimacy Burden Hope Challenge Spiritual Authority Transition Weakness Continuity	Unity Stability Spiritual Leadership Recrudescence By-Pass	Hope Perspective Modeling Ultimate Perseverance	Training Focus Spirituality Servant Steward Shepherd Movement	Structure Universal Giftedness Word Centered Harvest

Figure 35.2 Overview Time-Line of Biblical Leadership

Six Biblical Leadership Eras—Overviewed   page 175

In Figure 35.2 above, macro lesson labels occur at the bottom in the six columns. Just above the macro lesson labels are given distinctive characteristics of each of the eras. Finally, above that occurs the outline of the sub-time periods and the major time-line with the six eras.

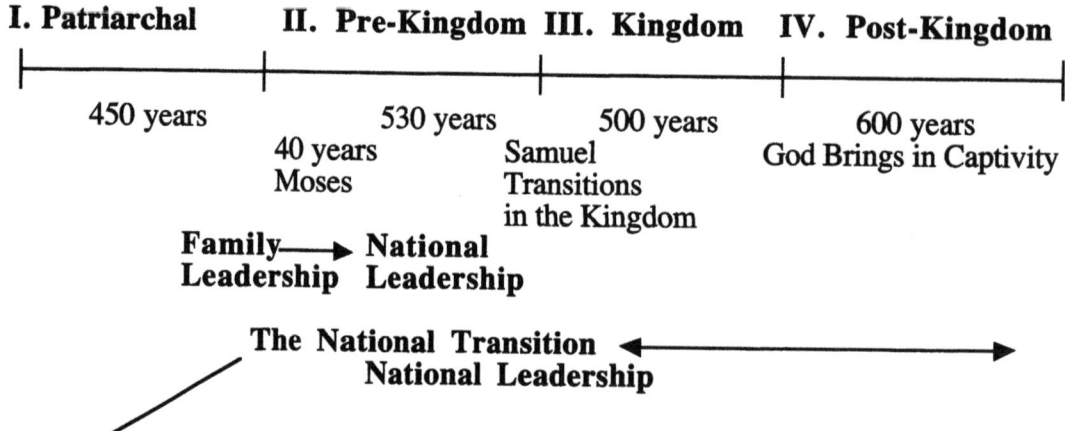

Crucial Macro Lessons: 3. Timing, 8. Intercession, 9. Presence, 10. Intimacy, 11. Burden, 12. Hope, 13. Challenge, 14. Spiritual Authority, 15. Transition.

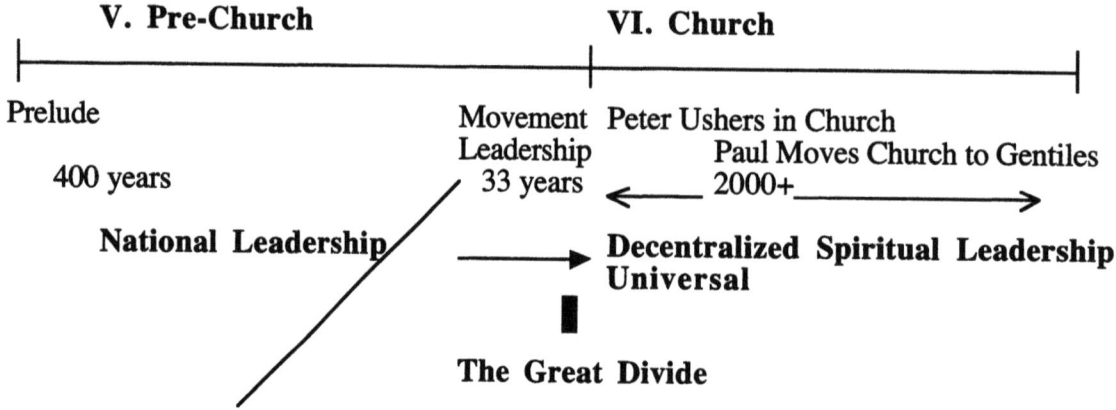

Crucial Macro Lessons: 28. Selection, 29. Training, 30. Focus, 31. Spirituality, 32. Servant, 33. Steward, 34. Harvest, 35. Shepherd, 36. Movement.

Figure 35.3 Two Major Transitions—The National Transition and The Great Divide

Note two things. These major transition times were short. God brought in major changes in a short period of time. Both transition times contain a large number of important macro lessons. For such short periods of time these are relatively large numbers of important leadership lessons.

Table 35.5 lists the transitions and key figures and the result of the transition.

Six Biblical Leadership Eras—Overviewed

Table 35.5 Transitions Along the Biblical Leadership Time-Line

Transition	Eras Involved	Key Figure/ Results
To God Directed Leadership	Begin Patriarchal Era	Abraham/ a God directed destiny involving an ethnic group and leaders from that group hearing God, getting revelation from Him, and obeying God.
Tribal to National	From the Patriarchal Era to the Pre-Kingdom Era	Moses/ A nation is established. God established concept of influential leader with spiritual authority to direct the nation; God reveals truth about Himself, life, and destiny for this nation. Major leadership guidelines (important macro lessons) flow through this transitional leadership.
Federation to Kingdom	Pre-Kingdom to Kingdom	Samuel/ A dispersed geographical/tribal society, each doing its own thing and basically not following God-given truth, is moved toward a centralized, unified national entity directed by one major leader—a king, who is to direct the nation with God's direction.
Babylonian Captivity	From Kingdom to Post-Kingdom	God/ God dismantles the kingdom structure. He disperses the followers. God by-passes the kingdom leadership altogether and begins a long preparation that will eventually emerge in spiritual leadership. In this era, individual spiritual leadership is highlighted in which God's perspective is crucial.
The Great Divide	From Post-Kingdom to Pre-Church. From a defunct national leadership to spiritual leadership which can be decentralized anywhere.	Jesus/ Jesus re-established God-directed leadership—the concept of the Kingdom of God. God by-passes the Jewish national leadership when they reject Him—i.e. His message through Jesus. Jesus at the same time of offering the kingdom also builds the foundational roots of a movement which will eventually contextualize the Kingdom of God in an institutional church form which can move into any culture on earth.
Universal Invitation	From Pre-Church to Church	Peter, Paul/ Peter ushers in the church to the Jewish followers of Jesus. Paul takes the church to the Gentiles. God's invitation of salvation and His truth for living God-directed lives become available (decentralized) to any people on the earth.

Note that that there are transition times between all the eras. Each of these are important in themselves but two stand out: Moses' Desert-Leadership; Jesus' Movement-Leadership. As is sometimes the case crucial transitions in the Bible are foundational. God focuses intently in these times and usually reveals foundational truth. Such is the case with all the transitions.

Tables 35.6 and 35.7 give the macro lessons discovered in these key transition times with suggested implications for today.

Table 35.6 Moses' Transition/ Lessons/ Implications

Timing— God's timing is crucial to accomplishment of God's purposes. **Implication**(s): Leaders today, especially in their complex ministries involving multi-cultural settings, must be more sensitive to the timing of God than ever before.
Intercession— Leaders called to a ministry are called to intercede for that ministry. **Implication**(s): Various prayer movements have gained tremendous momentum in our day testifying to the fact that God sees this as a very important aspect of leadership in our day.
Presence— The essential ingredient of leadership is the powerful presence of God in the leader's life and ministry. **Implication**(s): Much present day leadership misses the balance of this—God both in powerful ministry and in powerful life changing impact in the leader himself/herself.

Intimacy— Leaders develop intimacy with God which in turn overflows into all their ministry since ministry flows out of being. **Implication**(s): Doing and achievement dominate present day leadership. God through the various spirituality movements is calling leaders back to spirituality and beingness as the core of their ministries.
Burden— Leaders feel a responsibility to God for their ministry. **Implication**(s): Accountability is missing altogether in most cultures. This is true of Christian leadership as well. Sensitivity to this needed ingredient would avoid many of the leadership gaffes that are seen.
Hope— A primary function of all leadership is to inspire followers with hope in God and in what God is doing. **Implication**(s): This is especially true for leaders trying to reach Xers—generally without hope. But it is needed in all ministries as complex situations tend to take away hope for most Christians.
Challenge— Leaders receive vision from God which sets before them challenges that inspire their leadership. **Implication**(s): A leader must hear from God if that leader is to influence specific groups of people toward God's purposes—the basic definition of a leader. This is deeply needed especially in the many small churches which are floundering in our day.
Spiritual Authority—Spiritual authority is the dominant power base of a spiritual leader and comes through experiences with God, knowledge of God, godly character and gifted power. **Implication**(s): Abuse of power is one of the five major barriers facing leaders today. There are lots of leaders with all kinds of authority but few who exercise spiritual authority as a primary power base (with all its implications).
Transition—Leaders must transition other leaders into their work in order to maintain continuity and effectiveness. **Implication**(s): Every work of God is just one generation away from failure if it does not transition emerging leaders into its decision-making influential positions.

Table 35.7 Jesus' Transition/ Lessons/ Implications

Selection— The key to good leadership is the selection of good potential leaders which should be a priority of all leaders. **Implication**(s): Leadership selection is desperately needed in church and parachurch organizations. Recruitment is often haphazard at best, especially in local church situations.
Training—Leaders should deliberately train potential leaders in their ministry by available and appropriate means. **Implication**(s): If emerging new leaders are not developed they will exit organizations and go somewhere else, depriving churches and parachurch organizations of on-going leadership. Leading with a developmental bias is the key to seeing on-going recruitment and longevity in organizational life.
Focus— Leaders should increasingly move toward a focus in their ministry which moves toward fulfillment of their calling and their ultimate contribution to God's purposes for them. **Implication**(s): Focused leaders are few and far between. Most leaders are faddish leaders jumping on the bandwagon of other apparently successful leaders. What is needed is leaders, knowing their own focus, and following it. Focused leaders are the need of the hour.
Spirituality— Leaders must develop interiority, spirit sensitivity, and fruitfulness in accord with their uniqueness since ministry flows out of being. **Implication**(s): As previously seen with the intimacy lesson from Moses' era, spirituality is crucial to leadership. And what is true of intimacy, one aspect of spirituality, is true as leaders develop balanced spirituality. Doing and achievement dominate present day leadership. God through the various spirituality movements is calling leaders back to spirituality and beingness as the core of their ministries.
Servant— Leaders must maintain a dynamic tension as they lead by serving and serve by leading. **Implication**(s): Servant leadership is not naturally found in any culture. It requires a paradigm shift for any leader to move into this leadership model—which is what Jesus intended for leaders he developed. Because of accepted leadership patterns in some cultures (great power distance) this is really difficult for emerging leaders to see or accept.
Steward— Leaders are endowed by God with natural abilities, acquired skills, spiritual gifts, opportunities, experiences, and privileges which must be developed and used for God. **Implication**(s): Accountability is greatly needed in our generation where successful leaders dominantly self-authenticate their own ministries and heed little or nothing from outside resources which could hold them accountable.

Six Biblical Leadership Eras—Overviewed

Harvest— Leaders must seek to bring people into relationship with God. **Implication**(s): The outward aspect of the Great Commission must be carried out. God is focusing on this as He continues to raise up missionary movements from all over the world. The impetus of the missionary movement has already moved from the western world to the non-western world. We need to support this while at the same time bringing about renewal of missionary thinking in the western world.
Shepherd— Leaders must preserve, protect, and develop God's people. **Implication**(s): God still gets most of the leadership business done at local church level. Leaders who hold to the shepherd model concepts must in fact carry local church ministries—especially as cultures become more radically opposed to Gospel values. This means that more pastoral work will be necessary if we are winning those from deteriorating cultures.
Movement— Leaders recognize that movements are the way to penetrate society though they must be preserved via appropriate on-going institutions. **Implication**(s): New life can be instilled in parachurch organizations and churches when movement ideals are focused on. We see all around us movement leaders being raised up by God who are creating new ministries which God is blessing. This can be done more deliberately and proactively when movement dynamics are heeded.

Conclusion

The Six Leadership Eras and the seven leadership genre provide major perspectives for studying leadership in the Bible. This **Handbook** presents eight Bible books and applies these perspectives. Of particular importance are two of the leadership genre—the *macro lessons* across each leadership era and the Bible *books as a whole*. The macro lessons flowing from Moses' desert leadership and Jesus' movement foundations are particularly instructive. They apply with great force to today's leadership challenges.

See **Articles**, *Biographical Study in the Bible—How To Do; Bible Centered Leader; Leadership Act; Leadership Eras in the Bible—Six Identified; Leadership Genre—Seven Types; Macro Lessons Defined; Macro Lessons—List of 41 Across Six Leadership Eras; Principle of Truth.*

Article 36

Spiritual Authority Defined: Six Characteristics

Introduction

A Biblical leader is a person with God-given capacities and with God-given responsibility who is influencing specific groups of God's people toward God's purposes for them. To influence, a leader must have some power base. I am indebted to Dennis Wrong[67] for helping me identify a taxonomy of concepts dealing with power. Wrong has influence as the highest level on his taxonomy, power next, and authority third. Influence can be unintended or intended. In terms of leadership we are interested in intended influence. Intended influence can be subdivided into four power forms, the second level: Force, Manipulation, Authority, and Persuasion. All of these are important for Christian leaders with the final two being the most important—authority and persuasion—since spiritual authority is related to both. Authority, the third level, can further be sub-divided into coercive, inducive, legitimate, competent, personal. A leader will need to use various combinations of these power forms to influence people. However,

> **Effective leaders value spiritual authority as a primary power base.**

This is one of seven major leadership lessons that I have identified from comparative study of effective leaders. This article defines spiritual authority and gives some guidelines about its use.

Spiritual Authority—What Is It?

Spiritual authority is the ideal power base for a leader to use with mature believers who respect God's authority in a leader. A simplified definition focusing on the notion of maturity of believers is:

Definition   *Extrinsic Spiritual authority* (ESA) is the
- right to influence,
- conferred upon a leader by followers,
- because of their perception of spirituality in that leader.

An expanded definition focusing on how a leader gets and uses it is:

---

[67] See Dennis H. Wrong, **Power—Its Forms, Bases, and Uses**. 1979. San Francisco, CA: Harper and Row.

Spiritual Authority Defined

Definition *Intrinsic Spiritual Authority* is that
- characteristic of a God-anointed leader,
- developed upon an experiential power base (giftedness, character, deep experiences with God),

that enables him/her to influence followers through
- persuasion,
- force of modeling, and
- moral expertise.

Spiritual authority comes to a leader in three major ways. As leaders go through deep experiences with God they experience the sufficiency of God to meet them in those situations. They come to know God. This experiential knowledge of God and the deep experiences with God are part of the experiential acquisition of spiritual authority. A second way that spiritual authority comes is through a life which models godliness. When the Spirit of God is transforming a life into the image of Christ those characteristics of love, joy, peace, long suffering, gentleness, goodness, faith, meekness, temperance carry great weight in giving credibility that the leader is consistent inward and outward. A third way that spiritual authority comes is through gifted power. When a leader can demonstrate gifted power in ministry—that is, a clear testimony to divine intervention in the ministry via his/her gifts—there will be spiritual authority. Now while all three of these ways of getting spiritual authority should be a part of a leader, it is frequently the case that one or more of the elements dominates. From the definitions and description of how spiritual authority comes you can readily see that a leader using spiritual authority does not force his/her will on followers.

What Are Some Guidelines—To Maximize Use and Minimize Abuse

The following descriptive characteristics about spiritual authority sets some limits, describe ideals, warn against abuse and in general gives helpful guidelines for leaders who desire spiritual authority as a primary means of influence.

Six Characteristics And Limits Of Spiritual Authority

These six descriptions were derived from my own observations of leaders and from adaptations made from several writers on power such as Watchman Nee, R. Baine Harris, and Richard T. De George. Nee was a Chinese Christian leader. The other two are secular authorities on power and authority in leadership.

Table 36.1 Six Characteristics of Spiritual Authority

Character-istic	Statement
1. Ultimate Source	Spiritual authority has its ultimate source in Christ. It is representative religious authority. It is His authority and presence in us which legitimates our authority. Accountability to this final authority is essential.
2. Power Base	Spiritual authority rests upon an experiential power base. A leader's personal experiences with God and the accumulated wisdom and development that comes through them lie at the heart of the reason why followers allow influence in their lives. It is a resource which is at once on-going and yet related to the past. Its genuineness as to the reality of experience with God is confirmed in the believer by the presence and ministry of the Holy Spirit who authenticates that experiential power base.
3. Power Forms	Spiritual authority influences by virtue of persuasion. Word gifts are dominant in this persuasion. Influence is by virtue of legitimate authority. Positional leadership carries with it recognition of qualities of leadership

Spiritual Authority Defined

	which are at least initially recognized by followers. Such authority must be buttressed by other authority forms such as competent authority, and personal authority.
4. Ultimate Good	The aim of influence using spiritual authority is the ultimate good of the followers. This follows the basic Pauline leadership principle seen in 2Co 10:8.
5. Evaluation	Spiritual authority is best judged longitudinally over time in terms of development of maturity in believers. Use of coercive and manipulative forms of authority will usually reproduce like elements in followers. Spiritual authority will produce mature followers who will make responsible moral choices because they have learned to do so.
6. Non-Defensive	A leader using spiritual authority recognizes submission to God who is the ultimate authority. Authority is representative. God is therefore the responsible agent for defending spiritual authority. A person moving in spiritual authority does not have to insist on obedience. Obedience is the moral responsibility of the follower. Disobedience, that is, rebellion to spiritual authority, means that a follower is not subject to God Himself. He/she will answer to God for that. The leader can rest upon God's vindication if it is necessary.

Remember,

Effective leaders value spiritual authority as a primary power base.[68]

See power forms (various definitions), **Glossary**. See **Articles**, *Influence, Power, and Authority Forms; Leadership Lessons—Seven MajorIdentified*.

---

[68] They also know that it will take varied forms of power including coercive, inducive, positional, personal, competence and others to influence immature believers toward maturity. But the ideal is always there to use spiritual authority with mature believers.

Article 37

Spiritual Warfare—Two Extremes To Avoid

Introduction

Did Paul ever engage in spiritual warfare? Oh, yes! But when you read his epistles there is very little up front information, i.e. direct teaching, on doing spiritual warfare. There is Eph 6:10-17 and Col 2:13-15. But for the most part, spiritual warfare is incidental and remarks about it are asides simply woven into the fabric of a letter.[69] In my opinion, you can draw implications from them but not solid models that can be passed on authoritatively as to how to do spiritual warfare. And herein lies a model—two basics—that can help us approach spiritual warfare.

Two Extremes To Avoid

From a comparative study of all of Paul's epistles looking for spiritual warfare information I have drawn the following implications for leaders.

1. Spiritual warfare exists.
2. The spirit world is real and impinges on our world.
3. Leaders should be aware of spiritual warfare and their strengths[70] and limitations about it.
4. Paul is a model for how leaders ought to approach spiritual warfare in their ministries.

Paul deals with many problematic situations and people in ministry. Occasionally he will assert something about spiritual warfare as being involved in a problem or as the source of some person's situation. But for the most part Paul avoids two extremes:

Extreme 1. Overemphasis on Spiritual Warfare
Paul does not assign blame for everything that happens on spirit beings, demons, and spiritual warfare.

He sees the human side of things as being heavily involved in many of the problems.

---

[69] For example if you trace spiritual warfare content through 1,2Ti you will see only several asides: 1Ti 1:18-20; 3:6,7; 4:1; 2Ti 1:6. You will see little or none in most of Paul's epistles. The omissions speak loudly.
[70] See especially the **Article**, *Spiritual Warfare—Two Foundational Axioms*.

Extreme 2. Under Emphasis on Spiritual Warfare
   Paul does recognize that some problems and issues have at their heart spiritual warfare. Demonic influence must be countered.

Yes, there is spiritual warfare and it must be discerned and dealt with. But, no, not everything is spiritual warfare. Paul has a healthy balance.

Conclusion

In most of the evangelical world I have dealt with (Bible teaching ministries), **Extreme 2** is the norm. And most of those ministries do not discern or deal with spiritual warfare, even when most needed in their people or situations.

In the charismatic or pentecostal circles I deal with, **Extreme 1** is the norm.

When **Extreme 2** is the norm—great needs go unmet. When **Extreme 1** is the norm, abuse of power can abound. Frequently such a leader involved will fall by the wayside (many due to overpowering from the demonic world; many due to the power and pride barriers.)

Balance! How much we need it as leaders. Consistency in maintaining a middle ground and heeding both these dynamic extremes at the same time is needed. And Shakespeare said it well, "Consistency, thou art a jewel!"

See **Article**, *Finishing Well—Six Major Barriers*.

Article 38

Spiritual Warfare—Two Foundational Axioms

Introduction

Spiritual warfare is real. All leaders engage in it, knowingly or not. Spiritual warfare was introduced in the book of Da.[71] There we learned some initial truth about spiritual warfare.

1. The unseen spirit world is real and does affect a leader's world.
2. Leaders seemingly unanswered prayers may be delayed because of spiritual warfare in the unseen spirit world.
3. Leaders can know that God does protect them with supernatural beings.
4. Some renewal experiences can be via supernatural beings who will affirm, encourage, give physical strength and reveal God's working to leaders.
5. Progressive revelation[72] is needed before spiritual warfare in the heavenlies and our participation in it can be understood. That is, Daniel does not give the full picture or information about human leaders intervening in spiritual warfare.

Definition   Spiritual warfare refers to the unseen opposition in the spirit world made up of Satan and his demons and their attempts to defeat God's forces, angelic beings, and God's people, today called believers. It also involves the response by believers to these attempts.

This article identifies two fundamental axioms concerning spiritual warfare which are part of the progressive revelation given in the N.T. An axiom refers to a maxim widely accepted on its intrinsic merit. It is a statement accepted as true as the basis for argument or inference. It is an established rule or principle or a self-evident truth. To engage in spiritual warfare without these fundamental axioms is to invite defeat. To engage in spiritual warfare

---

[71] I refer to the commentary on Daniel. In the Bible spiritual warfare is introduced in Gen 3 with Satan's influence over Adam and Eve. It is explained further in Job which points out how the unseen spiritual world can influence the seen world. There are occasional allusions to it in other books (see 2 Kings 6:8-23; Note especially vs 16). Spiritual forces on God's side are mentioned throughout the Bible (Angels). And Da gives more information on spiritual warfare.

[72] Progressive revelation is a concept noted in the O.T. and N.T. that God is a God who continues to communicate and over time clarifies earlier revelation, expanding on it, filling in more details, helping later leaders see the relevance of it, etc. See especially prophetic ministry. Example: Daniel's prophecies in ch 2, 7, 8, 9, 10-12. There is progress in both content and methodology as observed in various genre in Old and New Testaments. See Job for further references to spirit world intervention in human affairs. See also Eph 6:10ff for basic teaching on spiritual warfare, particularly what human leaders can do. See also Jn 16:11 and Col 2:15 for the strategic basis of spiritual warfare.

Spiritual Warfare—Two Foundational Axioms

with these fundamental axioms lays the foundation for victory over those unseen spiritual forces representing Satan.

Axiom 1. Strategic Warfare

Jesus makes an unusual statement in Jn 16:11 as he looks forward to the Cross.

> 11 Judgment is certain, because the ruler of this world is judged."[73] Jn 16:11

Removing the figurative language and expressing the meaning in a powerful statement we have the foundation for Axiom 1 on Strategic Warfare.

> 11 **At the Cross I will defeat Satan and his forces; this judgment on them is sure. Jn 16:11**

This aside on spiritual warfare concerns an aspect of the Cross not usually stressed. Besides dealing with sins, sin and righteousness, the Cross also was a strategic victory over Satanic forces. This is the single most important truth for leader's using power ministry in spiritual warfare.

Paul gives the basic teaching on this foundational axiom in Col 2:13-15.

> 13 And you, Gentiles, were dead in your sins. God gave you life through Jesus' death, having forgiven you all your wrongdoings; 14 All our failures to meet the law's demands were taken care of at the Cross. 15 At the same time He openly triumphed over those spirit beings which powerfully oppose God. They are defeated. Col 2:13-15

Axiom 1. Strategically, Jesus Has Already Defeated All Spiritual Forces Opposed To God. The War Was Won At The Cross. It Only Remains That This Strategic Victory Be Appropriated And Won Tactically.

This is fundamental to any believer's spiritual warfare. It is a truth that must be believed and acted upon.

Axiom 2. Tactical Warfare

Though the Commander-in-Chief has declared the overall war won there are still battles going on all around us. It doesn't always appear won. A defeated army can still inflict many casualties. So it is in spiritual warfare. Satan has not acknowledged defeat and still fights on. A fundamental axiom basic to this continued warfare is introduced by John.

> 1 Beloved, believe not every spirit, but try the spirits whether they are of God. Because many false prophets are gone out into the world. 2 But here is how you can know the source is by the Spirit of God: Every spirit that affirms that Jesus Christ is come in human form is of God: 3 And every spirit that does not affirm that Jesus Christ came in human form is not from God. Such a source is a spirit against Christ and already is in the world. 4 You are of God, little children, and have overcome these spiritual forces,

---

[73] This is a certainty idiom, the *prophetic past*. A future event is spoken of as if it had already happened (the **TEV** and **NLT** translate—*has already been judged*) because it is so certain, in this case the Cross and one result of it. *Captured: At the Cross I will defeat Satan and his forces; this judgment on them is sure.* See *capture*, *certainty idiom*, **Glossary**. See **Article**, *Figures and Idioms in the Bible*.

> **because greater is he that is in you, than he that is in the world.**

In a context dealing with spiritual warfare (trying the spirits) John gives the encouraging statement which enables tactical victory.

Axiom 2. A believer has within himself/herself, the Spirit of God which is much more powerful than Satanic forces.

Conclusion

Victory is certain, it was potentially won at the Cross. It will be won totally in history. In the meantime, a believer has the indwelling Holy Spirit who will enable victory in everyday skirmishes over spirit forces. Count on these axioms.

See **Articles**, *Spiritual Warfare—Satan's Tactics; Spiritual Warfare—Two Extremes to Avoid; Daniel—Supernatural Beings and Spiritual Warfare.*

Haggai

CLINTON'S BIBLICAL LEADERSHIP COMMENTARY SERIES

Restoring A Work of God
Inspirational, Task-Oriented Leadership

Glossary and Bibliography

Glossary—Leadership Definitions

The following leadership related definitions occur throughout the **Haggai Leadership Commentary**. They are listed here alphabetically for convenience in referencing. SRN stands for Strong's Reference Number. These numbers can be used to look up the definitions of these words in the **Strong's Exhaustive Concordance** containing Hebrew and Greek dictionaries. These numbers are now also used by many other Bible study aids.

Item	Definition
Absolutes	*Absolutes* refer to replicated truth in leadership situations across cultures without restrictions. Failure to follow or use will normally result in some stirrings of conscience.
Affect	a learning domain, that is, a term describing learning which primarily moves the feelings and emotions.
Bible Centered Leader	a leader (1) whose leadership is being informed by the Bible and (2) who personally has been shaped by Biblical values, (3) who has grasped the intent of Scriptural books and their content in such a way as to apply them to current situations and (4) who uses the Bible in ministry so as to impact followers.
Capture	a technical term used when talking about figures of speech being interpreted. A figure or idiom is said to be captured when one can display the intended emphatic meaning of it in non-figurative simple words. e.g. not ashamed of the Gospel = captured: completely confident of the Gospel.
Certainty Continuum	a horizontal line moving from suggestions on one extreme to requirements on the other extreme which attempts to provide a grid for locating a given statement of truth in terms of its potential use with others and the degree of authority with which it can be asserted.
Civil Leadership	refers to followers of God, sold out on following God, yet impacting the society in which they exercise two types of roles often needed in society—1. Governmental or political roles sanctioned by the society and 2. Military roles sanctioned by the society.
Cognitive	a learning domain, that is, a term describing learning which primarily focuses on the transmittal and understanding of knowledge and ideas.
Destiny Pattern	a leadership pattern. The development of a sense of destiny usually follows a three fold pattern of destiny preparation, destiny revelation, and destiny fulfillment. That is, over a period of time God shapes a leader with experiences which prepare, reveal, and finally brings about completion of destiny.
Destiny Processing	refers to the shaping activities of God in which a leader becomes increasingly aware of God's Hand on his/her life and the purposes for which God has intended for his/her leadership. This processing causes a sense of partnership with God toward God's purposes for the life and hence brings meaning to the life.

Glossary of Leadership Definitions

Divine Affirmation	a concept from leadership emergence theory. The shaping activity of God whereby God makes known to a leader his approval of that leader. This is a major motivating factor to keep one serving the Lord.
Divine Contact	from leadership emergence theory. One of 51 process items that God uses to shape a leader. A <u>divine contact</u> is a person whom God brings in contact with a leader at a crucial moment in a development phase in order to accomplish one or more of the following to: affirm leadership potential, encourage leadership potential, give guidance on a special issue, give insights which may indirectly lead to guidance, challenge the leader Godward, open a door to a ministry opportunity, other insights helping the emerging leader to make guidance decisions.
Double Confirmation	from leadership emergence theory. One of 51 process items that God uses to shape a leader. <u>Double confirmation</u> refers to the unusual guidance in which God makes clear His will by giving the guidance directly to a leader and then reinforcing it by some other person totally independent and unaware of the leader's guidance.
Figure	the unusual use of a word or words differing from the normal use in order to draw special attention to some point of interest. The more important figures (100s used in Bible) include: metaphor, simile, metonymy, synecdoche, hyperbole, irony, personification, apostrophe, negative emphatics (litotes and tapenosis), rhetorical question. See individual definitions for each of these. See **For Further Study Bibliography, Figures and Idioms** by Dr. J. Robert Clinton.
Flesh Act	from leadership emergence theory. One of 51 process items that God uses to shape a leader. A <u>flesh act</u> refers to those instances in a leader's life where guidance is presumed and decisions are made either hastily or without proper discernment of God's choice. Such decisions usually involve the working out of guidance by the leader using some human manipulation or other means and which brings ramifications which later negatively affect ministry and life. See Genesis 16 for an example in Abraham's life. See Joshua's treaty with Gibeonites in Jos 9. See Isa 39:4 for Hezekiah's action with Babylonian envoys.
Guidelines,	a term used to define a position on the Certainty Continuum. *Guidelines* are truths that are replicated in most leadership situations and should only be rejected for good reasons though there will be no loss of conscience.
Idiom	the use of words to imply something other than their literal meanings. People in the culture know the idiomatic meaning of the words. Example: *I smell a rat*. Some idioms are patterned in which case you can reverse the pattern to get the meaning. Others must simply be learned in the culture from contextual usage of them.
Inspirational Leadership	a description of one of three major high level generic leadership functions that a leader of an organization is responsible for producing. It describes the motivational force for developing the relational base and for achieving the task. The ability to get and motivate toward vision, the ability to see God's presence in a work, and to believe and challenge toward hope—God's future

Glossary of Leadership Definitions

working in the organization—are all part of inspirational leadership. Whereas some leaders are by personality either task-oriented or relationally-oriented in their leadership, inspirational leadership appears both in task and relationally oriented leaders. All three functions are necessary for healthy ministry. Haggai's ministry was dominantly task and inspirational leadership.

Integrity — the top leadership character quality. It is the consistency of inward beliefs and convictions with outward practice. It is an honesty and wholeness of personality in which one operates with a clear conscience in dealings with self and others.

Integrity Check — from leadership emergence theory. One of 51 process items that God uses to shape a leader. The <u>integrity</u> check refers to the special kind of process test which God uses to evaluate heart –intent, consistency between inner convictions and outward actions, and which God uses as a foundation from which to expand the leader's capacity to influence. The word check is used in the sense of test—meaning a check or check-up. See also testing patterns.

Leadership Coalition — A *leadership coalition* in Biblical literature refers to a partnership, whether formal or informal, which exists between civil leaders, mainstream religious leaders and/or peripheral religious leaders, for a temporary period of time in order to accomplish some God-directed task(s).

Leadership Committal — a special shaping activity of God observed in leadership emergence theory which is usually a spiritual benchmark and produces a sense of destiny in a leader. It is the call to leadership by God and the wholehearted response by the leader to accept and abide by that call. Paul's Damascus road experience, the destiny revelation given by Ananias, and Paul's response to it as a life calling provide the New Testament classic example of leadership committal.

Leadership Functions — a technical term which refers to the three major categories of formal leadership responsibility: task behavior (defining structure and goals), relationship behavior (providing the emotional support and ambiance), and inspirational behavior (providing motivational effort).

Left Hand of God — in contradistinction to the phrase *the right hand of God* which refers to an evident manifestation of God's power in a situation, usually through His people or His leaders, this phrase, *the left hand of God*, refers to God's use of people, nations, events not necessarily recognizing Him or what He is doing for His own purposes (e.g. Cyrus). See also Jn 11:49-51.

Macro-Lesson — a high level generalization of a leadership observation (suggestion, guideline, requirement), stated as a lesson, which repeatedly occurs throughout different leadership eras, and thus has potential as a leadership absolute. Macro lessons even at their weakest provide at least strong guidelines describing leadership insights. At their strongest they are requirements, that is absolutes, that leaders should follow. Leaders ignore them to their detriment. Example: *Prayer Lesson: If God has called you to a ministry then He has called you to pray for that ministry.*

Metonymy — a figure of speech in which one word is substituted for another word to which it is related. This is to emphasize both the word and call attention to

Glossary of Leadership Definitions

the relationship between the two words. e.g. Philemon 6 *communicate your faith* to *communicate what you believe and on which you have strong convictions*.

Ministerial Formation	the shaping activity in a leader's life which is directed toward instilling leadership skills, leadership experience, and developing giftedness for ministry.
Ministry Affirmation	a concept from leadership emergence theory. The shaping activity of God whereby God makes known to a leader his approval of that leader's ministry efforts. This is a major motivating factor to keep one serving the Lord.
Negative Preparation	from leadership emergence theory. One of 51 process items that God uses to shape a leader. <u>Negative preparation</u> refers to the special guidance process involving God's use of events, people, conflict, persecution, or experiences, all focusing on the negative, so as to free up a person from the situation in order to enter the next phase of development with a new abandonment and revitalized interest.
Obedience Check	from leadership emergence theory. One of 51 process items that God uses to shape a leader. An <u>Obedience checks</u> refer to that special category of process items in which God tests personal response to revealed truth in the life of a person.
Pivotal Point	A *pivotal point* is a critical time in a leader's life in which processing going on will be responded to in such a way that one of three typical things may happen: The response to this processing can: 1. curtail further use of the leader by God or at least curtail expansion of the leader's potential. 2. limit the eventual use of the leader for ultimate purposes that otherwise could have been accomplished, 3. enhance or open up the leader for expansion or contribution to the ultimate purposes in God's kingdom, that is, it may be a springboard to future expanded use by God of the leader.
Power Base	a term referring to the means which enable a leader's influence. Force, manipulation, authority, and persuasion enfold various power means.
Principle (of truth)	refers to generalized statements of truth which reflect observations drawn from specific instances of leadership acts or other leadership sources.
Progressive Calling	the recognition that most leaders will receive on-going leadership challenges from God throughout their lifetimes and not just some initial call; such challenges will bring renewal, divine affirmation, ministry affirmation and will continue to give strategic guidance to a leader's ministry.
Promise	or more specifically, a *promise from God* is an assertion from God, specific or general or a truth in harmony with God's character, which is perceived in one's heart or mind concerning what He will do or not do for one, and which is sealed in that one's inner most being by a quickening action of the Holy Spirit, and on which that one then counts. See Jn 14 where six such promises are used to inspire the disciples in a crisis moment.
Prophecy	one of the 19 spiritual gifts. It is in the *Word Cluster* and *power cluster*. A person operating with the <u>gift of prophecy</u> has the capacity to deliver truth

Glossary of Leadership Definitions

(in a public way) either of a predictive nature or as a situational word from God in order to correct by exhorting, edifying or consoling believers and to convince non-believers of God's truth. **Its central thrust is To Provide Correction Or Perspective On A Situation.**

Prophecy (genre)	refers to the genre of Scripture in which the thrust of the passage is an authoritative revelation from God usually through a spokesperson, called a prophet or prophetess, to correct a given historical situation or to warn of a future situation.
Recruitment	refers to the deliberate efforts to challenge potential leaders and to engage them in on-going ministry so that they will develop as leaders and move toward accomplishment God's destiny for them.
Relational Oriented Leadership	a description of one of three major high level generic leadership functions that a leader of an organization is responsible for producing. It describes those activities which a leader does to affirm followers, to provide an atmosphere congenial to accomplishing work, to give emotional and spiritual support for followers so that they can mature, in short, to act relationally with followers in order to enable them to develop and be effective in their contribution to the organization. All three functions are necessary for healthy ministry.
Religious leadership, Mainstream	refers to officially recognized religious roles sanctioned by the society and religious structures.
Religious leadership, Peripheral	refers to those roles, mostly outside the mainstream religious structures, which attempt to speak for God to bring about change in religious groups, structures, and society in general.
restoration (corporate)	refers to God's attempts to restore the people of God as a viable channel through whom He can work to carry out His Biblical purposes.
restoration (crisis)	refers to the period of time from 539 B.C. to 430 B.C. and which covers the activity of God in bringing His people back into the land and establishing a testimony there. His providential care of His people (both in the land and outside it) is also shown.
Restoration (individual)	the process whereby a fallen leader is transitioned back into leadership. It usually involves repentance, restitution where appropriate, correction of the aberrant leadership dysfunctionalities, and recognition by other leaders of the restoration process and their stamp of approval for the leader to renew ministry.
Restoration Leaders	refer to the important leaders, civil, religious, and prophetical, who worked during the restoration crisis years to bring some kind of recrudescence to God's people.
Rhetorical Question	a figure of speech in which a question is <u>not</u> used to obtain information but is used to indirectly communicate an affirmative or negative statement, the importance of some thought by focusing attention on it, and/or one's own feeling or attitudes about something. 1 Tim 3:5 For if anyone knows not

Glossary of Leadership Definitions

	how to rule his own house, how shall that one take care of the church of God. Captured: A person who can not lead his/her own family can't lead people in a church.
Sense of Destiny	an inner conviction arising from an experience or a series of experiences in which there is a growing sense of awareness that God has His hand on a leader in a special way for special purposes. See destiny pattern.
Sentness	a term capturing the divine backing of Jesus' intervention in the world to represent and reveal God to our world. It carries the notion of anointing and appointment by God for a mission, but in Jesus' case—more since it was the incarnation of God in human form. The closest functional equivalent for leaders today is divine appointment.
Sovereign Mindset	an attitude demonstrated by the Apostle Paul in which he tended to see God's working in the events and activities that shaped his life, whether or not they were positive and good or negative and bad. He tended to see God's purposes in these shaping activities and to make the best of them. Haggai demonstrates this when He sees God's Hand involved in the setbacks of the people.
Sphere of Influence	refers to the totality of people being influenced and for whom a leader will give an account to God. The totally of people influenced subdivides into three domains called direct influence, indirect influence, and organizational influence. Three measures rate sphere of influence: 1. Extensiveness—which refers to quantity; 2. Comprehensiveness—which refers to the scope of things being influenced in the followers' lives; 3. Intensiveness—the depth to which influence extends to each item within the comprehensive influences. Extensiveness is the easiest to measure and hence is most often used or implied when talking about a leader's sphere of influence.
Spiritual Authority	from the standpoint of the follower, Spiritual authority is the right to influence, conferred upon a leader by followers, because of their perception of spirituality in that leader. Technically this is called extrinsic spiritual authority (ESA). From the leader's perspective Spiritual Authority is that characteristic of a God-anointed leader, developed upon an experiential power base (giftedness, character, deep experiences with God), that enables him/her to influence followers through persuasion, force of modeling, and moral expertise. Technically this is called intrinsic spiritual authority (ISA).
Spiritual Formation	the shaping activity in a leader's life which is directed toward instilling godly character and developing inner life.
Spiritual Warfare	refers to the unseen opposition in the spirit world made up of Satan and his demons and their attempts to defeat God's forces, including believers. It also involves the response by believers to these attempts.
Strategic Formation	the shaping activity in a leader's life which is directed toward having that leader reach full potential and achieve a God-given destiny.
Suggestions	a term used to describe a position on the Certainty Continuum. It refers to truth observed in some situations and which may be helpful to others but they are optional and can be used or not with no loss of conscience.

Glossary of Leadership Definitions

Task Oriented Leadership	a description of one of three major high level generic leadership functions that a leader of an organization is responsible for producing. It describes the thing to be accomplished by the organization, its raison d'être, reason for being. Some leaders by personality and processing are highly task oriented and tend to prioritize everything in terms of getting the task done; this means frequently using people. All three functions are necessary for healthy ministry.
Volitional	a learning domain, that is, a term describing learning which primarily focuses willful decisions that are made in response to learning. Haggai's ministry focuses on this very strongly.
Word Check	from leadership emergence theory. One of 51 process items that God uses to shape a leader. A word check is a process item which tests a leader's ability to understand or receive a word from God personally and to see it worked out in life with a view toward enhancing the authority of God's truth and a desire to know it.
Word Gifts	a category of spiritual gifts used to clarify and explain about God. These help us understand about God including His nature, His purposes and how we can relate to Him and be a part of His purposes. These include: teaching, exhortation, pastoring, evangelism, apostleship, prophecy, ruling, and sometimes word of wisdom, word of knowledge, and faith (a word of). All leaders have at least one of these and often several of these.
Word of Knowledge	one of the 19 spiritual gifts. It is primarily in the *Power Cluster* but can be in the Word Cluster and Love Clusterde pending upon what is revealed. The *word of knowledge gift* refers to the capacity or sensitivity of a person to supernaturally perceive revealed knowledge from God which otherwise could not or would not be known and apply it to a situation. **Its central thrust is Getting Revelatory Information.**
Word of Wisdom	one of the 19 spiritual gifts. It is primarily in the Power Cluster but can be in the Word Cluster and Love Cluster depending upon what is revealed. The **word of wisdom gift** refers to the capacity to know the mind of the Spirit in a given situation and to communicate clearly the situation, facts, truth or application of the facts and truth to meet the need of the situation. **Its central thrust is Applying Revelatory Information.**

For Further Study Bibliography—Resources

Alford, Henry
   1871   **The Greek Testament in Four Volumes, Vol III.** 5th Edition. London: Deighton, Bell, and Co.

(Bratcher, Robert G. et al)
   n.d.   **Good News Bible—Today's English Version.** New York: American Bible Society.

Bruce, A. B.
   1929   **The Training of the Twelve.** 3rd Edition. Garden City, N.Y: Doubleday, Doran & Co.

Butt, Howard
   1973   **The Velvet Covered Brick: Christian Leadership in An age of Rebellion.** New York: Harper and Row.

Clinton, Dr. J. Robert
   1977   **Disputed Practices.** Redone in 1994. Altadena, Ca: Barnabas Publishers.

   1977   **Interpreting The Scriptures: Figures and Idioms.** Altadena, Ca: Barnabas Publishers.

   1983   **Interpreting The Scriptures: Hebrew Poetry.** Altadena, Ca: Barnabas Publishers.

   1986   **A Short History of Leadership Theory.** Altadena,Ca: Barnabas Publishers.

   1986   **Coming to Conclusions On Leadership Styles.** Altadena,Ca: Barnabas Publishers.

   1987   **Reading on the Run—Continuum Reading Concepts.** Altadena,Ca: Barnabas Publishers.

   1988   **The Making of A Leader.** Colorado Springs, Co: Navpress.

   1989   **Leadership Emergence Theory.** Altadena,Ca: Barnabas Publishers.

   1989   *The Ultimate Contribution.* Altadena,Ca: Barnabas Publishers.

   1993   *Getting Perspective—By Using Your Unique Time-Line.* Altadena,Ca: Barnabas Publishers.

   1993   **Leadership Perspectives.** Altadena,Ca: Barnabas Publishers.

   1993   **The Bible and Leadership Values.** Altadena,Ca: Barnabas Publishers.

   1993   *Social Base Processing—The Home Environment Out of Which A Leader Works.* Altadena,Ca: Barnabas Publishers.

   1994   **Focused Lives—Inspirational Life Changing Lessons from Eight Effective Christian Leaders Who Finished Well.** Altadena,Ca: Barnabas Publishers.

   1995   *Gender and Leadership.* Altadena,Ca: Barnabas Publishers.

   1995   **Strategic Concepts That Clarify A Focused Life.** Altadena,Ca: Barnabas Publishers.

1995   *The Life Cycle of A Leader*. Altadena,Ca: Barnabas Publishers.

1998   **Having Ministry That Lasts.** Altadena,Ca: Barnabas Publishers.

Clinton, Dr. J. Robert and Dr. Richard W.
1991   **The Mentor Handbook—Deatiled Guidelines and Helps for Christian Mentors and Mentorees**. Altadena,Ca: Barnabas Publishers.

1993   **Unlocking Your Giftedness—What Leaders Need To Know To Develop Themselves and Others**. Altadena,Ca: Barnabas Publishers.

Davis, Stanley B.
1982   Transforming Organizations: The Key To Strategy Is Context in Organizational Dynamics, Winter, 1982.

1987   **Future Perfect**. New York: Addison Wesley.

Doohan, Helen
1984   **Leadership in Paul**. Wilmington, Del.: Michael Glazier, Inc.

Gerlach, L.P. and Hine, V.H.
1970   **People, Power, Change: Movements of Social Transformation**. New York: Bobbs-Merrill Co.

Harville, Sue
1976   **Reciprocal Living**. Coral Gables: West Indies Mission.

1977   **Walking in Love.** Coral Gables: West Indies Mission.

Hersey, Palul and Ken blanchard
1977   **Management of Organizational Behavior—Utilizing Human Resources**. Englewood Cliffs, N.J.: Prentice-Hall, 1977.

Kraft, Charles H.
1979   **Christianity and Culture**. Maryknoll, N.Y.: Orbis Books.

Kuhn, Thomas
1974   **The Structure of Scientific Revolutions**.

Leupold,
1961   **Psalms**. Minneapolis: Augsberg.

Mickelsen, A. Berkley
1963   **Interpreting The Bible**. Grand Rapids: Eerdmans Publishing Company.

Morgan, G. Campbell
1903, 1936   **The Crises of the Christ**. Old Tappan, N.J.: Fleming H. Revel Co.

1990   **Handbook for Bible Teachers and Preachers**. 5th Printing. Original 4 Volume Series, 1912. Grand Rapids, Michigan: Baker Book House.

Peterson, Eugene H.
1993   **The Message—The New Testament in Contemporary Language**. Colorado Springs, Co: Navpress.

For Further Study Bibliography—Resources

Stanley, Paul and J. Robert Clinton
   1992   **Connecting—The Mentoring Relationships You Need to Succeed in Life**. Colorado Springs, Co: Navpress.

Strong, James
   1890   **The Exhaustive Concordance of the Bible** (with Dictionaries of the Hebrew and Greek Words). Nashville: Abingdon Press.

(Taylor, Ken did original version; other Bible scholars the new version)
   1996   **Holy Bible—New Living Translation**. Wheaton, Il: Tyndale house Publishers, Inc.

Tippett, A. R.
           Solomon Island Christianity. Pasadena: William Carey Library.

Wrong, Dennis
   1979   **Power—Its Forms, Bases, and Uses**. San Francisco, CA: Harper and Row.

BARNABAS PUBLISHER'S MINI CATALOG

Approaching the Bible With Leadership Eyes: An Authoratative Source for Leadership Findings — Dr. J. Robert Clinton
Barnabas: Encouraging Exhorter — Dr. J. Robert Clinton & Laura Raab
Boundary Processing: Looking at Critical Transitions Times in Leader's Lives — Dr. J. Robert Clinton
Connecting: The Mentoring Relationships You Need to Succeed in Life — Dr. J. Robert Clinton
The Emerging Leader — Dr. J. Robert Clinton
Fellowship With God — Dr. J. Robert Clinton
Finishing Well — Dr. J. Robert Clinton
Figures and Idioms (Interpreting the Scriptures: Figures and Idioms) — Dr. J. Robert Clinton
Focused Lives Lectures — Dr. J. Robert Clinton
Gender and Leadership — Dr. J. Robert Clinton
Having A Ministry That Lasts: By Becoming a Bible Centered Leader — Dr. J. Robert Clinton
Hebrew Poetry (Interpreting the Scriptures: Hebrew Poetry) — Dr. J. Robert Clinton
A Short **History of Leadership Theory** — Dr. J. Robert Clinton
Isolation: A Place of Transformation in the Life of a Leader — Shelley G. Trebesch
Joseph: Destined to Rule — Dr. J. Robert Clinton
The Joshua Portrait — Dr. J. Robert Clinton and Katherine Haubert
Leadership Emergence Theory: A Self Study Manual For Analyzing the Development of a Christian Leader — Dr. J. Robert Clinton
Leadership Perspectives: How To Study The Bible for Leadership Insights — Dr. J. Robert Clinton
Coming to Some Conclusions on **Leadership Styles** — Dr. J. Robert Clinton
Leadership Training Models — Dr. J. Robert Clinton
The Bible and **Leadership Values:** A Book by Book Analysis— Dr. J. Robert Clinton
The Life Cycle of a Leader: Looking at God's Shaping of A LeaderTowards An Eph. 2:10 Life — Dr. J. Robert Clinton
Listen Up Leaders! — Dr. J. Robert Clinton
The Mantle of the Mentor — Dr. J. Robert Clinton
Mentoring Can Help—Five Leadership Crises You Will Face in the Pastorate For Which You Have Not Been Trained — Dr. J. Robert Clinton
Mentoring: Developing Leaders...Without Adding More Programs — Dr. J. Robert Clinton
The Mentor Handbook: Detailed Guidelines and Helps for Christian Mentors and Mentorees — Dr. J. Robert Clinton
Moses Desert Leadership—7 Macro Lessons
Parables—Puzzles With A Purpose (Interpreting the Scriptures: Puzzles With A Purpose) — Dr. J. Robert Clinton
Paradigm Shift: God's Way of Opening New Vistas To Leaders — Dr. J. Robert Clinton
A Personal Ministry Philosophy: One Key to Effective Leadership — Dr. J. Robert Clinton
Reading on the Run: Continuum Reading Concepts — Dr. J. Robert Clinton
Samuel: Last of the Judges & First of the Prophets–A Model For Transitional Times — Bill Bjoraker
Selecting and Developing Those Emerging Leaders — Dr. Richard W. Clinton
Social Base Processing: The Home Base Environment Out of Which A Leader Works — Dr. J. Robert Clinton
Starting Well: Building A Strong Foundation for a Life Time of Ministry — Dr. J. Robert Clinton
Strategic Concepts: That Clarify A Focused Life – A Self Study Guide — Dr. J. Robert Clinton
The Making of a Leader: Recognizing the Lessons & Stages of Leadership Development — Dr. J. Robert Clinton
Time Line —Small Paper (What it is & How to Construct It) — Dr. J. Robert Clinton
Time Line: Getting Perspective—By Using Your Time-Line, Large Paper — Dr. J. Robert Clinton
Ultimate Contribution — Dr. J. Robert Clinton
Unlocking Your Giftedness: What Leaders Need to Know to Develop Themselves & Others — Dr. J. Robert Clinton
A **Vanishing Breed:** Thoughts About A Bible Centered Leader & A Life Long Bible Mastery Paradigm — Dr. J. Robert Clinton
The Way To Look At Leadership (How To Look at Leadership) — Dr. J. Robert Clinton
Webster-Smith, Irene: An Irish Woman Who Impacted Japan (A Focused Life Study) — Dr. J. Robert Clinton
Word Studies (Interpreting the Scriptures: Word Studies) — Dr. J. Robert Clinton

(Book Titles are in Bold and Paper Titles are in Italics with Sub-Titles and Pre-Titles in Roman)

BARNABAS PUBLISHERS

Unique Leadership Material that will help you answer the question:
"What legacy will you as a leader leave behind?"

"The difference between leaders and followers is perspective. The difference between leaders and effective leaders is better perspective."
Barnabas Publishers has the materials that will help you find that better perspective and a closer relationship with God.

BARNABAS PUBLISHERS
Post Office Box 6006 • Altadena, CA 91003-6006
Fax Phone (626)-794-3098

www.ingramcontent.com/pod-product-compliance
Ingram Content Group UK Ltd.
Pitfield, Milton Keynes, MK11 3LW, UK
UKHW051300180426
11947UKWH00020B/1822